This book is a study of the relationship between full-time union officers and shop stewards across the whole of British industry (public and private, manufacturing and services) in 1986–91. It is the first major study of union officers for twenty years, and one of the most detailed studies of workplace collective bargaining and union organization following the recession of the early 1980s. In the wake of recession, union decline, industrial restructuring, anti-union legislation, and changes in union policies (towards a 'new realism'), Britain is said by some commentators to be entering 'a new industrial relations'. This book provides a unique body of evidence that throws new light on this claim, and casts serious doubt on its validity. It combines survey, interview, questionnaire and observation data and thus overcomes the well known limitations of both large-scale surveys and individual case studies.

*Cambridge Studies in Management 22*

# Working for the union

*Cambridge Studies in Management*

Formerly Management and Industrial Relations series

*Editors*
WILLIAM BROWN, *University of Cambridge*
ANTHONY HOPWOOD, *London School of Economics*
*and* PAUL WILLMAN, *London Business School*

The series focuses on the human and organizational aspects of management. It covers the areas of organization theory and behaviour, strategy and business policy, the organizational and social aspects of accounting, personnel and human resource management, industrial relations and industrial sociology.

The series aims for high standards of scholarship and seeks to publish the best among original theoretical and empirical research; innovative contributions to advancing understanding of the area; and books which synthesize and/or review the best of current research, and aim to make the work published in specialist journals more widely accessible.

The books are intended for an international audience among specialists in universities and business schools, undergraduate, graduate and MBA students, and also for a wider readership among business practitioners and trade unionists.

*For a list of titles in this series, see end of book*

# Working for the union
*British trade union officers*

John Kelly
*London School of Economics*
and
Edmund Heery
*Kingston Business School, Kingston University*

CAMBRIDGE
UNIVERSITY PRESS

Published by the Press Syndicate of the University of Cambridge
The Pitt Building, Trumpington Street, Cambridge CB2 1RP
40 West 20th Street, New York, NY 10011–4211, USA
10 Stamford Street, Oakleigh, Victoria 3166, Australia

First published 1994

Printed in Great Britain at the University Press, Cambridge

*A catalogue record for this book is available from the British Library*

*Library of Congress cataloguing in publication data*
Kelly, John E., 1952–
Working for the union: British trade union officers /
John Kelly and Edmund Heery.
    p.    cm. – (Cambridge Studies in management : 22)
Includes bibliographical references and index.
ISBN 0 521 38320 X (hc)
1. Trade-unions – Great Britain – Officials and employees.
I. Heery. Edmund.  II. Title.  III. Series.
HD6490.042G74   1994
331.87′33′0941–dc20   93–37384   CIP

ISBN 0 521 38320 X hardback

JK

CE

# Contents

# Figures and tables

# Preface

The research on which this book is based would not have been possible without the full cooperation of a number of trade unions and many of their local full-time officers. We would particularly like to thank the following: from the AEU (now AEEU) – Laurie Smith and Bill Young; from ASTMS (now MSF) – Chris Ball, Dave Barr, John Chowcatt, Donna Haber and Jim Mercer; from the GMB – Alan Cave, John Cope, Derek Gladwin, Alan Gordon, George Holland, Derek Horn, Derek Hunter, Paul Kenny, Ian Keys, George Little, Tony Lusby, Dave Ryland and Terry Tarling; from the T&GWU – Barry Camfield, Ron Connolly, Jacqui Ford, Ken Fuller, Fred Higgs, Terry Hurst, Peter Martindale, Tom O'Driscoll, Philip Pearson, Regan Scott, Fred Tooke and Ron Webb. We would also like to thank the Economic and Social Research Council for their financial support (Grant FOO 23 2201). A number of people helped with data preparation including Janet Heery, Louise Heery and Penny Page. Una Macauley collected our data on women officers. Finally we would like to thank the many people who have typed successive drafts of the book over the past few years, most recently Yvonne Curtis and Stephanie Wilson. None of the above is responsible for what we have written: this is all down to the authors.

# Abbreviations

| | |
|---|---|
| ACTT | Association of Cinematograph, Television and Allied Technicians (now BECTU) |
| AEU | Amalgamated Engineering Union (now AEEU) |
| AEEU | Amalgamated Engineering and Electrical Union |
| AMMA | Assistant Masters' and Mistresses' Association (now ATL) |
| APCT | Association of Polytechnic and College Teachers |
| APEX | Association of Professional Executive Clerical and Computer Staff (now GMB) |
| ASLEF | Associated Society of Locomotive Engineers and Firemen |
| ASTMS | Association of Scientific, Technical and Managerial Staffs (now MSF) |
| AUEW | Amalgamated Union of Engineering Workers (became AEU) |
| AUT | Association of University Teachers |
| BACM | British Association of Colliery Management |
| BALPA | British Airline Pilots' Association |
| BECTU | Broadcasting Entertainment Cinematograph and Television Union |
| BETA | Broadcasting and Entertainment Trades Alliance (now BECTU) |
| BFAWU | Bakers' Food and Allied Workers Union |
| BIFU | Banking Insurance and Finance Union |
| CATU | Ceramic and Allied Trades Union |
| CMA | Communication Managers' Association |
| COHSE | Confederation of Health Service Employees (now UNISON) |
| CPSA | Civil and Public Services Association |
| EETPU | Electrical Electronic Telecommunications and Plumbing Union (now AEEU) |
| EIS | Educational Institute of Scotland |
| EMA | Engineers' and Managers' Association |

| | |
|---|---|
| EQUITY | British Actors' Equity Association |
| FBU | Fire Brigades' Union |
| FDA | Association of First Division Civil Servants |
| FTAT | Furniture, Timber and Allied Trades Union |
| GEC | General Executive Council |
| GMB | General Municipal and Boilermakers' Union |
| GPMU | Graphical Paper and Media Union |
| HCSA | Hospital Consultants' and Specialists' Association |
| HVA | Health Visitors' Association (now MSF) |
| IPCS | Institution of Professional Civil Servants (now IPMS) |
| IPM | Institute of Personnel Management |
| IPMS | Institution of Professionals, Managers and Specialists |
| IRSF | Inland Revenue Staff Federation |
| ISTC | Iron and Steel Trades Confederation |
| MSC | Manpower Services Commission |
| MSF | Manufacturing Science and Finance Union |
| MU | Musicians' Union |
| NACO | National Association of Cooperative Officials |
| NACODS | National Association of Colliery Overmen, Deputies and Shotfirers |
| NALGO | National and Local Government Officers' Association (now UNISON) |
| NALHM | National Association of Licensed House Managers |
| NAPO | National Association of Probation Officers |
| NAS/UWT | National Association of Schoolmasters/Union of Women Teachers |
| NATFHE | National Association of Teachers in Further and Higher Education |
| NCU | National Communications Union |
| NGA (1982) | National Graphical Association (1982) (now GPMU) |
| NLBD | National League of the Blind and Disabled |
| NUCPS | National Union of Civil and Public Servants |
| NUDAGO | National Union of Domestic Appliances and General Operatives |
| NUFLAT | National Union of the Footwear Leather and Allied Trades (now NUKFAT) |
| NUHKW | National Union of Hosiery and Knitwear Workers (now NUKFAT) |
| NUIW | National Union of Insurance Workers |
| NUJ | National Union of Journalists |
| NUKFAT | National Union of the Knitwear Footwear and Allied Trades |

| | |
|---|---|
| NULMW | National Union of Lock and Metal Workers |
| NUM | National Union of Mineworkers |
| NUMAST | National Union of Marine Aviation and Shipping Transport Officers |
| NUPE | National Union of Public Employees (now UNISON) |
| NUT | National Union of Teachers |
| NUTGW | National Union of Tailor and Garment Workers (now GMB) |
| PAT | Professional Association of Teachers |
| POA | Prison Officers' Association |
| RCN | Royal College of Nursing |
| RMT | Rail Maritime and Transport Workers' Union |
| SOGAT '82 | Society of Graphical and Allied Trades '82 (now GPMU) |
| SPOA | Scottish Prison Officers' Association |
| STE | Society of Telecom Executives |
| T&GWU | Transport and General Workers' Union |
| TSSA | Transport Salaried Staffs' Association |
| UCATT | Union of Construction Allied Trades and Technicians |
| UCW | Union of Communication Workers |
| URTU | United Road Transport Union |
| USDAW | Union of Shop Distributive and Allied Workers |
| YTS | Youth Training Scheme |

*Part 1*

# Introduction

# 1    Introduction: trade unions and industrial relations

One of the major resources of any trade union movement is the cadre of full-time officers employed to service its membership. British trade unions currrently employ about 3000 full-time officers (FTOs) to represent the interests of members both collectively, through negotiations and consultation, and individually, through procedures and at tribunals. Full-time officers can play a key role in shaping the responses of union members to management initiatives; they can have an impact on workplace union organization; and they have often been seen as key recruiting agents for unions in unorganized companies. The salary costs of the officer workforce now make up the single largest item of total union expenditure. Yet despite their importance little is known about union full-time officers, and in the past 30 years they have been the subject of only three major studies: *Trade Union Officers* (Clegg, Killick and Adams, 1961); *Workplace and Union* (Boraston, Clegg and Rimmer, 1975); and *Managers of Discontent* (Watson, 1988). Industrial relations research in this period concentrated on a variety of other actors: shop stewards in the 1960s and 1970s, government incomes and legal policies from the early 1970s, and employers from the 1980s. The present study aims to fill this serious gap in our knowledge by presenting a wide range of data on the numbers, organization, activities and values of full-time union officers. To this end we used a variety of research methods – interviews, questionnaires and non-participant observation – in a cross-section of unions and employment sectors.

Our second aim was to contribute to theoretical debates about union organization in which the concept of 'bureaucracy' has played a prominent role. Whilst trade unions clearly do have bureaucratic organizational features they also have non-bureaucratic elements, and it is important to understand these two faces of union organization. Exaggeration of the bureaucratic elements of unionism is likely to produce misleading accounts of officer power and officer–member conflict. There are other theoretical approaches in the literature (discussed in chapter 2) and wherever possible we have tried to relate our findings to the analyses or hypotheses derived from theory.

Thirdly we also use the evidence from this study to contribute to broader debates in industrial relations. The decline of trade union membership in the 1980s, the loss of power experienced by many shop steward organizations and the adoption of 'new' management techniques by more assertive employers have led to fundamental questions being asked about the future trajectory of British industrial relations. Some foresee a slow steady decline of unionism whilst others see it being confined to the shrinking ghettos of private industry and the public sector. Union–management relations have been the subject of equally wide-ranging and intense discussion with some writers claiming to have discerned a new, more cooperative pattern of industrial relations amongst workers, unions and employers particularly, but not exclusively, in greenfield sites. Others by contrast have held fast to the view that compliance is a more accurate description of events and that labour's apparent acquiescence and 'cooperation' is a product of high unemployment and adverse product markets. We return to these issues in the concluding chapter (chapter 10) of the book.

## The research

Our research began in 1985 and was completed in 1991. Full details of the various phases and methods can be found in the Appendix (p. 208), and copies of the questionnaires and observation schedules can be obtained from the authors on request, but briefly we proceeded as follows. After pilot interviews with local full-time officers in four unions – ASTMS, AUEW, GMB and T&GWU – we then embarked on a period of intense observation of officers at work. After careful consultation with 27 officers we selected a number of companies from amongst the bargaining units they serviced and wherever possible tried to accompany them to all of the meetings dealing with a particular issue, whether it was pay, hours of work, equal opportunities or whatever. In other words, we tried to follow through the whole process of formulating a claim, negotiating it with the employers and reaching a final settlement. We tried to cover a wide range of issues, companies, sectors and officers rather than concentrating on particular issues or a particular sector. We also conducted a series of questionnaire surveys: of union Head Offices in 1986 and 1991, of individual full-time officers in 1987 and of women full-time officers in the same year. We used multiple methods as a way of cross-checking data collected in different ways, but mainly as a way of addressing different types of issues.

### The context

One of the questions that is always raised about empirical research is how far the findings are situation- or period-specific. This is a particularly acute problem in industrial relations because of the many political, social, economic and legal changes that have taken place in the past 20 years or so. In addition, there is an important theoretical reason for reflecting on the context of the present research. Some of the theories that we review in chapter 2, particularly theories of union bureaucracy, have identified powerful external pressures on unions that allegedly contribute to goal displacement and goal moderation. Insofar as unions are secondary organizations whose existence depends on the survival of companies and other employing organizations, they have an unavoidable interest in the objectives of employers. Full-time union officers have often been seen as peculiarly susceptible to pressures towards collaboration with or incorporation by employers (and the State) because their own interests are tied so heavily to the survival of union organization. Other formulations of bureaucracy theory emphasize the officer's intermediary role, caught between rank and file pressures on the one hand and incorporationist pressures from employers on the other. The context of our research has an important bearing on these arguments. Throughout the 1980s unions steadily lost members, particularly but not exclusively in the two recessions. The level of strike activity fell sharply and the balance of power shifted towards employers. Union officers found themselves having to work in an extremely inhospitable environment dominated by mass unemployment, adverse product markets, restrictive labour laws and pronounced State hostility to trade unionism. Membership pressures towards militancy were therefore weakened at the same time as external pressures for cooperation with employers were strengthened. The context of our research was therefore one in which the bureaucratic tendencies of unions and their officers were given their freest rein for some time. If such tendencies are as pervasive as has sometimes been claimed, then the 1980s was an ideal period in which to observe them. But this argument has an important corollary. If we failed to confirm or strongly support the predictions and analyses of bureaucracy theory under such ideal conditions then we could be confident that the theory was indeed seriously flawed and our findings could not be explained away as situationally-specific.

The account of our research is organized as follows. In chapter 2 we review the different theories of union organization, from the Webbs onwards, and examine the concepts of bureaucracy, oligarchy and polyarchy. In different ways these theories all attempt to derive a model of officer goals and interests from their structural location in the union hierarchy. Contingency studies, such as Boraston *et al.* (1975) have at least recognized variation amongst officers, but have also tried to explain this in terms of the structures of union organization and collective bargaining. We argue that structural properties of unions and bargaining systems are important in explaining many facets of officer organization, but are very much less useful when it comes to officer actions. Whilst recognizing structural constraints on officers, we stress the values of union officers themselves in determining their objectives and actions in particular settings, a perspective that owes much to the 'social action' approach in sociology. In part 2 (chapters 3, 4 and 5), we look at the organization of full-time officers within the union. Chapter 3 presents basic data on the numbers of union full-time officers and more importantly on their backgrounds and their route into the job. We trace the rather different routes of men and women, and of manual and non-manual officers, and also provide information on the terms and conditions of employment of officers. This data, the most complete available since 1961, is also analyzed as a function of union type and union size in order to try and explain the dramatic variations in officer salaries. Chapter 4 concentrates on the workloads of officers and presents data on officer–member ratios and on specialization and hierarchy in union organization. We examine variations between unions, and try to interpret shifts over time. Chapter 5 looks at a question that is critical for any organization: how do senior officers monitor, control and reward the activities of their subordinates? We present a wealth of detail on the control systems of trade unions and demonstrate the severe problems faced by the national officers of a democratic organization in exercising day-to-day control over full-time union officers in the field. Conversely, we also examine the degree to which field officers have an input into their union's policy-making process and we consider the links between officer involvement in policy formation and officer commitment to policy implementation.

Part 3 of the book focuses on the officer at work and looks in turn at organizing, bargaining and relations with management. Chapter 6 shows the critical role played by officers in maintaining and building strong workplace union organization. Officers were extremely anxious to encourage steward organization, independence from management, strong links with members and a high level of density. The main relationship between stewards and officers was one of inter-dependence, with stewards dependent on officers for their expertise and officers dependent on stewards for both information and for the implementation of union policy in areas like recruitment, a topic we explore in some depth. In chapter 7 we look at the process of formulating objectives in collective bargaining and assess the relative power of officers and stewards in placing items on the agenda. We also examine the important role of officers' own ideologies in shaping the objectives they seek to pursue and the criteria they use to decide on objectives in the first place. Chapter 8 looks at the bargaining process itself, and reveals the dominant role exercised by officers, a role for the most part fully accepted by stewards. We found a large measure of agreement between officers and stewards on the arguments used in bargaining and in their willingness to resist management arguments. However, we also found that the officers' own ideologies again played a key role in shaping their willingness to resist or comply with management pressure, and to moderate or to maintain stewards' own objectives. The chapter therefore explores the sources and variations in officer ideologies. In chapter 9 we look at relations with management and at the generally negative views of management promulgated by officers to their stewards. Part 4, and chapter 10, recapitulates our main conclusions and returns to the major debates about British trade unions and industrial relations through the 1980s and early 1990s.

# 2 Theoretical analysis and empirical studies of trade union officers

Chapter 1 explained why an analysis of the role, behaviour and values of full-time officers is integral to many of the debates about contemporary British industrial relations. In the present chapter we therefore set out to look at the theoretical and empirical literature on union officers with three aims in mind. First, we want to outline and evaluate the major theoretical approaches that have been used to understand trade union organization, and the role of the officer within the union. Secondly, we want to summarize the current state of knowledge about union full-time officers in Britain, though from time to time we shall also refer to comparative material. Finally, we shall outline the main features of our own approach to the explanation of union officer organization and behaviour.

Some of the most contentious issues in the study of trade union organization were first highlighted by the Webbs in their classic studies *Industrial Democracy* (1902) and *The History of Trade Unionism* (1920). The local craft societies of the early nineteenth century became transformed into large, national organizations, and with the change in size came a change in structure. The 'primitive democracy' of mass membership meetings gave way to the delegate conference, the elected executive committee and the full-time salaried officer with an increasingly sophisticated division of labour between them. This separation of functions between rank and file members, delegate conference, executive committee and full-time officers led the Webbs to raise two critical questions about trade union organization. What were the relations of power between these different groups within a trade union? And if it was the case, as the Webbs argued, that power was becoming concentrated in the hands of trade union officers, then to what ends would this power be used? Or to put it another way, had the division of functions inside trade unions also created a division of interests? The Webbs conceptualized these issues in terms of a potential conflict between the demands of democracy and efficiency, or what Child *et al.* (1973) later described as representative and administrative rationalities. We prefer to examine

8

these issues by looking at the behaviour of union officers and the networks of relationships within which they operate. This entails a focus on their objectives as officers, such as bargaining goals for example, and on the means used to attain them. And it also means focusing on the key industrial relations actors with whom they most frequently interact: shop stewards, management, and fellow officers within their own union.

Our knowledge of trade union officers is still insufficient to permit highly rigorous testing of precise hypotheses about their behaviour, and there are many gaps in our knowledge that must first be filled with basic descriptive data. But we also believe that social scientific inquiry must try to proceed beyond description towards the development and elaboration of theory and hypotheses, and towards the testing of hypotheses. In the following account of previous research we have therefore tried wherever possible to draw out the predictions and hypotheses that follow from a particular theoretical approach, so that we can then confront these propositions with empirical evidence.

## Theories of bureaucracy and oligarchy

The concepts of bureaucracy and oligarchy have frequently been deployed in analyses of trade union officers, though not always with a clear or consistent meaning (cf. Albrow, 1970, Heery and Fosh, 1990 on bureaucracy; Edelstein and Warner, 1979, chapter 2 on oligarchy). Modern usage derives from Weber who identified several features of an ideal–typical bureaucratic organization: appointment of officials on merit; precise definition of jobs; arrangement of jobs in a hierarchy of authority; regulation of officials' behaviour by rules (Clegg and Dunkerley, 1980). In the field of trade union organization Heery and Fosh (1990, and see below) were able to identify five distinct approaches to the concept of bureaucracy.

For the Webbs, a separate stratum of full-time salaried officers, a bureaucracy, was a necessity for two reasons: first, because of the growth in size and complexity of trade unions and their administration; but second, and more importantly, because of the tendency of rank and file trade unionists to engage in 'short-sighted' and 'irresponsible' actions. The Webbs' *History* is replete with examples of workers who went out on strike until their union was bankrupt; or meetings that voted for more union services but refused to raise subscriptions. For the Webbs workers were their own worst enemies, and they welcomed trade union officers as a means by which unions could make more 'rational' decisions about worker and union interests. By protecting union organization and the union's procedural rights in collective bargaining the officers were preserving the indispensable prerequisite for workers to improve the conditions of their working lives (Webb and Webb, 1920: 1). The preservation of organization was therefore a common interest of both officers and rank and file trade unionists. Nevertheless, the Webbs also recognized the possibility that officers could, and sometimes did, develop an entirely different set of interests and outlooks. The officers' income and working conditions removed them from the worst privations of manual labour, particularly once unions became consolidated and accepted by employers for collective bargaining (cf. also van Tine, 1973, on US union officials of the early twentieth century). The work of the officials brought them frequently into contact with employers and government functionaries, allegedly giving them less time for contact with rank and file members of their unions. It was claimed that their bargaining function, and their good relations with employers, led them increasingly to regard compromise as the essence of negotiations, and to view with impatience the ambitious and militant demands of their members. And their command over power resources, particularly their own expertise, facilitated the periodic imposition of their own views against rank and file dissent. The union officer had to walk a very finely balanced tightrope, taking care not to become too distant from the rank and file, whilst at the same time not being afraid to oppose the members and assert authority over them. Many of the Webbs' ideas were carried over into pluralist analyses of trade union organization and collective bargaining. Clegg (1979) and Flanders (1970) both wrote about the 'institutional needs' of trade unions and readily accepted that these would inevitably give rise to compromises in collective bargaining. Part of the role of the union officer was therefore to secure workers' acceptance of such agreements as being in their own long-term interests.

In all essential respects the Marxist theory of trade union bureaucracy is identical with that of the Webbs, a claim supported by the fact that several Marxist accounts of union bureaucracy have relied almost entirely on their work (e.g. Pearce, 1959; Cliff, 1971; and see also Kelly, 1988, chapter 7). What is distinctive about the Marxist theory of union bureaucracy is its value orientation. The rank and file militancy which struck the Webbs as irresponsible and short-sighted appeared to Marxists as the most exemplary manifestation of class struggle. Because of their position as exploited wage-labourers in the capitalist system of production, workers had a vested interest in combining together, at first to protect and advance their immediate economic interests, but ultimately to overthrow by revolution the system of exploitation and oppression which was the root cause of their problems and grievances. Given this expectation of working-class militancy it was perfectly reasonable for the classical Marxists to seek out an explanation for its absence, and in the figures of the trade union official and the 'labour aristocrat' they believed they had found it. Having satisfied their own ambitions for material privileges, job security, power and status, these leaders of the early trade unions were thought to have made their peace with capitalism, and their primary role was henceforth to secure accommodations and compromises between labour and capital.

Marxists have always differed amongst themselves as to the precise determinants of the behaviour of union officials (Kelly, 1988, chapter 7). Marx, Engels and Lenin emphasized the material privileges of office; Trotsky laid more stress on the incorporation of union leaders into the social networks of employers, State agencies and the middle classes; whilst Gramsci argued that the bargaining function of the union official led to him acting as an intermediary between labour and capital despite his formal employment by, and accountability to, workers. Finally, where the Webbs retained a relatively open mind about the outcome of the many different influences, both radical and conservative, on the behaviour and outlooks of union officials, the classical Marxists had no such doubts, and were convinced of the inexorable conservatism of union leaders.

With the growing involvement of the State in postwar economic growth a number of Marxist and radical analysts turned their attention to the implications of this trend for trade union organization (Heery and Fosh, 1990). According to one line of argument union officers were becoming increasingly involved in a process of 'political exchange' with the State in which they ensured wage restraint in collective bargaining in return for far-reaching procedural and substantive rights for the working class as a whole. These trade-offs eventually gave rise to internal conflict between union officers (particularly at national level) and their rank and file members and thus exacerbated some of the existing internal divisions in unions identified by Marxists and others (Kelly, 1988, chapter 9). For some contemporary Marxists the actions of the full-time officer are less stable and predictable than the classical Marxists supposed, because the officer is thought to play an intermediary role, caught between the conflicting pressures from union members on the one hand and from employers and the State on the other. Under conditions of worker militancy and strong shopfloor organization, union officers can be pressured to act in a more representative capacity and pursue the interests of their members (Bramble 1991, 1992; Callinicos, 1982). This formulation makes the theory somewhat more flexible and also generates an interesting prediction. During periods of labour quiescence, such as the 1980s, the conservatism of the officials will go largely unchecked by rank and file pressure and should therefore be at its most visible. Our own research, conducted in the latter half of the 1980s, would therefore be expected to uncover a pervasive conservatism on the part of union officers.

It is this belief in the conservatism of union officers which links Marxists closely to Michels' theory and to the 'iron law of oligarchy'. For Michels (1915), even those organizations which professed to be democratic were subject to powerful oligarchic tendencies. Leadership in trade unions was required because of the division and specialization of function occasioned by organizational growth, but once in post office-holders showed a pronounced tendency to remain there. They were able to deploy their expertise in union affairs against dissidents; they exploited their monopoly of the union's administrative resources – staff, newspapers, etc. – and finally they satisfied sufficient rank and file demands to induce in them feelings of loyalty and gratitude. For all these reasons rank and file opposition to bureaucratic leadership inevitably fell foul of the greater resources of the democratically elected but now oligarchic leadership. And where democratic measures were thought insufficient by a union leadership then a variety of mechanisms came into operation to preserve them in power: cooptation, patronage, nepotism, bribery, fraud, ballot-rigging (see for instance Benson, 1986, on the history of such practices in American trade unions). As Mills (1948) put it, the leadership's power to act *for* the members was turned into the exercise of power *over them*. Michelsian theory was given a curious twist in the 1980s by the British Conservative government. They fully accepted the view that union leaders exercised considerable power over their members, but far from being a restraining force against rank and file militancy such leaders were seen as the key instigators of militancy (Department of Employment, 1983). The government therefore legislated the introduction of secret ballots in union decision-making and officer elections in order to 'enfranchise' the moderate rank and file and help them to outvote their militant leaders.

### The role and behaviour of union officers

What are the implications of these arguments for the analysis of trade union officers?

(1) *Officers' organizational and bargaining goals:* union officers should espouse more moderate objectives than stewards and lay representatives, because of their distance from the rank and file, their contacts and relations with employers, and their commitment to bargaining procedures.

(2) *Union tactics:* union officers should be reluctant to sanction indus-

trial action, and willing to oppose it when suggested by stewards because of its threat to union organization and orderly bargaining.

(3) *Relations with stewards:* differences in interest and outlook between stewards/lay representatives and union officers should provide officers with a powerful incentive to control the behaviour and organization of stewards in order to shape their aspirations and values in a more 'moderate' direction.

(4) *Relations with management:* management can be used by officers as a valuable resource in bargaining and in the management of conflict with stewards, and officers will therefore develop close and friendly relations with their management counterparts.

(5) *Union officers and their superiors:* whether the union is conceptualized as a bureaucracy or an oligarchy, the local union officer comes under the 'command' of his/her national superior, and should thus function as an instrument of national policy. The common interests of all union officers in organizational preservation and stability should also ensure their compliance with national directives.

(6) *Variation within and between unions:* variations in the organization and behaviour of union officers could logically be explained by variations in the degrees of bureaucracy and oligarchy within and between unions. The behaviour patterns described in (1)–(5) above would all be reduced if, for instance, there was less social distance between officers and rank and file, if the material privileges of the job were curtailed, or if there were strong oppositional or factional currents within a union. On the other hand, Michels' pessimism about such devices (elections lead to oligarchy) suggests there should be little variation between or within unions.

### Critical evaluation

It is not difficult to find selected evidence from particular unions, industries or historical periods to support the predictions just outlined. The history of Britain's largest union, the T&GWU, contains examples from the 1930s until the 1950s of a national officer corps that was hostile to strikes and to the shop stewards that often organized them, avowedly moderate in their wage demands, and willing to work closely with managements in industry (Allen, 1957; Fuller, 1985, chapter 18; Lane, 1974, chapter 7). Similar examples can be found from a wide range of unions in more recent years (e.g. Undy et al., 1981). If we turn to the Michelsian arguments about oligarchy, it is a well established fact that very few prominent union leaders ever suffer electoral defeat, although it does happen (Allen, 1954, 1957; Chaison and Rose, 1977; Edelstein and

Warner, 1979; Maksymiw *et al.*, 1990; Mills, 1948: 64; Roberts, 1956; Undy and Martin, 1984). But the basic claim that bureaucratic union leaders tend to be 'moderate' and 'conservative' in their goals and tactics as compared to the more militant members seems implausible as a general thesis, whatever its validity in particular cases. There are simply too many instances and evidence of leadership militancy and radicalism and membership conservatism for these cases to be explained away as the exceptions which prove the rule (see for examples Edwards and Heery, 1989, chapter 6; Heery and Fosh, 1990; Kelly, 1988, chapter 7). The alleged correlation between the material privileges of a group of workers and their political outlook is equally unconvincing as a general thesis, given the history of industrial and political militancy amongst skilled manual workers (cf. Hinton, 1973, on the first shop stewards' movement). The idea that militancy is contrary to the interests of officers in preserving the union machine and orderly collective bargaining does have a ring of truth, and is consistent with the Webbs' account of the evolution of trade union administration in Britain. But the problem once more is that a proposition which may be valid in certain cases and under specific circumstances is elevated into a universal truth. For, as we shall show later, it is just as plausible to argue that officers have a positive interest in militancy because (a) it may increase union membership and therefore revenue, thus augmenting the funds which pay their salaries, and (b) because quite a number of officers have their salaries linked to those of the members, thus giving them a direct interest in boosting their members' wages and salaries.

It is rather more problematic to test the claim that officers are highly motivated to control shop stewards because of their incipient threat to the officers' own status, authority and interests. For it seems likely that officers may want to control shop stewards for a variety of reasons: they may be anxious to suppress sectionalism; to encourage office-holding by women and ethnic minorities in the face of white male disinterest and opposition; or to preserve the members' 'willingness to act' for a general pay claim, rather than let them exhaust their militancy in guerrilla skirmishes over local issues. Batstone *et al.*'s (1977, 1978) case study of strong workplace organization contains numerous examples where the quasi-elite of leader stewards and convenors suppressed the actions and initiatives of populist stewards. They did so to preserve the plant-wide organization that had been instrumental in securing higher earnings for those groups who accepted collective decisions and discipline as compared to the 'populists' and 'cowboys' who were often spoiling for a fight over purely local matters.

On a more fundamental point, it is not clear from the small amount of previous research that unions actually are organized bureaucratically. These studies suggested that selection on merit was comparatively rare; job descriptions were vague; training was practically non-existent; and field officers enjoyed a considerable amount of discretion in the conduct of their work (Boraston *et al.*, 1975; Clegg *et al.*, 1961; Roberts, 1956). In similar vein there is considerable evidence of factional activity inside trade unions sufficient to change or block the policies of current leaders, even if the leaders themselves cling to office (Hemingway, 1978; Undy *et al.*, 1981; Undy and Martin, 1984). As Gouldner (1955) once said, if there is an 'iron law of oligarchy', there also appears to be a counteracting 'iron law of democracy'. Factions provide one means by which oligarchic and bureaucratic tendencies can be held in check, and elections provide another, notwithstanding the pessimism of Michels (cf. Edelstein and Warner, 1979). Strong workplace organization and membership complaints are other mechanisms by which activists and rank and file union members may be able to hold their officers to account.

We can also question the view that strong workplace organization necessarily threatens the status, authority and interests of full-time officers. Again, this may be true in certain cases, but we can also conceive of several grounds on which union officers would want to *encourage* strong workplace organization: a strong steward body is likely to have an accurate view of members' aspirations and this will facilitate more effective negotiations by the officer; a strong steward body may even conduct its own bargaining and relieve the overburdened officer of some work; and supportive stewards may be an invaluable resource for an officer within the union's administrative and political system, particularly where officers are elected.

Our preliminary assessment of the theories of bureaucracy and oligarchy is thus that their predictions are unlikely to hold up across a range of unions, officers and situations, although this does not preclude them being valid in particular cases.

### The theory of polyarchy

Theories of trade unions as polyarchies have been advanced by Banks (1974), Crouch (1982) and James (1984) and the basic proposition of the theory is that unions consist not just of 'leaders and led', but of a variety of interest groups whose goals are sometimes shared, sometimes in conflict. Union organization is therefore to be understood as a political system in which different groups contend for power and influence, either as an end in itself, or because it enables them to pursue their particular group's objectives. In Banks' (1974) view the primary locus of competition is between officers and lay activists who both contend for the support of a largely apathetic membership. Crouch (1982) offered a more refined analysis based on two types of union goal – money goals and participation goals – pursued at two different levels, national and local, by three sets of actors – national union officers, shop stewards and members. With this framework it then becomes possible to analyze systematically the shifting alliances between different groups within a union, and to identify the many potential sources of internal conflict.

James' case study of the Manchester District Committee of the AUEW was based on the premise that different groups in the union compete 'to have legitimate control over individual decisions or whole areas of decision-making' (James, 1984: 19). This notion is similar to Hemingway's (1978) view of union democracy as conflict between different groups over substantive and procedural issues. Finally, and most recent, is the argument that unions are internally divided on lines of gender. The priorities of union officers are said to reflect the interests of male workers in the labour market, despite the fact that a significant proportion and sometimes a majority of their members are female. Male domination of union officialdom is reinforced by ideological views in which men are regarded as breadwinners and the male wage is seen as a 'family wage' (Heery and Fosh, 1990: 12–14; Rees, 1990).

### The role and behaviour of union officers

Since the theorists of polyarchy disagree over the issues and interests which bring intra-union groups into conflict, it is not that easy to specify any straightforward predictions or expectations about officer organization and behaviour. Nonetheless we shall try to do this where possible, and otherwise indicate where it is not.

(1) *Officers' organizational and bargaining goals:* union officers are likely to assign a higher priority to procedural than to substantive goals (Crouch, 1982). Whilst the procedural bias of officers is clearly argued by Crouch, it is not a proposition unique to the theory of polyarchy, since theorists of bureaucracy have advanced the same claim.

(2) *Relations with stewards:* union officers will be particularly anxious to maintain and extend their own involvement in collective bargaining, particularly as this constitutes the core component of their job. Local officers will therefore tend to oppose shifts in bargaining level which exclude them to the benefit of other union actors, whether national/regional officers above them or lay activists below them.

(3) *Union officers and their superiors:* it follows from point (2) that there is likely to be competition and hence conflict between different levels of union officer. And this suggests that local union officers may not function as the simple instruments of union policy portrayed in theories of bureaucracy. Implicit in the idea of the union as a polyarchy is the idea of coalitions between different interest groups within the union. Local officers, for instance, may collude with lay representatives to thwart or dilute a union's national initiative.

(4) *Relationships with management:* officers will endeavour to develop strong bargaining relationships with management in order to maintain their involvement in collective bargaining.

(5) *Variation within and between unions:* James (1984) suggested that variation between unions could be accounted for by structural differences in power and decision-making which facilitate or inhibit the existence and effectiveness of interest groups, whether occupational, regional or gender-based

### Critical evaluation

The theory of polyarchy has two principal strengths, namely its specification of the different interests and priorities of groups within a trade union (e.g. substantive and procedural), and its claim that intra-union cooperation and conflict can be generated by a variety of cleavages, and not just that of the bureaucracy/rank and file. These features render the theory very useful as a counterweight to the proponents of bureaucracy and oligarchy.

But the theory does have several deficiencies. James (1984: 19) contended that union interest groups vie for influence and 'legitimate control' over areas of decision-making, and that as a result 'conflict in trade unions is the rule rather than the exception' (1984: 115). He accepted that this account of the internal politics of trade unions may be particularly apposite to the AUEW, because of its complex internal system of checks and balances and its highly developed factionalism, and this suggestion sounds plausible. Indeed a study of the NUM found very little evidence of officer–lay representative conflict over bargaining spheres, with officers being strong enthusiasts of independent workplace bargaining (Edwards and Heery, 1989: 139–42). However, even if it were the case it would merely restrict the applicability of the concept of polyarchy, rather than invalidate it. But what are we then to say about union officers in situations and organizations where there is very little overt conflict or where the bargaining territories and objectives of different groups are stable and well established?

### Structural contingency theory

The final approach we want to consider can be labelled contingency theory, because its core proposition states that the organization and behaviour of union officers will vary as a function of several sets of circumstances and there is no reason to expect uniformity across unions or industries. The key issues for contingency theory are therefore, first: what are the circumstances or conditions on which officer behaviour is contingent? And, secondly: what forms or dimensions of officer behaviour will vary with these contingencies?

Structural contingency theory identifies the structural properties of collective bargaining, trade unions, workforces and workplace organization as the principal contingencies affecting the organization and behaviour of union officers. In Clegg (1976), it was the *structure of collective bargaining* that was used as the main explanatory variable. In contrast to the theories of bureaucracy and oligarchy, Clegg treated the 'interests' of workers and union officers as fairly simple and unproblematic: to improve terms and conditions of employment and to extend the scope of joint regulation. Using properties of collective bargaining such as level, scope, formality and depth, he argued that these attributes largely determined the distribution of power within unions. *Ceteris paribus*, centralized bargaining will concentrate power at the top of a trade union, amongst its national officers, whilst decentralized bargaining entails the devolution of power to the workplace, and presumably to the local trade union officers who service shop stewards (cf. also Batstone and Gourlay, 1986: 99). Other things may not be equal, however, and Clegg noted that union and management policies as well as union involvement in 'corporatism' may also place limits on the scope of workplace bargaining and on the power of shop stewards. The second main theme of Clegg's argument was that the structure of collective bargaining was itself largely, though not wholly, determined by the actions of employers. Employers will make 'strategic choices' about the structure of collective bargaining as well as their approach to industrial relations, which could in turn influence the actions and approaches of union officers. The literature in this area is replete with typologies and classifications, and until recently the best known was probably that of Purcell and Sisson (1983), itself derived from Fox (1974: 297–313). Purcell and Sisson divided managerial approaches to industrial relations into five categories: traditionalists (anti-union); sophisticated paternalists (union avoidance); sophisticated modern – consultors; sophisticated modern – constitutionalists; and standard moderns – opportunists. However by their own admission most organized firms in Britain fell into the last of these categories, so their typology is not especially useful for a study focused almost entirely on the unionized sector of the economy. Attempts to rework the typology into two orthogonal dimensions of individualism and collectivism have proved equally problematic when confronted with the complexities of managerial actions in industrial relations (Marchington and Parker, 1990: 230–9).

Undy *et al.* (1981) amongst others have argued that the *structure of a union* may help explain the role and actions of its full-time officers. Unions vary in the ratio of full-time officers to members, a point documented many years ago in descriptive studies by Roberts (1956), Clegg *et al.* (1961), and McCarthy and Parker (1968). Variations in the numbers of members per officer may explain different officers' roles and priorities. It has also been suggested that the heterogeneity of a union's membership will influence the autonomy and role of the full-time officer. Allen (1957) for instance suggested that a diverse membership would be associated with a high degree of centralization of union power in order to counteract the pressures of intra-union competition. Consequently, in unions such as the T&GWU local officers would be subject to more control from above than in more homogeneous craft unions such as ASLEF. Likewise unions which appoint their officers rather than have them elected by the membership may display a greater degree of central control over officer behaviour, whereas elected officers can mobilize membership support in their constituency as a shield against national control.

Brown and Lawson (1973) and Boraston *et al.* (1975) found a relationship between the spatial distribution of a union's membership and the dominant role of the full-time officer. Where membership was concentrated in large, well organized establishments, the officer role revolved around servicing collective bargaining. But where membership was dispersed or displayed higher rates of turnover, and lower levels of union density, then the officer was more likely to take on the role of organizer, recruiting new members and building up workplace steward committees. This distinction is consistent with some of the data in Boraston *et al.* (1975), who noted for instance that building union officers devoted considerably more time to recruitment and organization than their counterparts in other unions, reflecting the often temporary character of employment in the building industry (cf. also Frenkel and Coolican, 1984, chapter 10). It could also be argued, as noted earlier, that the character of a union's membership may influence both the opportunities available to the union's officers and the demands placed on them. The priorities of white-collar as compared with blue-collar workers, of women compared to men, of part-timers compared to full-timers: these and other attributes of a union's membership may shape the bargaining demands which the union's officers will be asked to process.

Finally, it has been shown that *strong workplace organization*, measured by the numbers, organization, abilities and resources of stewards, will result in fewer demands on full-time officers and facilitate greater independence from the external union (Boraston *et al.*, 1975; Fosh and Cohen, 1990; Willman, 1982: 83). On the other hand such sophisticated steward organization is likely to develop in large, strategic firms whose industrial relations outcomes have widespread repercussions for other groups of workers. Consequently the unions involved in such firms may be anxious that their officials *are* involved in workplace or company bargaining in order to exert union influence on these key collective bargaining rounds (Batstone and Gourlay, 1986: 99).

### The role and behaviour of union officers

Structural contingency theory has generated a wide range of propositions about factors that will influence the numbers, organization, power resources and priorities (organization vs. bargaining) of full-time officers. It has (to date) generated far fewer predictions about the actions of officers in particular settings and about their relations with other industrial relations actors. We can therefore say nothing about officer goals and tactics or relations with management. On relations with stewards, it could be argued that officer control over stewards is most likely to be found in small establishments where there are few workplace union resources, where the membership is inexperienced in trade unionism and lacking in cohesion, and where there is a high ratio of officers to members. Officer relations with their superiors are likely to vary as a function of centralization of power inside the union, which will itself be shaped by the structure of collective bargaining amongst the union's members. Contingency theory has most to say about variations between unions, with differing degrees of steward dependence on officers influenced by the factors set out above.

### Critical evaluation

Structural contingency theory may well prove useful in identifying some of the correlates of organization (such as numbers, officer–member ratios, etc.), but the central problem of the theory has already been alluded to, namely its failure to specify the goals of the industrial relations actors. Without such a specification, the theory merely tells us that some dimensions of officer behaviour, or officer–steward relations, are likely to vary between unions or industries, but that is all. In this form the contingency approach hardly qualifies for the title of a theory, and is best understood as a heuristic device, alerting us to the possibility of variation in officer behaviour and cautioning against universalistic theories that assume a uniform pattern of officer goals across unions.

A second problem is that the 'theory' has nothing to say about the values which officers themselves bring to the roles and which may influence the way they perform their job (Frenkel and Coolican, 1984: 230). Officers' values are likely to prove especially important in situations where they can exercise a high degree of discretion and where the 'requirements' of their role are vague or contradictory.

### Descriptive and analytical studies

We turn now to a number of studies of full-time officers that have espoused no general theoretical approach but which are nonetheless important. First there are purely descriptive studies that have presented information on the numbers of union officers, their workloads, backgrounds and training. The first and most detailed of this type was Clegg *et al.* (1961), but others include Roberts (1956), McCarthy and Parker (1968), Brown and Lawson (1973), Robertson and Sams (1976, 1978), TUC (1989), Fisher and Holland (1990) and IRRR (1992). Similar studies have been carried out for the US (Mills, 1948), Australia (Cupper, 1983; Callus, 1986) and continental Europe (Carew, 1976), and there are also detailed analyses of union officers' salaries (e.g. Applebaum and Blaine, 1975; Sandver, 1978; IDS, 1984). Broadly speaking these studies have demonstrated that most British trade union officers service between 3000 and 6000 union members and that most of their work consists of negotiations and maintaining workplace organization. They work longer hours than most of their members, but are also paid more than their members.

A second set of studies has looked in more detail at the job content of union officers (e.g. IRRR, 1992, 1993). Brown and Lawson (1973) for instance distinguished between an 'organizing role' and a 'negotiating role' on the basis of interview data about the predominant job content of local full-time officers. Jary (1990) tried to adapt Batstone *et al.*'s (1977) leader–populist distinction to the work of full-time officers, by distinguishing between organization-led and membership-led activities. He added a cross-cutting dimension of proactive and reactive to produce a $2 \times 2$ matrix of officer types. As most officers fell into just one of these four cells (reactive and membership-led, labelled fire fighters) it is not clear how useful the typology will prove to be. Other studies have presented evidence on the frequency of officer–steward contact, one of the main components of officers' jobs (e.g. Batstone and Gourlay, 1986;

Frenkel and Coolican, 1984; Millward and Stevens, 1986; Millward *et al.*, 1992) or on similarities and differences in officer and steward attitudes (e.g. Blumler and Ewbank, 1970; Dufty, 1979; Howells and Alexander, 1970; McCarthy and Parker, 1968; Parker, 1974, 1975).

Batstone *et al.*'s (1977, 1978) study of shop stewards however provided by far the most detailed and sophisticated analysis of full-time officers and their relations with shop stewards, although the confinement of the study to a single factory necessarily rendered the officer sample both small (N = 8) and perhaps atypical. The authors showed that there was a high degree of consensus over bargaining goals and tactics between officers and stewards, and that conflict between them was rare. Their relationship was characterized by a high degree of cooperation and interdependence: officers relied on stewards for information and used them as a resource in the achievement of their own, or the union's, objectives. Stewards in turn used officers, either as a source of legitimacy and identification with the wider labour movement (in the case of manual stewards), or as a source of bargaining skills and expertise (in the case of staff stewards). Officers were particularly keen to encourage strong leadership and self-reliance amongst stewards, to ensure that they had a strong bargaining relationship with management, and to stress the importance of retaining close links with their membership. The most significant difference amongst officers emerged in the analysis of their influence over bargaining goals and tactics, where the white-collar officers were found to exercise far more influence over their deferential and weakly-organized stewards than the manual officers did over their more powerful stewards. Many of these themes are ones we shall pursue in the course of our own discussion of findings.

Finally, there are a number of studies which have focused on officer perceptions of their role and of the problems they face in coping with the demands placed on them. The most sophisticated of these is Watson (1988) who used ideas from occupational sociology in her study of 28 union officers (and 25 personnel managers). She confirmed the predominance of negotiating and organizing in the officers' workload and found that entry to the job was often facilitated by a current officer acting as a 'sponsor' or by a union tutor. Once in the post, many officers came to regard excessive closeness to management as the main problem they had to deal with. More personal problems were reported in Miller (1988) in which officers described the stress under which they worked and its personal and family consequences (see also IRRR, 1992, 1993).

## General problems in the study of union organization

The various approaches and studies reviewed in this chapter have been criticized on a number of quite specific counts, but they also share (to varying degrees) a number of common and more general problems.

To begin with, there is a strong structural determinist bias running through much of the literature. Union officers are often portrayed as people who occupy roles in organizational structures which subject them to powerful and almost irresistible general imperatives. Authors who have recognized the variations in officer behaviour, or the discretion embodied in their job, have still sought to account for their observations in terms of structural factors in the officers' environment. What has been absent from many studies is an appreciation of the potential importance of officers' own values in shaping their perceptions and conduct of their job (although there are important exceptions, such as Frenkel and Coolican, 1984). Several factors suggest that officers' values could indeed be important: the absence of detailed job descriptions; the high degree of on-the-job discretion; the absence of formal training; and the decentralized character of much collective bargaining: all these structural factors are conducive to the operation and influence of officers' own values.

Second, much of the literature is ahistorical in one of two senses. Either the role and the social relations of the full-time officer are unaffected by historical trends, and remain the same whatever the historical period, and many theories of union bureaucracy and oligarchy fall into this camp. Alternatively, findings about officer–steward relations are not properly situated in their historical context, so that it is sometimes difficult to see how far any given set of findings are specific to, or transcend, a particular historical period. The main exception to this stricture is probably the contemporary pluralist school (insofar as such a school can still be identified). It can be argued that Flanders and Clegg subscribed to a 'Whiggish' view of history (as indeed did the Webbs) in which industrial relations systems have steadily and progressively evolved towards their modern form, based on collective bargaining between employers and independent trade unions and constituting the highest form of industrial democracy. Some Marxists would use the term 'historical regression', and diagnose the growth of incorporation, but it is clear that they and their pluralistic counterparts have similar processes in mind. What is missing from the literature so far is a view of history as a series, or cycle, of struggles between competing groups in which their relations and objectives change across historical periods.

**Towards an alternative**

Our own approach to the organization and behaviour of union officers has a number of elements. First we stress the importance of officers' own values in shaping the conduct of their work, but this point raises the question of how values and variations in values can be conceptualized. Batstone *et al.* (1977, 1978) distinguished four ideal types of shop stewards from two cross-cutting dimensions: pursuit of union principles (high–low) and relation to members (representative–delegate). In practice their analysis of shop steward action revolved mainly around the distinction between representatives (referred to as leaders) and delegates (known as populists), not least because of the problems of operationally defining 'trade union principles' (on which, see Williman, 1980). A second problem is that whilst there are clearly 'populist' shop stewards we could find no consistently populist union officers. Even those few officers who were consistently the most receptive to shop steward and member influence were also prepared to exercise leadership at key stages in the bargaining process based on their often considerable expertise. The populist category therefore cannot be applied to union officers. Third, union officers may also represent managerial interests, a point explored in the text of Batstone *et al.* (1977) but not incorporated into their typology. Another alternative would be to categorize officers on the basis of their general attitudes to industrial relations or to politics. Dufty (1979) divided his sample of Australian officers according to their views of the employment relationship, whether conflictual, cooperative, or a mixture of the two. As most British trade union officers see conflict as inevitable (albeit for different reasons) this is probably not a useful approach (Watson, 1988: 164–7). Classification based on views of the class structure may well discriminate amongst officers (cf. Frenkel and Coolican, 1984: 210–11), but the links between these abstract conceptions and the day-to-day conduct of industrial relations are likely to be complex. What we have chosen to do is classify officers' values at two levels of abstraction. First we shall use self-reported political position (far-left/left/centre-left/centre-right, etc.). This classification has the advantage of being used by trade union officers themselves and will therefore be meaningful. It also accords with descriptions of unions in the industrial relations literature as 'left' or 'right', differences that presumably will be reflected amongst their full-time officers. In addition we shall use a typology of three officer orientations to organizing and bargaining which (like that of Batstone *et al.*) emerged in the course of our research. Our claim is that these help to make sense of a lot of the data, not that they permit unambiguous classification of all facets of officer behaviour. These orientations are best

Table 2.1. *Officer orientations to union activity*

| Dimension | Managerialist | Regulationist | Leader |
|---|---|---|---|
| Goal ambition | Low | Medium | High |
| Sympathy for managerial goals and arguments | Strong | Variable | Weak |
| Willingness to moderate steward/member goals | Strong | Modest | Weak |
| Willingness to advocate industrial action | Low | Medium | High |

understood as the two ends and the middle of a set of inter-related dimensions, as follows: ambition of bargaining objectives; sympathy for managerial goals and arguments; willingness to moderate steward and member goals; and advocacy of militant tactics (see table 2.1).

The *managerialist* orientation corresponds in many ways to the stereo-type of 'the union bureaucrat'. The bargaining process often involves intra-union conflict as the officer seeks to adjust the 'unrealistic' aspirations of the stewards and members to the constraints and realities of the enterprise. These same factors also render industrial action futile. At the other end of the spectrum is the *leader* orientation, resting on a perception of worker–employer interests as antagonistic. Steward aspirations are endorsed or perhaps criticized for being too modest, and the bargaining process is seen as a power struggle whose outcome reflects the officer's capacity to mobilize the membership for industrial action. Between these two polar opposites we also need to distinguish a third orientation (*regulationist*) in which the bargaining process appears above all as one of joint *regulation*. The hallmark of this orientation is pragmatism, a capacity to respond in different ways to different issues and different groups of members. This is not to suggest that pragmatism is wholly absent from the other orientations, but only that it is less common. There is obviously some similarity between this typology and the threefold classification of unitarism, pluralism and Marxism/radicalism advanced by Fox (1966), but the similarity should not be pushed too far. Within Fox's unitarist category there is no place for trade unions at all, and strictly speaking therefore a unitarist orientation by a trade union officer is a contradiction in terms. Throughout this and the subsequent chapters we shall use this typology to examine variations between union officers, and we have therefore categorized all 27 officers from our observation sample into one of three orientations based on information about their constituent dimensions (further details are available from the authors on request).

Second, we must acknowledge the *historical* character of trade union organization. According to Offe and Wiesenthal (1980) union organization passes through a characteristic series of stages, beginning with struggles for recognition by the employer. Once recognition has been obtained and union organization placed on a reasonably stable footing, union officers increasingly become the guardians of the procedure agreements that guarantee the union's institutional survival. During periods of growth there may be no conflict between the procedural requirements of stable organization and the substantive demands of the membership, but this mutually beneficial state of affairs is eroded by the gradual onset of economic crisis. At this stage the union's officers trade concessions on terms and conditions of employment both with employers and with the state, in order to obtain guarantees of their organization's survival. The interests of the union and its members then begin to diverge, thus giving rise to rank and file revolts expressed in unofficial organization and in local, wildcat stoppages. If sustained and widespread, these revolts eventually generate changes in union policy so that the union must again seek to achieve gains through membership mobilization, rather than relying on the operation of procedures and agreements signed with employers, and on the legal rights guaranteed by the State. Officer–steward relations will therefore vary with the different stages of trade union development. Offe and Wiesenthal's notion of stages in the relations between officers and union members is a valuable corrective to historical accounts of union bureaucracy, but even their account is marred by the same type of motivational assumptions that we found in bureaucracy theory. In other words, all union officers guard procedures, and do so at the expense of the members' substantive interests if necessary.

Third, historical changes in the status of trade unions will be reflected in changing union goals, and the mechanisms linking these two features will include turnover and *generational change* amongst union officers (Jary, 1990; Brown, 1986). For example, the devolution of power in the T&GWU towards shop stewards was initiated by General Secretary, Jack Jones, formerly a steward and later a local officer in the Midlands car industry. Subsequently, district officers in the union came to be appointed largely on the basis of their record as shop stewards. So the district officers currently in post in the union come from the generation of stewards and convenors who were heavily involved in the resurgence of trade union power and militancy during the late 1960s and early 1970s. It is reasonable to suppose that union officers whose formative industrial experiences date from this period would enter full-time union work with a very different set of values from the generation of the inter-war Depression, or the Cold War of the 1940s and 1950s. It may well be the case that the values imported into a union by new officers are subject to erosion from fellow-officers, from superiors, from employers and from their own job experiences. Nevertheless, despite processes of socialization it remains highly plausible to argue that different generations of officers import different values into trade unions, and that these values have a considerable impact on their goals and on their relations with stewards, union members and employers.

Fourth, the relations between officers and stewards also need to be examined in the light of the *business cycle*. During the Depression of the early 1980s and again in the early 1990s we witnessed a downturn in the frequency of strikes, in other words a decline in worker militancy, and it seems reasonable to suppose that the adverse state of product and labour markets coupled with anti-union legislation reduced workers' bargaining aspirations. Under these conditions, an older generation of stewards now turned officers may find themselves wanting to pursue more ambitious goals and to use more militant tactics than their members. Their own values would incline them in these directions, and their actions would be less affected by the product and labour market pressures that influenced their members (cf. Brown and Wadhwani, 1990). Other officers might now find their moderate aspirations more in tune with those of their members.

Fifth, in examining the impact of union organization on the behaviour of full-time officers we have been strongly influenced by the view of polyarchy theory that trade unions are best seen as *coalitions of interest groups*, rather than bureaucracies *per se*. This is because the job of the full-time officer is generally ill-defined and officers may exercise considerable discretion over many parameters of their job, making it difficult for superior officers to exercise close and effective control. In addition officers are likely to be accountable to a number of different constituencies – such as the union's General Secretary, the Executive, regional or area officers and lay committees. These organizational properties mean that the degree to which unions actually do function 'bureaucratically' is a matter for empirical investigation and cannot be determined *a priori*.

Finally, in analysing the relations between officers and other actors – senior trade union officers, shop stewards, union members, and employers – we deploy the concepts of *power and power resources* (see Martin,

1992 for general discussion). Following Batstone *et al.* (1977) we have adopted Lukes' (1974) threefold classification of levels of power. The first level refers to the capacity of one party in conflict with another to persuade or force the other to adopt a course of action other than the one it originally intended. The second level refers to the capacity of a party to control the agenda of interactions such as meetings, and determine which issues are kept on or off the agenda in the face of opposition. The third level refers to the use of ideology, and refers to a situation in which one party is able to secure assent to its objectives by another group because of its successful diffusion of a hegemonic ideology. Subordinate groups thus come to define their interests in terms compatible with or identical to those of the superior group because of their acceptance of a dominant ideology. It follows that a research strategy based on this conceptualization needs to examine the attempts by officers and stewards to control bargaining agendas, and to diffuse ideological messages, as well as looking at the overt goal conflicts traditionally featured in research on power. Ideological messages need not be overt attempts at influence: we assume that ideology is embodied in the systems of argument officers deploy with managers, stewards and their own members. Batstone *et al.* (1977) distinguished systems of argument according to whether or not they embodied trade union principles, such as unity and collectivism and showed that there were striking differences in the types of argument used by leader and populist stewards respectively. As we have already argued, this steward dichotomy is not particularly useful in looking at full-time officers; it then follows that the classification of systems of argument is likely to prove equally unilluminating. In contrast Armstrong *et al.* (1981) proposed that different types of argument reflected different sets of interests in the workplace – those of the employers and the workforce respectively – whilst a third set of arguments reflected a negotiated version of managerial ideology. The distinction between worker and managerial arguments is potentially useful, but in our view it is difficult to disentangle a third set of arguments. The examples given by Armstrong *et al.* were actually cases in which workers opportunistically used managerial arguments to pursue their own interests. Rather than construct a third type of argument it seems more sensible to argue for two sets, based on the interests of employers and workers whilst recognizing that each side may also deploy the arguments of their opponents for tactical gain. In the study of power we have also found it helpful to analyze the resources available to the parties, and originally we had considered the classification of French and Raven (1959). They distinguished the following types of power resource: expertise (expert power), the relationships between power-holders (referent power), the authority vested in an office or role (legitimate power), the control of rewards and punishment (reward and coercive power respectively). Our initial work with full-time officers called into question the likely salience of reward and coercive power, and suggested that legitimate power was too vague an analytical category to prove illuminating. We have therefore developed a classification which distinguishes the following resources available to a trade union in seeking to achieve its ends: (1) the willingness of the membership to act; (2) the agreement and support of management; (3) procedural and other collective agreements reached between the union and the employer; (4) the support of other trade unions and their members; (5) the government, whether through intervention in disputes, legislation, etc.; (6) public opinion; (7) and finally the skills, knowledge and expertise of the officer himself. These resources are not necessarily exclusive, though they may be in particular cases, and are not always available to officers and stewards. Moreover one and the same resource can be deployed by officers for quite different purposes. This conceptualization allows us to analyze differences between officers and between unions, and ultimately to arrive at a more refined and theoretically grounded typology of union officers than has hitherto been advanced in the literature.

*Part 2*

The parameters of union work

# 3    Full-time officer organization

## Introduction

This chapter is concerned with the basic parameters of organization among full-time officers. It deals with officer numbers, ratios of officers to members and trends in officer employment, as well as with patterns of officer bureaucracy, the degrees of hierarchy, specialization and dispersal of officers. The aim is to describe each of these dimensions of officer organization and both to show and to account for variation in officer organization across unions. The intention is also to describe such variation over time and examine how full-time officer organization in British unions has been affected by the sustained period of union retreat and aggregate membership decline since 1979. One might hypothesize, for example, that decline would be accompanied by a shrinkage in the size of the total officer workforce, a reduction in the number of officer grades within unions, and possibly by an increase in specialization, as unions appointed recruitment and other specialists in response to the drop in membership.

In pursuing the theme of why union officers are organized as they are the group of hypotheses, claims and arguments we have labelled 'contingency theory' has greatest relevance. A key argument to be examined is Clegg's (1976: 8–11) contention that forms of union organization are powerfully determined by the structure of collective bargaining and by variations in the level of bargaining in particular. This would suggest that unions which are primarily engaged in industry-level bargaining, like those in the public sector, will have fewer officers, larger numbers of members per officer and more centralized, less spatially dispersed patterns of officer bureaucracy. Other contingencies, however, may also exert an influence. The degree of sophistication of workplace organization, for instance, may help determine officer–member ratios, with unions with a tradition of strong organization at the workplace employing proportionately fewer officers. Recent merger activity may also influence officer organization, either by increasing officer numbers or by producing a more complex officer hierarchy, as separate organizations are bolted together. There are a range of possible influences on officer organization, therefore, and the purpose of the chapter is to isolate and rank these in order of importance.

The other theoretical frameworks introduced in chapter 2, which are primarily models to account for officer behaviour, have less relevance to the material considered below. They are not completely without relevance, however, and clearly patterns of officer organization can have implications for patterns of officer behaviour. Bureaucratic control of stewards and members, for example, may be facilitated by a relatively high ratio of officers to members and attenuated where the officer workforce is relatively small and extensive representative responsibilities have to be delegated to lay activists. It may also be the case that the independence of local officers from central control, suggested by theories of polyarchy, is supported by particular forms of organization. Where officers are dispersed around the country, for example, or where they are responsible for servicing large concentrations of members, then they may acquire greater discretion and be better able to engage in competition with their seniors. The same conditions may also permit officers to interpret their role in accordance with their own values and ideologies. A final aim of the chapter, therefore, is to distinguish the possible consequences of union organization for officer behaviour.

### Officer numbers

The 67 unions upon which data were collected in 1991 employed a total of 2819 officers. This figure excludes a few fairly sizeable unions, such as RMT and NUKFAT, with substantial complements of officers, as well as excluding about 240 small, mainly non-TUC unions, each employing very few, if any, officers. If these are taken into account then it is likely that the total officer workforce in British unions in 1991 was between 2900 and 3000.[1] The majority of these were employed by a small number of very large unions. The five largest unions, for instance, employed 46.5 per cent of officers (T&GWU: 481; GMB: 275; NALGO: 230; AEU: 165; NUPE: 159), while 77.1 per cent (2174 officers) were employed by unions with more than 100,000 members. It follows from this that most unions in Britain employ very few officers and, in fact, 64.2 per cent of those surveyed employed fewer than 20 officers, while 40.3 per cent employed fewer then ten. Among the smaller unions excluded from the survey officer complements in the vast majority of cases will be even more modest, consisting of only a handful of officers, where they exist at all. A study of staff associations in building societies (Swabe and Price, 1984:

200), for example, found that only one of 23 associations examined 'had a full-time general secretary comparable to an outside official'.

These figures indicate both the small size of the officer occupational group and the modest scale of the organizational resources unions commit to servicing approximately 9.8 million members. It is clear that most unions, in employment terms, are equivalent to small businesses. The modesty of the unions' organizational resources is seen most clearly when they are contrasted with those of the other side of industry. Membership of the IPM, for instance, which attracts only a minority of personnel specialists into membership, stood at 46,543 in 1991.

There are a number of reasons for the small size of the officer workforce. Perhaps the most important is the modest scale of union finances (cf. Kessler and Bayliss, 1992: 146–7; Willman et al., 1993: 10–17). The net worth of the entire union movement at the end of 1990 was £636 million (£64.80 per member), gross assets were £778 million and gross income was £562 million (Certification Officer, *Annual Report*, 1991). Total expenditure in the same year was £555 million (98.7 per cent of income), 88 per cent of which was spent on administration, including officer and support staff salaries. Moreover, of the 23 unions with 100,000 members or more, which employed the majority of officers, nine (39 per cent) reported total expenditure in excess of total income in 1990. Given this financial position, it is clear that there is limited scope to expand the officer workforce.

The modesty of union finances, in its turn, has often been linked to the low level of union subscriptions in Britain relative to those in other countries. In Britain average subscriptions are approximately 0.4 per cent of average, full-time male manual earnings compared to 1 per cent in Germany and between 0.6 and 1 per cent in France and Italy (*Labour Research*, June 1988; Visser, 1990: 170; Willman, 1989: 268). This is important because income from members, principally through subscriptions, is the main source of union finance, accounting for 82.4 per cent of total income in 1990. Low subscriptions themselves have typically been explained in terms of the overlapping job territories of many British unions and consequent competition for members. It is notable that *per capita* subscription incomes are well below the average in industries like health, finance and education, where competition for members is intense (Willman, 1989: 268).

A further reason for the small size of the officer workforce is the strength of workplace trade unionism in Britain, which arguably obviates the need for a substantial complement of officers. British unions are voluntary organizations, not simply in the sense that membership is usually voluntary, but in that they depend to a disproportionate degree, especially when compared with unions in other countries, on the actions of volunteers. The 1984 Workplace Industrial Relations Survey estimated that there were some 335,000 shop stewards in British industry, although their numbers almost certainly declined between 1984 and 1990 (Millward *et al*. 1992: 116–17). They fulfil the role of maintaining union organization, representing union members and negotiating with employers, often with infrequent contact with the external union (Millward and Stevens, 1986: 85; Millward *et al*., 1992: 129–30). The conventional explanation for the prominence of the shop steward in Britain, following Clegg (1976: 118), points to the structure of collective bargaining and the rise of workplace negotiations, first in engineering and then in other industries in the postwar period. This is not a sufficient explanation, however, as the spread of workplace bargaining could potentially have been accompanied by a large rise in the number of local officers, as was envisaged by the Donovan Commission (Hyman, 1989b: 152).

A number of additional factors served to prevent this development. First, the decades of steward growth, the 1960s and 1970s, were marked by weakening union finances which probably served to block any major expansion in officer numbers (Willman and Morris, 1988: 3–8, 15–27; Willman *et al*., 1993: 10–17). Second, there is evidence of management preferring to deal with shop stewards, rather than full-time officers, because of their availability, local knowledge and closeness to employees (McCarthy and Parker, 1968). This preference found tangible expression in employer subsidy of workplace trade unionism, through check-off, the provision of office facilities and the granting of time-off allowances for senior lay representatives. The 1984 Workplace Industrial Relations Survey estimated there were 4200 full-time shop stewards in British industry (Millward and Stevens, 1986: 84) and about the same number in 1990 (Millward *et al*., 1992: 113). Third, the State has also offered support for workplace unionism through legislation enshrining the rights of safety representatives and for paid leave for union business and by funding shop steward training. Fourth, there has been abiding suspicion of union officialdom among lay activists in many British unions, particularly those with a craft tradition, which has found expression in attempts to maintain tight control of administrative expenses, and therefore the number of officers, and a determination to maintain shop steward independence (cf. Clegg, 1985: 110; Clinton, 1984: 338; Pelling, 1987: 135). Fifth, in certain unions, the T&GWU being the most prominent, there has been a strong national policy commitment towards the promotion of workplace activism and steward autonomy, these being seen as defining characteristics of union democracy (Hyman, 1983: 41–4; Maksymiw *et al*., 1990: 333–4). In combination, therefore, these factors served to ensure that the multiplication of the unions' needs for representatives, arising from the changes in bargaining structure, would be met primarily by increased reliance on lay activists rather than by a major expansion of the officer workforce. Since the mid-1960s the size of the officer workforce has been remarkably stable: the Donovan Commission also gave an approximate figure of 3000 in 1968 (Coates and Topham, 1988: 82).

As was suggested above, differences in the numbers of officers employed by individual unions were largely due to differences in levels of membership. Across the unions surveyed in 1991, for example, there was a strong correlation between membership level and number of officers ($r = 0.96$, $p < 0.001$). There was also a strong association with union structure, with open, multi-industry and multi-occupational unions tending to employ more officers ($\chi^2 = 59.00$, $p < 0.001$). Union structure is, of course, related to union size, as open unions tend to have larger memberships. There were differences, however, in the numbers of officers employed by unions of equivalent size. UCATT, COHSE and UCW, with memberships of 207,232, 203,311 and 201,200, respectively, had officer workforces of 108, 59 and 13. Differences of this kind are best explored by examining officer–member ratios.

### Officer–member ratios

Table 3.1[2] shows the 1991 membership, number of officers and officer–member ratios for all unions and for individual unions with more than 100,000 members. The first thing to note is that the mean (1:3229) officer–member ratio is low in international terms. In Western Europe ratios of between 1:1000 and 1:2000 are the norm (Carew, 1976: 140–7; cf. Visser, 1990: 170). Table 3.1 also indicates considerable variation in officer–member ratios, with the range stretching from SOGAT '82 (1:1358), at one extreme, to UCW (1:15,476) at the other. These differences lend support to Clegg's dictum that union organization reflects the structure of collective bargaining, in that several of the unions with below average ratios operated primarily in parts of the public sector or privatized corporations with centralized systems of pay determination (AMMA, CPSA, NAS/UWT, NCU, UCW). Moreover, across the entire sample there was a statistically significant relationship ($\chi^2 = 9.38$, $p < 0.05$) between main sector of organization and officer–member ratios, with unions in public services and state enterprises tending to have more members per officer. This relationship was not present in the individual officer data, however, indicating that the structure of bargaining is not the sole influence on officer–member ratios.

A second influence is the sophistication of workplace and branch organization. Several of the unions with below average ratios were

Table 3.1. *Union membership, officers and officer–member ratios, 1991*

| Union | Membership | Officers | Officer–member ratio |
|---|---|---|---|
| T&GWU | 1 223 891 | 481 | 1:2544 |
| GMB | 933 425 | 275 | 1:3394 |
| NALGO | 744 453 | 230[a] | 1:3237 |
| AEU | 702 228 | 165 | 1:4256 |
| MSF | 653 000 | 130 | 1:5023 |
| NUPE | 578 992 | 159 | 1:3641 |
| EETPU | 366 650 | 143 | 1:2564 |
| USDAW | 361 789 | 117 | 1:3092 |
| RCN | 288 924 | 87 | 1:3321 |
| UCATT | 207 232 | 108 | 1:1919 |
| COHSE | 203 311 | 59 | 1:3446 |
| UCW | 201 200 | 13 | 1:15 476 |
| BIFU | 171 101 | 50 | 1:3422 |
| NUT | 169 007 | 45 | 1:3756 |
| SOGAT '82 | 165 635 | 122[b] | 1:1358 |
| NCU | 154 783 | 27 | 1:5732 |
| AMMA | 138 571 | 17[c] | 1:8151 |
| NGA (1982) | 122 834 | 13 | 1:9448 |
| CPSA | 122 677 | 22 | 1:5576 |
| NAS/UWT | 119 816 | 18 | 1:6656 |
| NUCPS | 113 488 | 36 | 1:3152 |
| All unions (n = 67) | 9 103 208 | 2819 | 1:3229 |

*Notes:* [a] NALGO figure taken from 1985/86 head office survey.
[b] SOGAT figure includes full-time branch officers.
[c] AMMA figure derived from Maksymiw *et al.* (1990: 50–1).
*Sources:* Certification Officer, *Annual Report*, 1991; Union Head Office Survey, 1991.

associated with strong workplace organization or reliance on full-time lay officers (AEU, MSF, NCU, NGA, UCW), while among those with high ratios were unions largely operating in industries with weak or recently established workplace organization (NALGO, NUCPS, RCN, UCATT, USDAW). This suggests that a high officer–member ratio may be used to compensate for poor workplace organization. In the cases of USDAW and UCATT, for example, the prevalence of temporary work in the building and retail trades makes it difficult to establish effective work-place trade unionism and renders members highly dependent on their officers (England, 1979: 3; Maksymiw *et al.*, 1990: 358, 384). Further evidence of this connection between officer–member ratios and workplace organization was provided by the officers' questionnaire which revealed a correlation ($r = 0.49$, $p < 0.001$) between number of members serviced and number of full-time convenors in the officer's allocation. The variable pattern in officer–member ratios both within and across unions, there-fore, appeared to be determined by a combination of two institutional contingencies, the structure of collective bargaining and the sophisti-cation of workplace and branch organization.

### Changes in officer numbers

Our research was carried out in the context of the longest continual decline in union membership since records began in 1892 (Metcalf, 1991: 19). Table 3.2 shows that unions have responded to this trend through the rationalization of officer workforces. It shows the absolute and percent-age changes in membership and officers between 1980 and 1991 and 1985 and 1991 for individual unions with more than 100,000 members and for all unions which provided data. It indicates, firstly, that several large unions, including T&GWU, GMB, AEU, NUPE, UCATT, USDAW, MSF and COHSE, responded to a decline in membership by making significant cuts in their officer workforces and that overall officer employ-ment dropped by 10.9 per cent between 1980 and 1991 and by 7.1 per cent between 1985 and 1991. Analysis revealed strong associations between the measures of absolute change in members and officers ($r = 0.93$, $p < 0.001$; $r = 0.60$, $p < 0.001$) and a more modest association between the measures of percentage change for the period 1980–91 ($r = 0.37$, $p < 0.05$). For a later period, 1985–91, the percentage measures were even more weakly correlated, and at a statistically non-significant level ($r = 0.18$, $p = 0.1$).

However, table 3.2 also indicates that the decline in officer employment was not proportionate to the decline in membership, at least for the period 1980–91, and that cutting employment was not universal, even among unions, like CPSA, NUCPS and NUT, which lost substantial numbers of members. Indeed, whereas 73.7 per cent of unions surveyed had experienced membership decline between 1980 and 1991 only 57.9 per cent had cut officer numbers, while the equivalent figures for the period between 1985 and 1991 were 68.6 per cent and 62.7 per cent.

There are a number of possible reasons why the decline in officers was not as steep as or as universal as might have been expected. One is that the experience of membership decline was not shared by all unions and those like BIFU, EETPU, NCU or RCN, which bucked the national trend for all or part of the period from 1980 to 1991 were in a position to maintain or expand their officer workforces. Second, successful reform of union finances may, in some cases, have served to cushion the jobs of officers from the effects of membership decline (cf. Willman and Morris, 1988: 96).

Table 3.2. *Absolute and percentage change in union members and full-time officers, 1980–91, 1985–91*

| Union | Membership | | Officers | |
|---|---|---|---|---|
| | Absolute change | Percentage change | Absolute change | Percentage change |
| *1980–91* | | | | |
| CPSA | − 93 738 | − 43.3 | 4 | 22.2 |
| TGWU | − 663 080 | − 35.1 | − 169 | − 26.0 |
| UCATT | − 104 768 | − 35.1 | − 42 | − 28.0 |
| NUT | − 63 390 | − 27.3 | 12 | 36.4 |
| NUCPS | − 40 977 | − 26.5 | 1 | 2.9 |
| USDAW | − 88 498 | − 19.7 | − 6 | − 4.9 |
| NUPE | − 120 164 | − 17.2 | − 6 | − 3.6 |
| GMB | − 139 580 | − 13.0 | − 52 | − 15.9 |
| NAS/UWT | − 4 466 | − 3.6 | 4 | 28.6 |
| UCW | − 1 093 | − 0.5 | 0 | 0.0 |
| NGA (1982) | 6 396 | 5.5 | − 7 | − 35.0 |
| NCU | 23 807 | 18.2 | 5 | 22.7 |
| RCN | 107 813 | 59.5 | 62 | 248.0 |
| All unions (n = 38) | − 1 255 666 | − 19.2 | − 205 | − 10.9 |
| *1985–91* | | | | |
| AEU | − 272 676 | − 28.0 | − 61 | − 27.0 |
| SOGAT '82 | − 40 281 | − 19.6 | 6 | 5.2 |
| NUT | − 38 644 | − 18.6 | 25 | 125.0 |
| UCATT | − 41 461 | − 16.7 | − 17 | − 13.6 |
| CPSA | − 23 860 | − 16.3 | 5 | 29.4 |
| TGWU | − 210 114 | − 14.7 | − 43 | − 8.2 |
| NUPE | − 84 784 | − 12.8 | − 21 | − 11.7 |
| NAS/UWT | − 8 796 | − 6.8 | − 5 | − 21.7 |
| USDAW | − 23 666 | − 6.1 | − 14 | − 10.7 |
| COHSE | − 9 669 | − 4.5 | − 7 | − 10.6 |
| NCU | − 6 532 | − 4.0 | − 1 | − 3.6 |
| NUCPS | − 4 578 | − 3.9 | 1 | 2.9 |
| NGA (1982) | − 3 240 | − 2.6 | − 11 | − 45.8 |
| GMB | − 12 400 | − 1.3 | − 62 | − 18.4 |
| NALGO | − 7 678 | − 1.0 | 0 | 0.0 |
| MSF | 7 041 | 1.1 | − 57 | − 30.5 |
| UCW | 6 956 | 3.6 | 0 | 0.0 |
| EETPU | 19 015 | 5.5 | 19 | 15.3 |
| BIFU | 13 633 | 8.7 | 0 | 0.0 |
| RCN | 43 924 | 17.9 | 37 | 74.0 |
| All unions (n = 51) | − 748 933 | − 8.1 | − 205 | − 7.1 |

*Note:* Figures given take into account union mergers and transfers of engagements.
*Sources:* Certification Officer, *Annual Report*, 1991; Union Head Office Surveys, 1986, 1991.

Third, in many smaller unions, where the percentage decline in membership was typically more severe, there may not have been scope for cutting already modest officer workforces if unions were to continue functioning effectively. Expressed differently, officer salaries represent fixed costs for many unions. Fourth, the employment practices of unions may have inhibited sharp reduction in officer numbers. Unions typically offer their officers a high degree of job security and reduction of numbers usually occurs through natural wastage, though *in extremis* early retirement and voluntary redundancy may also be used (see chapter 4 below; cf. Clegg, 1985: 350). Fifth, membership decline may itself have generated increased demand for officers, in that certain unions have been forced to adopt major recruitment initiatives which are heavily dependent on officer contributions (Kelly and Heery, 1989: 199), and the decline of large workplaces and traditional industries, the sites of shop steward strength, has meant that workplace trade unionism has become more reliant on officer support (Millward *et al.* 1992: 122). Finally, developments independent of membership decline have also generated demand for officers. The decentralization of collective bargaining, for instance, has increased the amount of bargaining required, particularly for public sector unions, while the increasing 'feminization' of unions has led to a demand for specialist representatives, not only to recruit but also to service women trade unionists (IRRR, 1992: 7). Analysis indicated that decline in officers was less steep in unions which had increased their proportions of female members ($r = 0.36$, $p < 0.05$) and women officers ($r = 0.36$, $p < 0.05$) between 1980 and 1991, and that these relationships were quite independent of the trend in total union membership.

The fact that the decline in officer numbers was not proportionate to the decline in membership in most unions has had two main consequences. On the one hand, it must have contributed to the rise in real expenditure *per capita* in unions in the 1980s, noted by Willman and Morris (1988: 96; Willman *et al.*, 1992: 12; cf. Kessler and Bayliss, 1992: 147). On the other hand, it led to a fairly widespread increase in officer–member ratios. Across the 38 unions for which data are available for the period 1980–91, for instance, the average officer–member ratio increased from 1:4465 to 1:3592, with 71 per cent of unions experiencing an increase. Similarly, for the 51 unions supplying data for the 1985–91 period, the average ratio rose from 1:3598 to 1:3385, and 63 per cent of unions recorded a rise. The period of membership decline, therefore, was marked by an improvement in the organizational resources of unions.

### Officer organization

*Dispersal*

A majority of unions surveyed (79.3 per cent, n = 58) reported that some of their officers worked from premises other than national headquarters. Dispersal of officers is, therefore, a significant feature of officer organization in many British unions, with approximately three-quarters of the total officer workforce operating from local offices in 1991.[3] These are the district officers, district secretaries, regional organizers and divisional officers who are the main focus of this study.

Most large unions disperse the majority of their officers to facilitate contact with members and local employers. This is not true of all unions, however, and the survey found that 20.7 per cent of unions concentrated all officers at headquarters, while a further 19 per cent dispersed less than half. The extent to which officers were dispersed was related to union size, whether measured by number of members (r = 0.38, p < 0.01) or number of officers (r = 0.40, p < 0.01). There was also a relationship with officer–member ratios, in that unions with high levels of dispersion tended to have fewer members per officer (r = 0.25, p < 0.05). These associations suggest that dispersion is a functional response to the need to service a large and varied membership (e.g. GMB, MSF, T&GWU), with the need to provide support for dependent workplace organization also having a role in some cases (e.g. RCN, UCATT, USDAW).

The structure of collective bargaining can also be influential, as the three unions with the least dispersed workforces (AMMA, NCU, UCW) all operated in industries with centralized systems of pay determination. Across the sample as a whole, however, there was no association between main sector of organization and the proportion of local officers. One might have expected public sector unions, engaged in national bargaining, to have more concentrated officer workforces, but although this was the case in 1985 it was no longer true in 1991, suggesting that the movement to more local bargaining in the public sector and in privatized industries has stimulated dispersal of officers. Examples of hitherto relatively centralized public sector unions which have established new local offices or expanded local services in recent years include IPMS, NUT and RMT. This trend has typically been driven by employer initiatives to delegate industrial relations responsibilities to regional and divisional managers.

*Hierarchy*

Full-time officers are also differentiated hierarchically. Table 3.3 shows the number of officer grades in unions with 100,000 members or more,

Table 3.3 *Numbers of officer grades, 1991*

| Union | No. of grades | Union | No. of grades |
|-------|---------------|-------|---------------|
| AEU | 12 | NUT | 6 |
| TGWU | 11 | UCATT | 6 |
| NUCPS | 8 | BIFU | 5 |
| COHSE | 7 | CPSA | 5 |
| NUPE | 7 | NAS/UWT | 5 |
| RCN | 7 | USDAW | 5 |
| EETPU | 6 | AMMA | 4 |
| GMB | 6 | NCU | 4 |
| MSF | 6 | SOGAT '82 | 4 |
| | | UCW | 3 |
| All unions (n = 64) | | | |
| mean | 4.5 | | |
| minimum | 1.0 | | |
| maximum | 12.0 | | |

*Source:* Union Head Office Survey, 1991.

together with figures for all unions. It indicates, firstly, that unions tend to have relatively tall organizational structures considering the number of officers they employ. According to Child (1984: 59), for example, six levels is the norm for organizations with 1000 employees or more, while four is typical below that figure. Among the sample of unions, however, none employed anything approaching 1000 officers, but 25 per cent had six or more organizational levels. While longitudinal data are lacking, this would suggest that the recent fashion for developing flatter organizational structures has yet to spread to trade unions. One reason for this could be the fact that union structures are commonly inscribed in rule books and therefore can be altered only through democratic, as opposed to managerial, decisions (Steele, 1990: 57). This, in turn, could provide the opportunity to delay or block rationalization by those opposed to change.

Table 3.3 also indicates that there is considerable variation in the degree of officer hierarchy across unions. At one extreme there are unions with a single officer grade (APCT, NUDAGO) and at the other are the baroque structures of the AEU and T&GWU. These differences are primarily due to size. All but four of the large unions listed in table 3.3, for example, had more than the average number of grades, while analysis demonstrated strong positive associations between the number of grades and union membership (r = 0.63, p < 0.001), number of officers (r = 0.61, p < 0.001) and number of local officers (r = 0.63, p < 0.001). This indicates that larger and spatially differentiated unions are more likely to appoint managers and coordinators.

Other possible causes of variation, such as main sector of organization (used as a proxy for bargaining structure) and union structure, failed to show statistically significant levels of association across the sample, though they may influence patterns of hierarchy in individual unions. The four large unions listed in table 3.3 with flatter than average structures, for instance, (AMMA, NCU, SOGAT '82 and UCW) all operated in industries with traditionally centralized patterns of pay determination, while the complexity of the T&GWU's hierarchy was due to its open structure and combination of regional and trade group patterns of organization.

A second way in which officer hierarchies can be differentiated is in terms of the ratio of 'front-line' to senior officers, whether based at national or regional headquarters, a useful measure of the flatness of officer organization.[4] Across the sample there was considerable variation in the shape of the officer hierarchy, with some unions, such as NAS/UWT, NCU and NUCPS, having an inverted pyramid, with the majority of officers in senior positions, and others, like EETPU, MSF and T&GWU, having a more conventional organizational structure, with the hierarchy resting on a broad base of front-line officers. What was striking, though, was the top-heaviness of the majority of unions and the high ratio of senior to front-line officers. The ratio across all unions was 1:2.3, and 61.9 per cent had half or more of their officers in senior positions.

Unlike the number of officer grades, the ratio of senior to front-line officers was not related to union size. However, statistically significant relationships were found with the dispersal of officers ($r = 0.48$, $p = 0.01$), with method of officer selection ($r = 0.30$, $p < 0.05$) and recent merger activity ($\chi^2 = 12.04$, $p < 0.01$). Unions with flatter structures tended to have a high proportion of local officers, to rely on election and not to have engaged in merger activity. The latter two associations are particularly instructive. They suggest that the election of officers may act as a brake on bureaucratic growth at the centre, possibly because it endows front-line officers with more authority, while merger appears to have the opposite effect and promotes the duplication of officer functions at a senior level. A possible dysfunctional consequence of union mergers, therefore, may be an over-concentration of officer resources in senior positions (cf. Undy *et al.*, 1981: 185, 218; Willman *et al.*, 1993: 96–100). This could well reduce the economies of scale, which are usually given as the principal advantage of union mergers (cf. Coates and Topham, 1988: 62–3).

### Specialization

Although the main focus of our research was on the generalist at the base of the officer hierarchy, the local full-time officer, information was also

Table 3.4. *Specialist functions, specialist officers and specialist–bargainer ratios, 1991*

| Union | No. of specialisms | No. of specialists | Specialization ratio[a] |
|---|---|---|---|
| COHSE | 14 | 21 | 0.356 |
| NCU | 13 | n/a | n/a |
| NUCPS | 13 | n/a | n/a |
| EETPU | 12 | n/a | n/a |
| GMB | 12 | n/a | n/a |
| USDAW | 12 | 12 | 0.103 |
| NAS/UWT | 10 | 11 | 0.611 |
| NUPE | 10 | 30 | 0.189 |
| NUT | 10 | 49 | 1.089 |
| RCN | 9 | 80 | 0.919 |
| TGWU | 9 | n/a | n/a |
| AEU | 8 | n/a | n/a |
| BIFU | 8 | n/a | n/a |
| NGA (1982) | 8 | n/a | n/a |
| SOGAT '82 | 8 | 8 | 0.066 |
| CPSA | 6 | 8 | 0.364 |
| UCATT | 6 | 10 | 0.093 |
| MSF | 5 | 20 | 0.154 |
| UCW | 4 | 4 | 0.103 |
| *All unions* | | | |
| mean | 7.1 | 13.8 | 0.710 |
| median | 7.0 | 8.5 | 0.392 |
| minimum | 0 | 0 | 0 |
| maximum | 14 | 80 | 2.667 |
| | N = 52 | N = 38 | N = 38 |

*Note:* [a]The specialization ratio was computed by dividing the total number of specialists by the total number of bargainers.
*Source:* Union Head Office Survey, 1991.

collected on the various specialist officers whose work serves to supplement and support that of negotiators and organizers. Table 3.4 shows the number of specialist functions, the number of specialist officers and the ratio of specialists to bargainers in large unions, together with descriptive statistics for the sample as a whole. It indicates that a degree of specialization is the norm in British unions, with only one union reporting that it had no specialist officers whatsoever, and a mean of 7.1 specialist functions across the 52 unions which provided data. The most widely used specialists (see table 3.5) were research officers, journalists, finance officers, office managers and education officers, in that order. In many cases, however, the size of the specialist function was decidedly modest, with many unions, including relatively large ones like USDAW, SOGAT '82 and UCW, employing only one officer per function. This underlines the point made earlier about the limited scale of the human resources available to British unions (cf. *Labour Research*, June 1988). Although in-house specialists may be supplemented by those employed by the TUC and by academics and consultants, the findings support Lane's (1986) contention that the modesty of specialist resources within British unions limits their capacity to train their members and representatives and imposes a constraint on the development and implementation of policy.

The degree of specialization, measured by the number of specialist functions per union, like the degree of dispersal and the degree of hierarchy, was positively correlated with union size, measured either by membership ($r = 0.34$, $p < 0.01$) or by number of bargainers ($r = 0.32$, $p < 0.05$). The total number of specialists was positively associated with the same variables ($r = 0.39$, $p < 0.01$; $r = 0.36$, $p < 0.05$). Larger unions, therefore, were better able to resource a greater number of specialist functions and support a larger complement of specialists. The third measure of specialization, the ratio of specialists to bargainers, however, was inversely related to the same two measures of union size ($r = -0.26$, $p = 0.06$; $r = -0.34$, $p < 0.05$).

This third measure, essentially an indicator of the proportion of resources unions commit to specialist services, was positively associated with union structure ($\chi^2 = 23.70$, $p < 0.01$), main sector of organization ($\chi^2 = 14.70$, $p < 0.01$) and TUC affiliation ($\chi^2 = 8.67$, $p < 0.05$). That is, a higher proportion of resources were committed to specialist services in relatively closed, public sector unions, involved in centralized collective bargaining, and in unions which were not members of the TUC. The last of these associations suggests that non-TUC unions may have to commit a larger proportion of resources to specialist functions because they are denied the services and economies of scale made available by the TUC's education, organization, economic and other departments. The other two associations, by contrast, suggest that participation in centralized bargaining and a relatively closed structure may release funds for the employment of specialists, essentially because fewer bargainers are required and negotiation can be handled more cost-effectively. The additional specialists which can be employed in such unions can be used either in lobbying or campaigning, important activities for all public sector unions, or to provide services to members, in the way that a very full legal service is provided by the teaching unions.

This pattern of associations has implications for the analysis of union mergers. It has been argued, for instance, that the greater ability of large unions to offer a range of specialist services is a significant stimulus to merger activity (cf. Hyman, 1983: 38; Undy *et al.*, 1981: 214–15). Smaller unions, less able to maintain a range of specialist officers, it is assumed, will be less able to compete on the basis of service to members and therefore will come under pressure to seek defensive mergers with larger unions. However, the inverse relationship between size and the specialization ratio and the associations with union structure and sector suggest that smaller unions may well be able to provide specialist services to their members, provided they have a relatively homogeneous membership or are engaged in centralized bargaining. Such unions may be able to economize in the areas of basic representation and bargaining in a way that enables them to offset the diseconomies of smaller scale.

Comparison of the 1991 data on specialization with that collected for 1985 and 1980 indicates that there has been a trend towards greater specialization of officer resources in British unions over the past decade. Among the 35 unions which provided information for all three years, for instance, the mean number of specialist functions increased from 5.4 in 1980, to 5.8 in 1985, to 6.6 in 1991. The equivalent figures for the 26 unions which provided information on numbers of specialist officers were 9.7, 10.9 and 13.3. Finally, the specialization ratio also showed an increase, though in this case only 19 unions provided data for all three years and the increase was apparent only in the period from 1985. The figures were 0.56 for 1980 and 1985 and 0.60 for 1991. Further information on this trend is contained in table 3.5, which shows the proportion of unions with different categories of specialists for each of the three years. This indicates a general trend towards greater use of specialists, which has affected virtually every category listed. Particularly marked increases, however, are registered in five areas: computing, public relations, health and safety, recruitment and equality.

There are a number of possible explanations for this trend towards specialization. First, where there has been an increase in the specialization ratio, this may reflect the fact that it is easier to make economies by reducing the negotiating workforce than it is to do away with specialists, essentially because there are fewer of the latter. Second, however, there is evidence that in some unions increased reliance on specialists is a deliberate alternative to investment in the negotiating workforce. An increase in the number of specialist functions over the 1980s, for instance, was inversely related to the percentage of bargaining officers sent on training courses ($r = -0.34$, $p < 0.05$). Third, the declining trend in union membership has encouraged specialization. A percentage decline in membership since 1985, for example, was associated with an increase in the specialization ratio, though not at a high level of statistical significance ($r = 0.36$, $p = 0.07$). The introduction or strengthening of several of the

Table 3.5. *Types of specialist officer, 1980, 1985 and 1991*

| Specialism | 1980 | | 1985 | | 1991 | |
|---|---|---|---|---|---|---|
| | | | Unions | | | |
| | No. | Per cent | No. | Per cent | No. | Per cent |
| Journalism | 27 | 71.1 | 30 | 69.8 | 42 | 75.0 |
| Research | 25 | 67.6 | 29 | 67.4 | 42 | 75.0 |
| Finance | 24 | 63.2 | 27 | 62.8 | 42 | 73.7 |
| Office management | 26 | 68.4 | 28 | 65.1 | 40 | 71.4 |
| Education | 20 | 52.6 | 24 | 57.1 | 36 | 65.5 |
| Health and safety | 13 | 35.1 | 15 | 35.7 | 30 | 55.6 |
| Legal | 20 | 52.6 | 21 | 48.8 | 29 | 53.7 |
| Recruitment | 11 | 29.7 | 12 | 28.6 | 28 | 52.8 |
| Equality | 7 | 18.9 | 12 | 28.6 | 27 | 50.9 |
| Computing | 8 | 21.6 | 13 | 30.2 | 26 | 47.3 |
| Public relations | 12 | 31.6 | 15 | 34.9 | 26 | 47.3 |
| Compensation | 10 | 27.0 | 9 | 21.4 | 14 | 26.4 |
| Other | 7 | 18.9 | 9 | 21.4 | 14 | 26.9 |

*Source:* Union Head Office Survey, 1991.

specialist functions listed in table 3.5 could form part of a union response to membership decline, including computer specialists, to maintain better records of membership; finance officers, to ensure the better management of finances in a context of reduced subscription income; and equality, public relations and recruitment specialists, to promote union services to prospective members. Fourth, specialization has arisen as part of the 'feminization' of unions and the greater engagement of union policy with equality issues. The widespread introduction of equality specialists is the clearest indicator of this (cf. SERTUC, 1992), though the increase in specialist health and safety officers may be another. The establishment of a specialist health and safety function, for example, was strongly correlated with a relatively high female union membership ($r = 0.50$, $p < 0.001$) and this may be due to the high priority a number of unions have attached to the promotion of women's health issues in recent years.

Finally, and more speculatively, the trend towards specialization may form part of a broader change in the internal administration of unions and the adoption of a more 'managerial' approach to the conduct of union business (Willman *et al.*, 1993). This can be seen in three areas where there has been considerable innovation across the trade union movement in recent years and where change has stimulated demand for specialist expertise, either provided by specialist officers within unions or by external consultants. The first is union finance, where reform has included increasing the real value of subscriptions, improved management of union investments and the strengthening of internal financial controls (Willman, 1990: 324). These developments are likely to have bolstered the position of the finance function within unions and may also have supported the appointment of computing specialists. The second is policy development and the increasing use by unions of market research and opinion poll techniques to enable services to be matched to members' aspirations. It is in this area that the use of external consultants is most apparent, but work of this kind has also been carried out by internal research departments. The third area is policy implementation, where unions have increasingly made use of high-profile, planned campaigns either to support recruitment activity, communicate and elicit support for policy from activists and members or to influence public opinion. Examples include the T&GWU's Link Up campaign, the GMB's FLARE and 'Winning a Fair Deal for Women' campaigns, USDAW's 'Shopwatch' and 'Reach Out' campaigns and the joint union campaign against water privatization (cf. Ogden, 1991; Upchurch and Donnelly, 1992). Initiatives of this kind have drawn on a range of specialist functions including research, recruitment, public relations and education. In each of these three areas, therefore, a more planned or 'managed' approach to union administration has created a demand for specialist expertise.

### Discussion and conclusions

The patterns of organization described in this chapter have a number of implications for theories of officer behaviour. Perhaps the central finding is the modesty of the human resources, both negotiators and specialists, which unions are able to commit to servicing more than 9 million members. The total officer workforce is less than 3000 strong, and even substantial unions service their members with a relatively small complement of professional representatives. In the light of this it seems that the strong officer control of activists and members posited in theories of union bureaucracy is unlikely. Where individual officers in large unions commonly have an allocation of more than 5000 members, often spread across different establishments, firms and industries, then the material basis for bureaucratic control is likely to be absent, particularly in the context of a fragmenting collective bargaining structure.

However, a caveat should possibly be entered against this judgement. The effect of membership decline since 1979 has been to increase officer–member ratios in the majority of unions. A similar change occurred in the previous period of sustained membership decline between the wars which, according to Wrigley (1987: 120; cf. Clegg, 1985: 350), contributed to a strengthening of officer control over collective bargaining and the union rank and file. Commentators on the present period (cf. Brown and Wadhwani, 1990; Fairbrother and Waddington, 1990) have argued that a similar shift in power, from activists to officers, occurred in many unions in the 1980s and it is conceivable that the increase in officer–member ratios contributed to this. For this to be so, however, increase in officer–member ratios would have to have produced a reduction in officer workload, so that officers became able to intervene more consistently in workplace trade union organization and assume responsibilities previously delegated to shop stewards. In some cases this may have occurred, but in many others a reduction in the number of members serviced will not have meant a reduction in the number of bargaining groups or establishments serviced. In addition, the 1980s imposed many new burdens on full-time officers, not least being a requirement to spend more time on recruitment. For these reasons we would question whether the increase in ratios has facilitated significantly greater officer control, and would stand by our initial diagnosis that the limited scale of officer resources renders British unions peculiarly dependent on activist participation.

A second proposition which can be drawn from the literature on union bureaucracy is that the officer hierarchy itself will be centralized. There is some evidence to support this belief, most notably the large proportion of officers in senior positions and the relatively top-heavy structure of many unions. However, many senior officers are managers only in the loosest sense (see chapter 5) and there are a number of other features of officer organization which are not conducive to tight central control. First, low officer–member ratios in many unions are likely to require considerable delegation of authority. Second, the dispersal of the majority of officers around the country will further encourage delegation and facilitate the acquisition of autonomy by local officers. And third, the complexity of the officer grade structure is likely to have the same effect. Child's (1984: 61–5) assessment of the effects of the kind of tall, thin organizational structures favoured by many unions is that they lead to communication problems, the dilution of central control and confusion as to the relative responsibilities of adjacent levels.

While these findings may not provide strong support for theories of union bureaucracy they are supportive of two of the main alternatives we have identified, the theory of union polyarchy and theories which stress officer values and ideology. The latter rest on the assumption that officers are able to interpret and develop their role as representatives in accordance with their own values. Delegation, dispersal and organizational complexity are likely to provide officers with the opportunity to do this. The former rests on the assumption that unions consist of competing interest groups, often constituted at different organizational levels. Delegation, dispersal and organizational complexity, again, are likely to provide opportunities for the crystallization and expression of such interests.

The evidence provides strongest support, however, for the fourth approach to the analysis of union officers, contingency theory, in that variation in patterns of officer organization were related to a number of institutional and environmental 'contingencies'. The most important of these was union size. Larger unions employed more officers, were more likely to disperse officers, had more hierarchical levels but a smaller proportion of senior officers and employed more specialists in more specialist functions. A second influence was the structure of collective bargaining, in that public sector unions, which have typically been party to industry-wide collective agreements, displayed a number of distinctive features. These included a relatively large number of specialist officers, more members per officer, and reliance on a more top-heavy organizational structure. There was evidence, therefore, to support Clegg's proposition that union organization and behaviour are influenced by the structure of collective bargaining. There was also evidence, moreover, that the distinctive organizational patterns of public sector unions may be eroding as the structure of collective bargaining changes in public sector industries. In 1985, for instance, public sector unions were significantly less likely to disperse their officers than their private sector equivalents, but this difference had disappeared by 1991.

Three other contingencies also had an impact on officer organization. Officer–member ratios were influenced by the degree of sophistication of workplace trade unionism, so that unions with a tradition of strong workplace organization or of full-time branch officers employed a smaller complement of full-time officers. Methods of officer selection were also influential. In electing unions, for example, there were relatively fewer officers in senior, managerial positions, suggesting that election, and the legitimacy it bestows on front-line officers, has endowed them with greater influence and restricted bureaucratic growth at the centre. The final contingency, participation in recent merger activity, appeared to have the reverse effect and to produce a relatively top-heavy union structure. This finding casts doubt on the claim that merger promotes greater efficiency and more cost-effective delivery of union services. Other factors, not listed above, undoubtedly also influence forms of officer organization. The health and structure of union finances, for example, are likely to be potent influences, but paucity of data prevented us from examining their effects. Our analysis is not offered as a complete interpretation of union organization, therefore, but we are nevertheless confident that we have identified some of the principal factors which lead unions to organize their officers the way they do.

The final issue we have sought to address in this chapter is that of change in officer organization through the 1980s and the extent to which decline in aggregate union membership has prompted reform. The main developments in officer organization highlighted by the research were: a reduction in total officer numbers, though not in proportion to the decline in membership; a consequent improvement in officer–member ratios; and an increase in officer specialization. There did not appear to have been a major shift towards the removal of entire tiers from officer structures, though admittedly our evidence was limited on this point. Each of these developments in organization bore some direct relationship to membership decline. So, for example, reduction in officer numbers formed part of a programme of economy, prompted by reduced subscription income; increase in officer–member ratios was partly driven by the expanded need for officers to engage in recruitment; and the growth of at least some specialist functions, such as public relations, recruitment and equality, was prompted by the need to expand and better promote union services to potential members. Not all changes in officer organization, however, were prompted by the need to respond to membership decline. A significant change in a number of public sector unions, such as IPMS and NUT, for example, was the dispersal of officers in response to the decentralization of collective bargaining. Greater specialization and improvement in officer–member ratios were also encouraged by factors other than membership decline. These included the changing composition of union membership, shifts in union values and ideology, so as to endow equality issues with greater weight in policy-making and the adoption by at least some unions of a more 'managerial' model of organization, which has emphasized the role of specialists in the development of organizational strategy. Membership decline has undoubtedly been the primary organizational problem confronting trade unions since the early 1980s, therefore, but it has not been the sole influence on the reform of officer organization.

# 4   Employment relations

The purpose of this chapter is to describe, analyze and account for the employment relationship experienced by full-time officers. Accordingly, it reviews recruitment and selection practices, training and development, career opportunities and rewards and employment termination for officers employed by British unions. It also contains information on the personal characteristics of officers who are recruited through and experience these practices. The primary reason for this examination is that the literature on trade unions is replete with claims that officers acquire and advance their distinctive interests as representatives through their employment relationship. For example, within the Marxist tradition the alleged conservatism of officers and their unresponsiveness to members has been related to several features of their employment relationship: appointment, rather than election to office, relatively generous salaries and benefits, considerably in excess of those of their members, and training and socialization in the norms of 'good industrial relations practice' (see Kelly, 1988: 161–78). Employment relations may also condition officer interests and behaviour indirectly, by facilitating the selection of officers with particular characteristics. The neglect of 'equality bargaining' by British unions, for instance, has been related to the absence of women from officer positions, which in turn has been related to methods of recruitment and the absence of equal opportunities policies within unions (Colling and Dickens, 1989: 29–31). Given arguments of this kind, therefore, it was considered necessary to examine the employment relations and characteristics of officers before turning to an examination of how they actually discharge their role.

### Selection

The view that the employment relation of officers determines their behaviour in the job is encountered most forcefully in the debate over methods of officer selection. Since the Webbs, for example, appointment of officers has been advocated on the grounds that it enables unions to make use of professional expertise and thus raises their effectiveness as bargaining agents, provides scope for the exercise of 'leadership' by officers, who retain their independence from the union rank and file, and also ensures the independence of representatives from management. Election, in contrast, has been primarily advocated as a way of ensuring the accountability of officers to the workers they represent and a means of holding bureaucratic domination of unions in check. The requirement for unions periodically to re-elect through secret ballot all officers with seats on trade union governing bodies, introduced by the Conservative government of the 1980s, for example, was intended to reduce the power of officers and render them more responsive to the broad mass of non-activist union members (Heery and Fosh, 1990: 17).

These claims as to the link between methods of selection and officer behaviour have been criticized in a number of ways. One line of criticism has been to argue that methods of selection do influence officers' approach to the job and their relations with members, but not in the ways commonly suggested. Undy and Martin (1984: 153), for example, have pointed out that officers in the electing AEU were less likely to test collective agreements through a membership ballot than their colleagues in the appointing T&GWU. Election, that is, might endow officers with more power and greater autonomy *vis-à-vis* the membership than appointment. A second line of criticism is based on the argument that methods of selection are not a major determinant of officer behaviour, and that variation in the way officers perform their role is best explained by other factors. Kelly (1988: 168), for instance, has argued against the conventional Marxist claim that appointed officers are conservative on the grounds that opposition to incomes policy in the 1970s was maintained by an assortment of unions with both elected and appointed officers.

In this chapter we want to raise three further points in criticism of the orthodox view. The first is simply that trade union selection procedures are more complex than the bald opposition between election and appointment suggests, and are best seen as a continuum of practice. At one extreme are unions where periodic re-election of officers is required (e.g. AEU, ASLEF, FBU, FTAT, UCW, UCATT); next come unions in which, once elected, officers then hold office for life (e.g. BFAWU, NUM); third come unions where officers are appointed, normally by the union's national executive, but the pool of candidates is restricted to existing members with one or more year's seniority (e.g. COHSE, EETPU, SOGAT, T&GWU, TSSA); and finally come unions whose adherence to representative principles in selection is minimal and who recruit from beyond their own membership (e.g. AUT, BIFU, EMA, IRSF, NCU, NUJ, NUPE, USDAW).[1]

Table 4.1. *Trade union selection procedures*

| Selection Practice | Trade unions | | FTOs[a] | |
|---|---|---|---|---|
| | No. | Percentage | No. | Percentage |
| *Closed* | | | | |
| Periodic re-election | 8 | 11.9 | 333 | 11.8 |
| Single election | 4 | 6.0 | 59 | 2.1 |
| Appointment from | | | | |
| existing members | 11 | 16.4 | 1189 | 42.2 |
| *Open* | | | | |
| Appointment from internal | | | | |
| and external | | | | |
| labour market | 44 | 65.7 | 1238 | 43.9 |
| Totals | 67 | 100.0 | 2819 | 100.0 |

*Note:* [a] The figures for officers include senior officers, such as general secretaries, who may be selected through different procedures.
*Source:* Union Head Office Survey, 1991.

Our second point, however, is that it is possible to classify union selection procedures on alternative criteria. For example, methods of selection can be distinguished in terms of the degree to which recruitment of officers is open or closed. In the former case, unions recruit at least a proportion of their officers in an external occupational labour market, comprising officers and experienced lay activists in other unions, while in the latter constitutional rules restrict the pool of potential candidates to a proportion of the existing union membership. For these latter unions, officers are drawn from the stock of experienced and able lay activists who have secured the sponsorship either of organized factions or existing office-holders.[2] Of course this classification overlaps with the first, in that unions with minimal commitment to representative principles of selection are also the most open, but the overlap is not total and the category of closed unions embraces some which elect and some which appoint their officers. The distribution of practice across the movement is given in table 4.1, which shows the proportions of unions using each of the various methods and the proportions of officers employed by those unions.

Our third point relates to the significance of these different methods of recruitment and, in particular, the distinction between open and closed recruitment. This lies, we feel, not in any direct influence on officer behaviour but in that different methods lead to the selection of officers with different personal characteristics. It is through these differences – in gender, age, education, experience and ideology – that selection procedures exert influence over the interpretation and performance of the officer's role. Before considering officer characteristics and their link with selection procedures, however, we want to examine which methods are used by which unions and why.

The survey indicated that differences in method of officer selection between unions were primarily associated with differences in the occupational status of union members ($\chi^2 = 36.0$, p < 0.001). All of the unions using election, of whatever type, for example, represented manual workers and among those using restricted appointment only NUT, SPOA and TSSA had a predominantly white-collar membership. Open recruitment, in contrast, though it was found in a small number of manual unions, such as GMB, NUPE and USDAW, was a practice associated overwhelmingly with white-collar unionism. More than 90 per cent of non-manual unions used this method.

The principal reasons which are usually given for these differences are the characteristics of the varying occupational groups which unions represent and the circumstances in which different types of union were founded. Election, for instance, has been said to reflect the strong occupational consciousness and egalitarianism of the traditional manual crafts and the fact that craft unionism emerged from the unilateral regulation of labour supply, wages and working practices by groups of skilled manual workers (James, 1984: 20–1). Appointment in the unions of the less skilled, in contrast, has been linked to the relative absence of collective organization among these groups prior to the new unionism of the late nineteenth century and the fact that unions of dockers, labourers, transport workers and others were largely established by external activists, such as Tom Mann or John Burns (Coates and Topham, 1991: 97; Hinton, 1983: 47–50). Appointment of officers in white-collar unions, however, probably reflects the adoption by these organizations of the bureaucratic employment practices experienced by the bulk of their members, together with a concern to guarantee the independence of the union and its officers from employers. Studies of BIFU (Morris, 1986: 136–7) and the FDA (O'Toole, 1989: 115), for instance, have shown that appointment of officers has served as an alternative to reliance on seconded representatives who may be vulnerable to undue managerial pressure.

Once unions have adopted a particular method of officer selection it generally endures, regardless of subsequent changes in union structure, and only a minority of unions have fundamentally revised their selection procedures. The EETPU, for instance, abandoned the election of officers in 1969 and the CPSA introduced election for its senior officers (though not Assistant Secretaries) in 1981. Where changes have been introduced they have typically not reflected shifts in membership composition or characteristics but have been instigated by factions seeking advantage in internal union politics (Undy and Martin, 1984: 107). In the EETPU, for instance, the abandoning of elections formed part of the purge of Communists from the union and the consolidation of right-wing control, while the introduction of elections in the CPSA was promoted by the left. In the main, however, unions appear to be wedded to their traditions and officer selection procedures, where they remain untouched by the regulatory powers of the law, largely reflect the structure and circumstances of unions at their point of foundation.

### Methods of selection and officer characteristics

The research revealed three types of association between union selection procedures and officer characteristics. The first was that the small minority of female officers (302 or 11.8 per cent) were more likely to work for unions practising open recruitment.[3] Female officers were also more likely to work for unions with large female memberships, but the effect of officer selection procedures appeared to operate independently of this additional factor. The proportion of female officers employed, for example, was positively correlated with the openness of officer selection procedures, even when the level of female union membership was controlled for ($r = 0.3392$, $p < 0.05$). Examples of open recruiting unions with relatively low female membership levels but relatively high female employment included AUT, CMA, FDA, NACO, NAPO, NATFHE and NCU, all of which reported at least 20 per cent women officers in 1991. The likely explanation for this association is that open recruitment by unions makes it possible for them to recruit women activists, as well as officers, from other unions, so expanding the pool of female talent on which they can draw. It also enables them to give greater weight in appointments to formal qualifications and prior job experience at the expense of lay activist experience, which women trade unionists may be less able to acquire (Heery and Kelly, 1989). Finally, where officer selection is a 'managerial', rather than a democratic, decision, as is the case in open unions, then it is easier for a union to formulate and apply an equal opportunities policy.

The significance of this association between recruitment practices and the employment of women officers lies in the fact that women may interpret the role differently to their male colleagues. Elsewhere (Heery and Kelly, 1988) we have shown that women officers are more likely to promote the interests of women trade unionists in collective bargaining and more likely to make a priority of recruiting and organizing women workers. Trade union selection procedures may influence officer behaviour indirectly, therefore, by making it either easier or harder for women with such concerns to achieve full-time office.

Table 4.2 illustrates the second link between union selection procedures and officer characteristics: that open and closed unions tend to recruit officers with rather different qualifications and experience. It indicates that open unions were more likely to appoint younger officers and officers with higher educational qualifications and experience of professional and managerial work. Significantly this was as true of NUPE and, to a lesser extent, the GMB, as it was of NALGO and ASTMS, suggesting that this pattern was not solely a reflection of the characteristics (manual vs. non-manual) of union members. Closed unions, with representative selection procedures, in contrast, were more likely to appoint officers at a later stage in their union careers, who had extensive experience of lay activism and who previously worked in manual or technical jobs. The material suggests, therefore, that there were two groups among the officer workforce who brought different qualifications and experiences to the job and who tended to enter through different selection procedures.

The significance of this difference is likely to lie, in the first instance, in the skills and competences of the two groups. It can be hypothesized that the strength of the older group will lie in extensive experience of negotiation, detailed knowledge of particular industries and empathy with their workers. The younger group, in contrast, are likely to have more formal skills, such as information processing and written communication, and are also likely to be more accustomed to the office environment and work disciplines experienced by officers.

A second difference, however, is likely to lie in the values and commitment of the groups. Australian research by Callus (1986), for example, comparing elected negotiators with specialist officers, such as researchers, found that the latter, more educated group, held 'a broad, idealistic commitment to the values of the labour movement and to social issues extending beyond the workplace'. The loyalties of negotiators, in contrast, were more particularistic and their priorities focused more on 'helping individuals or workers on the shopfloor'. Within our sample of negotiators the same pattern was discernible. Highly educated officers were much more likely to describe their politics as left-wing, rather than centre-left or centre-right ($\chi^2 = 18.6$, p < 0.01). They were also more likely to be members of political pressure groups, such as the Campaign for Nuclear Disarmament (CND) ($\chi^2 = 7.0$, p < 0.05). Officers who had served as convenors, in contrast, and who had typically been selected through representative procedures, were significantly less likely to place themselves on the political left ($\chi^2 = 9.7$, p < 0.05), to be members of

Table 4.2. *Personal characteristics of officers employed by 'open' and 'closed' unions*

| | Open | | | | Closed | | |
| | ASTMS | NALGO | NUPE | GMB | TGWU | EETPU | AEU |
|---|---|---|---|---|---|---|---|
| Mean age at appointment | 30 | 29 | 29 | 34 | 36 | 39 | 44 |
| Percentage of officers with degrees | 33 | 37 | 16 | 18 | 20 | 11 | 0 |
| Percentage of officers without educational qualifications | 7 | 0 | 0 | 36 | 48 | 11 | 58 |
| Percentage of officers from professional or managerial occupations | 38 | 14 | 33 | 9 | 0 | 0 | 0 |
| Percentage of officers from manual occupations | 19 | 0 | 0 | 59 | 93 | 100 | 78 |
| Percentage of ex-convenors | 40 | 15 | 33 | 61 | 47 | 73 | 75 |
| | N = 16 | 16 | 6 | 23 | 16 | 11 | 13 |

*Note:* Across the sample the openness of officer selection procedures were inversely related to age at appointment (r = $-0.43$, p $<$ 0.001) and experience as a convenor (r = $-0.24$, p $<$ 0.01) and positively related to level of education (r = 0.39, p $<$ 0.001) and experience of professional or managerial work (r = 0.26, p $<$ 0.05).
*Source:* Officers' questionnaire.

political groups, other than the Labour Party ($\chi^2$ = 5.0, p $<$ 0.05), or to declare that they had a strong interest in politics ($\chi^2$ = 11.8, p $<$ 0.01). Trade union selection procedures, therefore, may indirectly determine the values of officers and the nature of their commitment to their work.[4] The implications of this for their behaviour will be explored more fully below, but it can be suggested that those with a broader, more explicitly 'ideological' commitment to the labour movement will pursue a broader and more ambitious set of goals in negotiations and will aspire to use the power of the union movement to assist relatively disadvantaged groups, such as the low-paid or ethnic minorities.

The third association between methods of selection and officer characteristics also concerned officer values, but within a specific union, the EETPU. The officers of the EETPU appeared to subscribe to a distinctive set of beliefs. More than half (55 per cent) described themselves as 'centre-right' in their politics, none were members of political pressure groups, like CND, and they were more likely than officers from other unions to disagree with the statement, 'The full-time officer should always seek to educate members in the politics of the wider Labour movement'. In other words, their attitudes provided a strikingly coherent reflection of the ideology of 'business unionism' propounded by the union's national leadership. The basis for these homogeneous and distinctive attitudes was the tight central control of officer appointments within the EETPU (Undy and Martin, 1984: 74).

The effectiveness of these arrangements in ensuring consistency in officer values can be further demonstrated by comparing officers in the EETPU with those in the AEU, a similar ex-craft union with a right-wing leadership. The AEU was marked by plurality in ideology, with officers ranging from the far-left to the centre-right in their politics and with some according high priority to the politicization of the membership while others felt that this was unimportant. In the AEU election of officers and associated factional competition had resulted in the selection of a more diverse set of officers. A further issue to be explored below, therefore, is whether the distinctive values of EETPU officers translated into distinctive behaviour. It might be expected, for example that, given their espousal of business unionism, EETPU officers would pursue a narrow range of economic objectives in collective bargaining, would be more accepting of the interests of management and would be resistant to attempts to use union power to aid minorities and other groups who fell outside the immediate membership.

### Training

Full-time officers have occasionally been described as labour movement professionals, equivalent to professional workers in other spheres (e.g. Perkin, 1989: 180–2). As most definitions of professionalism refer to the exclusive possession of expert knowledge and preparation through formal education and training (Crompton, 1990), it seems appropriate to examine the extent to which officers are trained for their role. A further question concerns the significance of officer training and its consequences for officer behaviour and relationships with members. According to one view, what might be called the 'innocent' or 'functional' account of officer training, the effect of training is to improve the expertise of officers and consequently the effectiveness of unions. This argument was first adumbrated by the Webbs, who referred to the need for professional representatives to handle complex negotiations in industries like cotton, and continues to be made within the labour movement today. The TUC's consultative document, *TUC Towards 2000*, for example, identified the reform of officer training as a 'priority task' for the 1990s and spoke of the need for unions to 'provide training of the quality and frequency essential to a profession' (TUC, 1991: 21; cf. T&GWU, 1992).

There is an alternative argument, however, which suggests that union members are not well served by the creation of a trained and professional officer corps. This 'power' view of officer training argues that the function of professional expertise is to foster client dependence and bolster the power of the professional worker (Abbott and Wallace, 1990: 3). Hyman (1989b: 150), for example, has said that among officers 'there is a natural tendency to define trade union purposes in a manner which emphasises officials' own expertise and activities: stressing "professional" competence in collective bargaining rather than militant mass action'. The training of officers, therefore, may promote professional domination of unions and diminish the scope for what Hyman (1989c: 181) has referred to as the 'mobilization and self-activity' of the rank and file.

To what extent, then, are officers prepared for their role through formal education and training? The data in table 4.2 indicate that, unlike the established and even many newer professions, trade union work is not a graduate-entry occupation. Only 21 per cent of officers surveyed had degrees while 25 per cent had no educational qualifications whatsoever. It is also the case that, although some unions require prospective candidates for officer posts to pass an examination, there is no generally accepted corpus of theoretical and practical knowledge, no standard training for entrants and no professional qualification for trade union work. Perhaps the main reason for this is that officers derive much of their expertise from an alternative source, by serving a lay apprenticeship. The length and precise detail of this may vary from individual to individual and between open and closed unions, but virtually without exception a proven record of lay activism is a requirement for appointment to an officer post.

For example, of the officers surveyed, 88 per cent had held union branch office for at least a year, 89 per cent had served as a shop steward, 65 per cent had held a senior shop steward position and 49 per cent had spent at least a year as a convenor. As a result of acquiring this experience many were quite old when they were first appointed to officer positions. The mean age at appointment was 34 and a quarter of officers were aged 40 or over when they first assumed office. For these latter officers appointment to an officer position represented the culmination, not the beginning, of a union career.

It is primarily through the lay apprenticeship, therefore, that officers acquire the skills and attributes required for the job (cf. Allen, 1954: 196; Watson, 1988: 80–1). These include competences such as the ability to negotiate or handle disciplinary and grievance cases. They also include a detailed knowledge of union constitutional rules, union administration and the informal political life of their organizations, the latter being particularly important in unions with representative procedures for selection. Finally, it is through service as a shop steward, branch or executive officer that prospective officers demonstrate their commitment either to a particular union or to the labour movement at large. Lay activism is the testing ground of the dedicated officer and dedication is important in Britain's under-resourced trade unions.

Although unions rely heavily on the lay apprenticeship to equip their officers with expertise it has become common to supplement this with formal training. The 1991 Head Office Survey, for instance, found that 39 per cent of unions had sent at least a quarter of their officers on training courses in the previous year and 48 per cent had sent more than half in the previous five years. The most frequently used source of training was the TUC Education Department and its programme of national short courses and regional briefings for officers. These courses constituted the bulk of officer training for TUC affiliates, 89 per cent of whom made use of them, and underline the extent to which the TUC discharges one of the traditional functions of an employers' association for its members, providing employment services to a level which few individual unions could afford.

The extent and depth of officer training, however, should not be exaggerated. Few unions develop a strategic approach to training, in which there is an attempt to specify the objectives of training policy, identify officers' training needs and provide a system of release and cover for officers involved in training (cf. Fisher and Holland, 1990: 19; T&GWU, 1992). Among those surveyed in 1991, for example, only 16 per cent operated a formal system of performance appraisal, the normal channel for the identification of training needs in many organizations, and an indicator that training tends to be offered on an *ad hoc* basis in unions. This, in turn, reflects the fact that the main aims of officer training are to supplement, deepen and update knowledge and skills which have been acquired through lay apprenticeship and experience in the job. Officer training, in other words, is oriented towards the refinement rather than the creation of expertise.

### Evaluation of officer training

The limited extent of officer training suggests that the concerns of those who have adumbrated the 'power view' are exaggerated. Full-time officers are not formally qualified in the manner of more established professions and do not have exclusive possession of a body of specialist expertise. Rather, there is a gradation of expertise within unions stretching up from the least experienced activists to the apex of the officer hierarchy. This, in turn, is likely to militate against the formation of a strong professional identity among officers and make it difficult for them to arrogate decision-making powers to themselves on the grounds of superior qualification.

The fact that most officers undergo a lay apprenticeship is also likely to colour their perceptions of the respective roles of officers and members. Unlike many other professions, virtually all union officers have stood on the client side of the fence, and this may incline them to support independent action by workplace trade unionists. It is perhaps significant that three-quarters of officers surveyed were first appointed or elected to office in the late 1960s and 1970s, when shop steward influence was being extended in major unions. The experience of these years, and the participation of many officers in the upsurge of rank and file activity, is likely to have shaped their attitudes towards lay activism and the prerogatives of the full-time officer to a substantial degree.

There is also evidence that the content of the lay apprenticeship shifted in these years so that an increasing proportion of officers came to have shop steward experience. Where at least a year's experience as a shop steward and as a branch official was the norm among our sample of officers, among Clegg et al.'s (1961: 51) 1959 sample only 35 per cent had served as shop stewards immediately prior to assuming office, as against 77 per cent who had held branch office. Even allowing for differences in the questions asked, the change in the proportion of officers with workplace representative experience is striking and indicative of the growth in importance of workplace unionism in the intervening period. The significance of this finding lies in the fact that shop stewards have often been identified as the major challenge to the autonomy and prerogatives of official unionism, and precisely for this reason were occasionally bitterly resisted by officers of the generation studied by Clegg and his colleagues.

Finally, it cannot be assumed that the formal training which officers do receive will foster an approach to the job which emphasizes member and steward dependence on professional expertise. Although officer training is intended to develop skills and knowledge which can be used directly on behalf of members, such as bargaining research, work study, pensions or industrial tribunals, it also covers education methods and union organizing. Officers, that is, are trained as facilitators as well as representatives, for whom a key task is disseminating skills and knowledge among lay representatives to enable them to handle their own problems. The TUC's national five day course in education methods, for example, is the third most heavily attended by officers and has the highest approval rating (TUC, 1989: 6).

Endorsement of training by officers provides some indirect evidence in support of the alternative, 'functional' view of officer training. The 1989

TUC survey of union officers found that almost two-thirds of officers attending TUC national courses felt they were 'very useful' and there was a strong demand for further training, particularly in the areas of technical knowledge and skills development (TUC, 1989: 6–7; cf. T&GWU, 1992). Officers also generally endorsed the need for formal induction for newly appointed officers. A number who were interviewed, for example, described the difficulties they encountered in making the transition from lay activism because of the absence of any significant preparation or support from their unions. Several spoke of arriving for work on their first day, being shown their desk and an unopened pile of their predecessor's mail and being told to wait for the telephone to ring (cf. Watson, 1988: 94–5). Proper induction and basic training in office skills, time management, research and communications, it was suggested, would have led to fewer errors and a more rapid adaptation to the demands of the officer role.

It is also the case that a number of unions have come to value officer training to a greater degree. Comparison of results from the 1986 and 1991 Head Office Surveys found a significant increase in the proportions of officers being sent on training courses and several large unions, including the GMB, NUPE, T&GWU and USDAW, have reviewed and extended officer training in recent years. In part, this enthusiasm for training is due to the notion of human resource development taking root within unions, the belief that core employees, like officers, should be the subject of investment and conscious development. However, it also represents a belief that there is a mismatch between the existing competencies of officers and the rapidly changing environment in which unions find themselves. As a T&GWU Regional Organizer put it: 'How do you turn an officer with 25 years experience in the docks into a recruiter for MacDonald's workers?' (cf. Fisher and Holland, 1990: 5–12). The answer to such problems in some unions has been to expand training and identify effective training as increasingly necessary or 'functional' for union success.

## Rewards

The final aspect of officers' employment relations that we want to examine and which is widely considered to condition officer behaviour is pay. It has been claimed both by academic commentators and by activists within trade unions that the level of officer salaries can influence officers' approach to their work and relations with shop stewards and members. Marxist critics of union bureaucracy, for example, have repeatedly traced the alleged conservatism of officers to their receipt of salaries considerably in excess of those of their members (Kelly, 1988: 161–6) and the proposal to tie officers' salaries to members' earnings has been a frequent demand of left-wing activists in British unions (Clinton, 1984: 331–8). According to this view the payment of a relatively generous salary and the development of a 'middle-class' lifestyle by officers has the effect of removing them from the deprivation and insecurity experienced by their members and defusing their militancy. That is, the material interests of the 'bureaucracy' become disjunct from those of the members, and this leads to a divergence in objectives and preferred tactics.

An opposing argument focuses on officer salaries not in relation to those of members but in relation to those of personnel managers. The key claim here is that there is a labour market rate for the expertise deployed by officers and that a failure to pay that rate will lead to recruitment, retention and motivational problems within unions (Roberts, 1956: 307–8). A related argument, which is often encountered in white-collar unions, is that officers have to be paid attractive salaries if talented activists are to be persuaded to give up their careers and work full-time for the union. According to this view, it is not the objectives of officers which are influenced by the level of salary offered, but the competence and commitment which is brought to the job.

Table 4.3 shows the annual salaries of field officers in fifteen unions in 1991, together with average earnings figures for some of the main occupational groups represented by those unions taken from the 1990 *New Earnings Survey*. Data are also included for all manual and non-manual unions and occupations. Table 4.3 indicates, firstly, that there is considerable variation in officers' salaries across the trade union movement, with non-manual unions tending to offer more generous rewards. It also indicates, however, that in the majority of cases officers earn considerably more than the workers they represent. There are exceptions. Industrial Relations Officers in the BMA, for example, are paid substantially less than the average earnings of medical practitioners, while university academics and civil service professionals earn more on average than at least some of their unions' field officers. It is also the case that in most unions there are pockets of highly-paid members who earn more than officers. It remains, however, that the vast bulk of officers enjoy a substantial differential over their members, that this differential widens considerably if officers' salaries are compared with the earnings of female members, and that the differential is greater for senior officers, such as General Secretaries, 61 per cent of whom earned more than £30,000 per year in 1991.

It cannot be assumed, though, that this officers' differential leads to radically different interests and objectives. One reason for this is that,

Table 4.3. *Earnings of full-time officers and union members, 1991*

| Officer grade | Salary (£000) | Occupational group | Earnings (£000) |
|---|---|---|---|
| *AEU* District Secretary | 20.5 | Machine tool setter-operators | 13.5 |
| | | Toolmakers, tool fitters, etc. | 14.8 |
| | | Maintenance fitters | 13.4 |
| | | Repetitive assemblers | 11.5 (8.0)[a] |
| *AUT* Regional Official | 16.8–24.1 | Academic and related staff in universities | 20.8 |
| *BIFU* Area Organizer | 15.0–16.7 | Finance and insurance clerks | 12.6 (10.0) |
| *CPSA* Assistant Secretary | 17.1–25.0 | Civil service clerks and data processors | 9.0 (8.6) |
| *FTAT* District Organizer | 15.4 | Timber and furniture industry manuals | 11.8 |
| *IPMS* Negotiations Officer | 15.6–20.7 | Civil service professionals and technologists | 17.9 |
| *MSF* Regional Officer | 20.0 | Laboratory technicians | 13.3 |
| | | Supervisors of clerks | 14.7 (12.4) |
| | | Foremen metalmaking | 16.4 |
| | | Engineering technicians | 16.8 |
| *NCU* Assistant Secretary | 25.8–27.3 | British Telecom Engineers | 14.0 |
| | | British Telecom Clerks | (11.2) |
| *NUPE* Area Officer | 15.1–18.9 | Local authority manuals | 10.0 (7.5) |

Table 4.3. (*cont.*)

| Officer grade | Salary (£000) | Occupational group | Earnings (£000) |
|---|---|---|---|
| **NUT** | | | |
| Regional Officer | 21.0–21.9 | School teachers | 17.3 (15.1) |
| **T&GWU** | | | |
| District Officer | 17.0–18.5 | Chemical, gas and plant operatives | 15.6 |
| | | HGV drivers | 13.1 |
| | | Packers, | 10.7 |
| | | bottlers, etc. | (7.7) |
| | | Storekeepers | 10.4 |
| | | General labourers | 10.4 |
| **UCATT** | | | |
| Regional Organizer | 15.4 | Civil engineering manuals | 15.4 |
| | | Building trade operatives | 12.0 |
| **UCW** | | | |
| Assistant Secretary | 30.0 | Post Office manipulative grades | 12.1 |
| **USDAW** | | | |
| Area Organizer | 16.1–18.4 | Sales assistants | 9.2 (6.6) |
| | | Roundsmen | 11.2 |
| **BMA** | | | |
| Industrial Relations Officer | 20.7–28.5 | Medical practitioners | 32.2 |
| *All non-manual unions*[b] | 19.8–22.7 | *All non-manual occupations* | 18.5 (11.2) |
| *All manual unions*[c] | 17.9–18.8 | *All manual occupations* | 12.3 (7.7) |

*Notes:*
[a] Female earnings in brackets.
[b] Based on data from 27 unions.
[c] Based on data from 14 unions.
*Sources:* Union Head Office Survey, 1991; *New Earnings Survey*, 1990: Part B, Analyses by Agreement; Part D, Analyses by Occupation.

despite higher earnings, many officers exist in the same social milieu as their members. Officers responding to the questionnaire, for example, were asked to list the occupations of three close friends. Of 261 friends listed 22 per cent were clerks, sales staff or technicians, 21 per cent had manual jobs, 21 per cent were lay or full-time trade union representatives, 18 per cent had professional jobs, 9 per cent were managers and 9 per cent were not in paid employment. Less than a third of officer friendships, therefore, were with people in identifiably 'middle-class' jobs and many of these were with members of the unionized and politically radical welfare professions. It was also the case that officer friendships reflected the characteristics of their unions' memberships, so that AEU officers were more likely to report skilled workers as friends, T&GWU officers were more likely to report semi-skilled friends and NALGO officers were more likely to report friendships with clerks. This, in turn, reflects the fact that many officers have served a lay apprenticeship among the workers they represent, which serves to minimize the social distance between themselves and their members.

A second reason for questioning the claimed link between officer earnings and objectives is that, although the vast majority of officers enjoy a differential, there are considerable differences in ideology and work orientation among officers. On the central issue of the relative objectives of officers and members, for instance, 9 per cent of officers surveyed said that they frequently or very frequently disagreed with lay representatives over the substance of collective bargaining claims, 40 per cent said that they 'sometimes' had such disagreements while 51 per cent said that this happened only occasionally or 'almost never'. Moreover, these differences were not associated statistically with differences in officer earnings. Among the questionnaire sample, for example, annual income in 1987 ranged from £11,000 to £19,000 but analysis failed to reveal any significant associations between officer income and political values, the degree of reported conflict with shop stewards over bargaining objectives, attitudes to independent steward-led bargaining, the need to support members or the use of the strike weapon. This is scarcely surprising. The argument that higher earnings for officers leads to an abandoning of members' interests is a crudely materialist one, which seems inapposite to employees of value-driven organizations like trade unions. Trade union officers, as has been made clear, have generally found their way to office by displaying commitment and dedication to the trade union movement. Given this, it seems one-sided to construct a theory of their interests and motivation which is based solely on the amount they are paid relative to their members.

While officers typically earn more than their members it is common for them to earn less than their equivalents in personnel management. According to the *New Earnings Survey*, median yearly earnings for personnel and industrial relations specialists stood at £22,000 in 1990. Two-thirds of unions surveyed paid maximum salaries below this figure to their most heavily populated officer grade, including most large unions with sizeable complements of officers. As personnel specialists with an industrial relations responsibility tend to be relatively senior (Sisson, 1989: 12), and are therefore likely to be paid at or above the median rate for their profession, it can be assumed that most officers will earn less than their negotiating partners in management. The same is true of senior officers, such as General Secretaries, most of whom earn less than those at the apex of the personnel profession. In only 28 per cent of unions, for example, was the maximum officer salary above the highest decile earnings figure for personnel managers of £38,200.

According to the argument outlined above the effect of this 'underpayment' of officers should be an adverse impact on union performance and the appearance of recruitment, retention and motivational problems amongst officers. The research revealed little evidence of these. On the issue of retention, for example, only 51 per cent of unions responding to the 1991 survey reported officers resigning to join another organization in the last five years and of a total of 257 officers who had left their jobs in this period, only 29 per cent were said to have done so to make a career move. Some officers do resign, therefore, to take up better paying positions in management or consultancy, but the bulk of the union workforce is stable, and most officers either retire or die in service. The research also found little evidence of motivational problems. Indeed, the reverse seemed to be the case. Officers who were observed at work, for example, generally attended a hectic schedule of meetings, worked long hours and, in the main, were receptive to the demands on their time of members and shop stewards. Confirming evidence was provided by the women officers' survey which revealed that women officers worked an average of 50.4 hours per week, 1.8 evenings per week and 1.2 weekends per month (cf. Robertson and Sams, 1978: 61).

There are two main reasons why the relative under-payment of officers does not appear to generate serious labour supply or motivational problems for trade unions. First, many trade union jobs do not comprise part of a national labour market for industrial relations expertise. This is most apparent for unions with closed selection procedures, which use an internal labour market to fill officer posts, but it is also true for many formally open unions which recruit officers from their own activists. The effect of these procedures, essentially, is to shelter trade unions from external labour market forces and give them greater freedom in setting

officers' pay. For unions, like other organizations which recruit internally, pay setting is 'an administrative and not a market process' (Brown,
1989: 250).

The second reason has to do with the distinctive characteristics of
officers themselves. Officers are distinguishable from other industrial
relations professionals in terms of their commitment to the values and
institutions of the labour movement. One indicator of this is their level of
support for left-wing political parties. 84 per cent of officers surveyed
were members of the Labour Party, a further 5 per cent were members of
the Communist Party and 87 per cent declared they had either a 'very' or
'fairly strong' interest in politics. The consequence of this commitment is
a tolerance, not just of relatively low pay, but also of long hours, inferior
working conditions and inadequate administrative support (cf. Watson,
1988: 108). Like the employees of charities and other voluntary agencies,
officers are both willing and expected 'to work longer hours for less pay
than those in comparable jobs in other sectors because they are also
expected to have altruism and commitment' (Harris, 1990: 127). The
strong value orientation of officers to their work, therefore, can explain
why low pay relative to personnel specialists does not generate labour
supply and performance problems within unions, in the same way that it
can explain why high pay relative to members does not lead to the
adoption of conservative objectives and the neglect of members' interests.

Although most discussion of officers' rewards has focused on salary
levels, an additional topic which deserves attention is the wage-form,
particularly as systems of payment have been widely identified as major
influences on employee behaviour (e.g. Smith, 1989). One striking feature
about the wage-form of union officers is that very few receive incentive
payments.[5] Only four unions, employing 3 per cent of officers, NULMW,
FDA, IPMS, IRSF, reported their use in 1991. With a few exceptions,
therefore, union officers have escaped the extension of performance-
related pay, which has spread to many other professional groups in recent
years (LACSAB, 1991). The evidence on officer commitment and work
patterns above suggests that this neglect of incentive payments does not
give rise to any noticeable performance problem within unions. An
intriguing question, though, is whether the performance of officers would
be further enhanced by greater use of incentives. One of the reasons given
by organizations for introducing performance payments, for example, is
that they can support the implementation of new business strategies and
ensure that core objectives are incorporated in the work routines of
employees (LACSAB, 1991: 24). In recent years several of the large
general unions in Britain have effected precisely this kind of change in
strategy and have placed greater emphasis on the task of organizing new

groups of employees outside their traditional membership. It is possible that the wider use of performance-related pay could ensure these initiatives are 'cascaded' down the union hierarchy and that recruitment is given greater priority by officers. It cannot be assumed, however, that incentives would have this effect. The research literature is replete with examples of incentive schemes which have either failed to work or which have generated fresh and unforeseen problems for organizations which have used them (e.g. Mitchell *et al.*, 1990: 64–7). Two obvious problems with the adoption of recruitment bonuses by unions, for example, are that they could lead to the neglect of other aspects of the officer's job, generating complaints from existing members, or to the recruitment of new members with little regard to their organization and retention.

The lack of incentives for officers is of a piece with a number of other aspects of their reward package. Virtually all union officers receive the kinds of reward which are said to be typical of the relatively diffuse employment relationship of the professional worker (cf. Fox, 1985: 97; Goldthorpe, 1982: 169). Thus, all unions surveyed paid their officers annual salaries; in 50 per cent of cases officers also received service-related increments; full use of a company car and the right to claim expenses are standard practice across most unions; and occupational pensions and sick pay for officers have been the norm since the early 1950s (Roberts, 1956: 310–11). Unions also typically offer their officers career opportunities and employment security, where constitutional and legislative requirements for re-election do not apply. While career opportunities may not be as extensive as those in managerial organizations (Watson, 1988: 107), for example, there are a significant proportion of promotion posts in most unions, which are generally filled by internal applicants. The provision of employment security, meanwhile, is demonstrated by: the considerable seniority of most officers (an average of 14.8 years in post among officers surveyed); the large proportion of vacancies in unions which are caused through retirement (63 per cent); the fact that union membership decline has not been accompanied by an equivalent decline in the numbers of officers; and the use of natural wastage, early retirement and voluntary redundancy to effect workforce reduction where this is unavoidable.

It is this set of practices which is arguably the most important feature of the rewards of officers, but which has been almost completely neglected in earlier writing on trade unions. Union officers, it can be said, typically offer a 'vocational' commitment to their work and display considerable dedication in its execution (Watson, 1988: 103–9). In recognition of, and in order to maintain, this commitment unions offer their full-time officers rewards, like employment security and career opportunities, which reflect acceptance of the obligations of the 'good employer'. Officers, therefore, may not be as well rewarded as equivalent professional and managerial employees outside the trade union sector, but they receive the same types of reward, which are essentially designed to cement a long-term and high-trust relationship between employer and employee.

## Conclusions

This chapter has provided some initial evidence in support of the common view that union officers can legitimately be viewed as labour movement bureaucrats or professionals, in that the employment relations of officers are similar to those of other professional employees working in manager-ial and State bureaucracies. Thus, the majority of officers are appointed, at least formally on merit, all are salaried employees and most are provided with secure, superannuated employment with opportunities for career development. In certain important respects, however, the employ-ment relationship of officers diverges from that of non-union pro-fessionals and reflects the nature of unions as representative and volun-tary organizations. General indicators of this are the absence of relevant qualifications for union work, the peculiar nature of officer careers, including late entry into the occupation, limited emphasis on formal training and relatively poor salaries.

The chapter has also demonstrated that officers' employment relations are highly variable, and diverge from conventional bureaucratic and professional employment relations to differing degrees, depending on union constitutions and traditions. Divergence is sharpest, for example, in manual, and particularly ex-craft, unions which make use of election and re-election, restrict officers' salary differential over members and are unable formally to offer employment security and career opportunities to their officers. In these unions employment relations reflect a strongly representative conception of the officer's role which over-rides more conventional employment practice. In white-collar unions, in contrast, and in a number of unions which have traditionally represented less skilled manual workers, employment relations conform more closely to the bureaucratic or professional model. These unions practise open recruitment, pay better wages and offer more secure employment. Employment in this second, and larger group of unions, reflects a concep-tion of the officer as an expert, a trade union civil servant, who exercises professional judgement and aptitudes on behalf of union members.[6] There is a continuum of employment practice within unions, therefore, which reflects the strength of adherence to representative or professional understandings of the officer's role.

Regarding the link between officers' employment relations and the performance of their role, the evidence contains three prime messages. The first is that the non-bureaucratic, representative elements in officers' employment relations may paradoxically contribute to administrative efficiency and be highly functional for unions as organizations. Thus, selection of officers from among the ranks of lay activists ensures a supply of experienced and knowledgeable representatives, and reduces both the training investment which unions are required to make and the need to compete for expertise on the open labour market against other, wealthier organizations. It is particularly noteworthy that officers selected through 'closed' procedures generally have greater representative experience than those who enter through 'open' competition.

The second is that there is little support for the view that bureaucratic employment relations foster a conservative orientation to their work among officers. Thus, appointed officers were more likely to espouse a broader, ideological commitment to the labour movement and place themselves on the political left and women officers were more likely to gain office through open appointment, possibly leading to a higher priority for women's interests in unions which use this method of selection. It was also demonstrated that although most officers earn substantially more than their members, this does not appear to influence their orientation to collective bargaining or their relationship with members.

The third message is that the employment relations of officers reflect the fact that they constitute a committed workforce and have been designed, whether consciously or not, to support and maintain commitment. Various aspects of officer employment relations, such as stable, secure and superannuated employment, express organizational recognition of officer commitment and are intended to maintain a diffuse, high-trust relationship between officer and union. Full-time officers' employment relations, therefore, derive in very large part from the nature of trade unions as value-driven organizations which attract committed activists into employment.

# 5    Work relations

Having examined employment relations of full-time officers in chapter 4, the 'structure of control' (Littler, 1982: 42) over their work is now examined. We look at the mechanisms trade unions use to guide and monitor the work of officers and hold them to account, estimate the degree of autonomy they exercise at work and review their role as conduits for national union policy. We also examine officers' views of their accountability to lay members and their superiors. Our purpose is the same as in chapter 4. The structure of control over officer work may determine officer behaviour and relations with members, and is therefore deserving of investigation. This can be illustrated by reference to the theoretical models of union officialdom set out in chapter 2. A recurrent theme in the literature on trade union bureaucracy, for example, is the ineffectiveness of member and lay officer control over union 'bureaucrats', whose expertise and influence within internal administrative and political systems enable them to set the agenda for union policy (Webb and Webb, 1902, 1920). Less frequently articulated, but derivative from the assumption of tight central control of union organization which is contained in this tradition, is the belief that officers will be subject to fairly strict supervision from their superiors within the hierarchy (cf. Bamber, 1986: 59–62; Lester, 1958: 26–7).

The reverse of this belief, however – that officers have considerable autonomy and the opportunity to order their priorities and activities – lies behind two of the other models described, those emphasizing union polyarchy and the influence of officer values over behaviour. For both of these models officers are typically possessed of considerable discretion to be employed, in the first, in maximizing their power and influence *vis-à-vis* other actors within trade unions, including national officials and, in the second, in the selection of goals and tactics congruent with their own values. Finally, the contingency approach would suggest that the structures of lay and superior control over officers will be influenced by a range of environmental factors. It is possible, for example, that lay controls over officers will be more or less effective depending on the sophistication of workplace unionism and the extent of workplace bargaining, the extent to which district and regional committees to which officers are accountable possess a collective bargaining function or formal powers to direct, monitor and discipline officers. Control by superiors, in turn, may be influenced by patterns of officer bureaucracy, officer–member ratios and the complexity of officers' jobs and the officers' employment relations, particularly the method of selection, as elected officers have often been thought to possess greater autonomy than their appointed colleagues (Donaldson and Warner, 1974: 53; Roberts, 1956: 304). In examining the nature and extent of control over trade union officers at work, therefore, our aim is test the validity of each of these models of union officialdom.

### Accountability to lay representatives

Most full-time officers are formally accountable to committees or councils of elected lay members, constituted at national, regional or district levels. The 1991 Head Office Survey, for instance, found that 89 per cent of unions required officers to make verbal reports to lay committees, while 71 per cent also required them to make written reports. Examples of this kind of 'constitutional' accountability included the requirement on ASTMS Divisional Officers to submit monthly reports on their activities to the union's Divisional Councils, the requirement for AEU District Secretaries to submit similar, regular reports to District Committees and divisional shop steward meetings and the requirement for T&GWU District Officers to attend and report to branches and regional trade groups.[1]

The extent to which these reporting systems constitute a significant control on officers' activities, however, and particularly their conduct as negotiators and organizers, is debatable. An ASTMS Divisional Officer, for instance, described reporting to Divisional Council as 'an institution-alized courtesy', and attendance at one of these meetings suggested this was an accurate description as there was no attempt to question officers on their work. A similar impression of rather empty formalism was gathered from AEU District Committee meetings. At one, for example, the District Secretary positively raced through his report on his activities, which was accepted *nem. con.* without comment. In another, the report did stimulate some discussion, but this was of a rather academic kind in which the negotiations reported by the officer were dissected for their own interest rather than as a means of checking on the District Secretary's behaviour.

These examples support the view found in theories of union oligarchy that, despite their formal subordination to elected lay committees, union officers retain considerable independence. However, this impression must be qualified in a number of ways. First, although formal reporting procedures may be little more than 'an institutionalized courtesy' in the majority of cases, on occasion they may be used to exert effective control over officers, particularly in situations of conflict between officers and groups of members. James' study (1984: 57) of the engineers, for instance, suggests that District Committee ratification of collective agreements negotiated by officers is not always automatic and that on occasion District Secretaries are instructed to re-open negotiations. Second, lay committees have other powers over officers which may be used to limit their autonomy. Union branches and other lay bodies, for instance, can instruct or request officers to undertake a range of activities and may also have the power to exclude officers from involvement in their affairs. In NALGO, for example, District Officers can act on a branch's behalf only if invited to do so, and a case was described to us of a District Officer being excluded from pay negotiations because the branch felt that his abrasive style was counterproductive. Finally, lay committees, and ordinary members, have potential sanctions over officers. In both T&GWU and ASTMS, for example, formal member complaints about officer behaviour are taken extremely seriously, are investigated and may result in disciplinary action. Such procedures are infrequently used, but they are activated on ocasion and two T&GWU District Officers were the subject of investigation at the time we interviewed them.

The formalism of reporting relationships to District, Divisional and similar committees largely arises from the fact that the concerns of such committees are often remote from the core, representational activities of officers. An indicator of this was that, in the small number of Branch, District and Divisional meetings which were attended, there was a tendency for pay and conditions of employment not to feature in the issues discussed. The failure of lay representatives to scrutinize officers' work behaviour rigorously at these meetings, therefore, was primarily due to the fact that the content of such behaviour was not 'normatively central' to the work of their committees (Willman, 1982: 19).

In addition to accountability to formally constituted union committees, most officers are also accountable to groups of members for whom they negotiate. Indeed, the two forms of accountability may overlap where union branches are based on the workplace or where company and branch membership is coterminous with a bargaining group. This latter arrangement is the norm for public sector and white-collar workers (Daniel and Millward, 1983: 83–4; Millward *et al.*, 1992: 140–1). The 1991 Head Office Survey found that in 90 percent of unions officers were required to make verbal reports to the groups on whose behalf they negotiated and 59 per cent were required to make written reports. The fact that fewer unions require written reports to bargaining groups than to lay committees reflects the fact that the collective bargaining function of unions is less formalized than internal policy-making and administration.

All the negotiations we observed passed through a similar set of stages in which officers met with shop stewards to formulate bargaining objectives, stewards accompanied officers to meetings with managers and contributed to negotiations and agreements were provisionally accepted by officers and stewards prior to referral to members. Lay participation in the bargaining process exposes the work of officers to scrutiny and imposes real constraints, which are not so apparent in meetings without a collective bargaining function. For example, we observed a number of instances where officer suggestions for inclusion in negotiations or for the adoption of particular tactics were rejected by stewards. In one case, an ASTMS officer, bargaining on behalf of workers in a financial services company, was unable to persuade stewards that they include a demand for equalizing male and female pension entitlements, while in another, a second ASTMS officer, bargaining on behalf of technicians, was unable to win steward support for industrial action. We also observed a number of cases where negotiations were extended because representatives were not prepared to give their assent to what they perceived as inadequate settlements.

This pattern of lay involvement in the bargaining process reflects the 'radical democratization' (England, 1981: 27) of most large unions, facilitated by Jack Jones and others in the late 1960s and 1970s. Despite greater formal powers for lay representatives to regulate bargaining, however, the research revealed that officers retain considerable influence over the bargaining process. Table 5.1 shows estimates of the relative influence of officers and stewards over the initiation, handling and outcome of issues raised at collective bargaining sessions. Table 5.1 indicates that while lay representatives generally exert greater or equivalent influence to officers over the setting of bargaining goals, tactical decisions and the conclusion of bargaining lie much more securely in the officers' hands. Similar findings were obtained through the officers' survey. For example, 50 per cent of officers reported that the most common method of setting pay claims was for members and stewards to decide without formal officer input and a further 23 per cent said that they were usually consulted but that stewards took the final decision. The survey also revealed, however, that 87 per cent of officers felt that their suggestions for inclusion in negotiations were 'usually' or 'always' accepted and 75 per cent said that they exercised 'quite a lot' or 'a great deal' of influence over the acceptance of offers from management.

Table 5.1. *The relative influence of officers and stewards over the initiation, handling and outcome of bargaining issues*

|  | Officer more influence | | Equal influence | | Stewards more influence | |
|---|---|---|---|---|---|---|
|  | No. | Per cent | No. | Per cent | No. | Per cent |
| Initiation of issues | 87 | 37.0 | 55 | 23.4 | 93 | 39.6 |
| Handling of issues | 159 | 65.2 | 40 | 16.4 | 45 | 18.4 |
| Outcome of issues | 180 | 76.6 | 25 | 10.6 | 30 | 12.8 |

*Source:* Observation.

These figures provide support for the theory of union bureaucracy. It must be stressed, however that the bulk of workplace bargaining does not involve full-time officers (Batstone and Gourlay, 1986: 126) and that their domination of bargaining, where they do become involved, is tempered by fairly extensive lay influence over the setting of negotiating objectives. Moreover, the basis for officer control of negotiations is generally steward acceptance of the greater expertise of officers, rather than immunity from member pressure. For example, the assessments of officers voiced by stewards at meetings tended to dwell on their expertise or lack of it, rather than their degree of responsiveness to members and the pattern of relative officer influence, with most being exerted over the handling and outcome of issues and least over their initiation, which is what one would expect if officers were accepted by stewards as skilled experts.

Variation in officer reporting relations to lay committees and bargaining groups across unions was primarily related to differences in officer organization. The requirement for officers to make written reports to lay committees, for example, was inversely related to the number of senior regional officers ($r = -0.29$, $p < 0.05$) and to the proportion of officers based away from head office ($r = -0.40$, $p < 0.01$). Similar results were obtained for the other measures of accountability and they suggest, as a whole, that in more differentiated unions formal accountability to lay bodies tends to be concentrated at senior levels of either national or regional hierarchies. A second source of variation, appeared to lie in the internal employment relations of different unions, in that unions that were less likely to train their officers had a stronger commitment to formal accountability in bargaining ($r = -0.33$, $p < 0.05$). This suggests that attachment to a representative, rather than a professional conception of the officer role, expressed in a lower commitment to staff development, may increase the importance of formal reporting relationships to lay members. Further evidence to support this view lay in the fact that a requirement for formal accountability to bargaining groups tended to be found in unions with a relatively large proportion of ex-shop stewards among their officers ($r = 0.36$, $p < 0.05$), that is among those which relied heavily on lay activism as a preparation for office.

The survey of individual officers suggested that officer characteristics further determine relations with members. Officers who reported that they had considerable influence over the formulation of pay claims tended to be on the right politically ($r = 0.25$, $p < 0.01$), to have fewer educational qualifications ($r = 0.19$, $p < 0.05$) and to have a background in manual work ($r = 0.19$, $p < 0.05$), while those who claimed they had greatest influence over the acceptance of agreements tended to have most seniority ($r = 0.25$, $p < 0.05$) and, again, to have a background in manual work ($r = 0.19$, $p < 0.03$). As most of these individual characteristics were related to the use of closed selection procedures they perhaps provide further indirect evidence of the significance of employment relations for officer behaviour. There was no direct statistically significant association, however, between methods of officer selection and reported relations with members.

The observation research also indicated that officer orientations influence the relationship with members, in that those officers with a 'leader' orientation to their work were more likely to initiate issues in collective bargaining ($\chi^2 = 9.0$, $p = 0.06$). Officer orientations, however, exercised no influence over the handling or outcome of bargaining, where variation was more closely related to the sophistication of workplace trade unionism. Officer influence over the outcome of bargaining tended to be greater where there was an absence of hierarchy among stewards attending the meeting ($r = 0.10$, $p < 0.06$), where unionization was lower among the bargaining group ($r = 0.19$, $p < 0.05$), at smaller establishments ($r = 0.17$, $p < 0.01$) and in industries, like food processing, electrical engineering, financial services and retail, which do not have a tradition of strong workplace trade unionism ($\chi^2 = 10.98$, $p > 0.05$). These findings indicate that officer expertise serves as a substitute for strong workplace unionism in parts of the economy.

The observation research also indicated that officer control was related to the subject matter of bargaining. In particular, where issues at bargaining sessions were more important to officers, there was a strong tendency for them to exert greater influence over their introduction ($r = 0.58$, $p < 0.001$), handling ($r = 0.35$, $p < 0.001$) and outcome ($r = 0.28$, $p < 0.001$). These findings suggest that, notwithstanding formal patterns of accountability, the boundary of officer and member influence over collective bargaining shifts according to the salience of the negotiating agenda for either party. Union officers may therefore be able to acquire greater purchase over the bargaining process where they feel it is necessary but, by the same token, it seems that lay members can equally increase their influence when it is important for them to do so.

### Accountability to superior officers

In the large unions which were the focus of the study, officers are organized in bureaucratic hierarchies in which front-line organizers and bargainers are formally accountable to superiors occupying managerial positions at regional and national headquarters. The 1991 Head Office Survey revealed that 78 per cent of unions required their officers to make regular verbal reports to superiors while 71 per cent required regular written reports. The survey also indicated that 69 per cent of unions issued their officers with job descriptions but only 15 per cent made use of performance appraisal and only 7 per cent used performance-related pay, increasingly common instruments of management control for professional and bureaucratic employees in other organizations. Finally, the majority of unions (72 per cent) declared their officers had 'almost complete' or 'a great deal' of autonomy in their daily work. These figures indicate that in most unions full-time officers are subject to dual systems of formal control, from lay representatives and superiors, but suggest that controls exerted by the latter are not particularly extensive or intrusive. This impression was confirmed by the officers' survey and the interview and observation research.

The officers' survey found that while 25 per cent were informally in contact with their superiors on a weekly basis, a full 33 per cent reported such contact less than once a month. In the observation research we were struck by the extent to which the routine work of officers was initiated, processed and concluded without reference to superiors. Very occasionally, officers referred to the need to inform or involve their superiors (9.6 per cent of meetings) or complained about head office restricting their freedom of action (6.4 per cent of meetings), but generally the work of field officers and their regional and national superiors appeared to proceed on parallel paths which only intermittently came together.

A similar impression was obtained from the interviews with officers in ASTMS, AEU, GMB and T&GWU, most of whom reported that they enjoyed considerable autonomy at work. An ASTMS officer, for example, remarked that, 'Most Divisional Officers are left to get on with it', and said of herself, 'I'm pretty free', while a colleague informed us that, 'no national officer can instruct me to do anything. I decide my own diary.' Even stronger statements of autonomy were obtained from AEU District Secretaries. One, for example, remarked that, 'When I come in, no-one from general office tells me what I can and cannot do', and a second, contrasting his position with that of appointed officers, referred to 'the powers of the rank and file ... this makes you very confident ... working for the boss you have to watch the boss. I can tell the executive to fuck off.'

However, it would be wrong to conclude that officers are free agents or that their superiors exert minimal influence over them. In the same way that control by lay committees could intensify in particular circumstances, so could control by superiors and it was clear that there were definite constraints on officer autonomy, even in the AEU. As one T&GWU officer put it, 'occasionally the Monty Python boot comes down'.

More intense management control of officers' work appeared to arise in three kinds of situation. First, their portfolio of responsibilities is often set by superiors. The allocations of T&GWU District Officers, for example, were fixed either by Regional Trade Group Secretaries or by the Regional Organizer, while in the GMB this power lay in the hands of the Regional Secretary. In one of the GMB regions which was studied this power had recently been exercised by a newly appointed Regional Secretary who had re-allocated work between officers to ensure a fairer distribution of workload and to free certain officers for priority tasks, such as recruitment. This exercise was keenly resented by those who had experienced an increase in workload as a result, but despite complaints and a tendency by some to work without enthusiasm in their new allocations, they could not prevent it. The situation in the other two unions was rather different, in the AEU because of the District Committee structure, and in ASTMS because divisional offices operated on a 'collegiate' basis, with work being allocated by Divisional Officers themselves. Even in ASTMS, however, it was reported that national headquarters was trying to erode such self-management and achieve greater control of work allocation.

The second situation in which superiors tended to intervene was the crisis in the officer's work with the potential to affect the union's reputation, role, organization or finances. This might be a crisis in the officer's relations with members, such as a complaint about undemocratic or unprofessional behaviour, or a crisis in relations with employers, such as a strike or threat of legal action. A number of examples of this kind of intervention were given in interviews. A T&GWU District Officer with responsibility for bus-workers, for example, was instructed by his Trade

Group Secretary to attend a coroner's inquest on a driver who had been killed and build up a file on similar accidents. Industrial conflict, particularly where the possibility of legal action arose, was an area where officer autonomy was constrained by permanent regulations. In the GMB, for instance, officers are unable to initiate action or strike ballots without securing the support of the Regional Committee, effectively the Regional Secretary, and similar controls exist in the T&GWU. There is also evidence that such regulations have been tightened as the legal risks of industrial action have grown. In the AEU, for example, the right of District Committees to call strikes was restricted in the mid-1980s, providing support for the view that recent changes in labour law have encouraged the centralization of decision-making within unions (Brown and Wadhwani, 1990: 62).

The third situation where senior officers exerted greater control was a national campaign or policy initiative. The interview research, for example, was carried out shortly after the T&GWU and ASTMS campaigns to ensure retention of political funds, and officers in both unions had been directed to organize ballots and rally member support for a 'yes' vote. This had imposed a considerable extra workload on top of the routines of negotiation and representation. Other initiatives at about the same time were 'intensive' recruitment campaigns, organized by ASTMS, GMB and T&GWU, the multi-union campaign against water privatization and a regional T&GWU initiative in the chemical industry, designed to coordinate resistance to techniques of employee involvement. Policy initiatives could also result in greater direction of officers' work, through their impact on the collective bargaining agenda. Several instances were provided by officers of negotiating objectives which had been set at industry or national levels and which they were supposed to pursue in enterprise bargaining. Examples included the elimination of sleeper cabs and blacking of agency labour in road transport (T&GWU), the preservation of four year apprenticeships in engineering (AEU) and promoting the specific interests of female and part-time workers (ASTMS, GMB, T&GWU).

In a number of unions national concern with campaigning, particularly in the linked fields of recruitment and equality, has led to attempts to institute new and permanent controls over the officer workforce. The best example is the self-consciously new unionism of the GMB, which has resulted in a series of initiatives, embracing selection, training, work allocation, and supervision. Under the leadership of John Edmonds the GMB embarked on a deliberate and high-profile strategy to organize the 'new service class' and institute a 'fair deal' for women workers, and attempts to secure greater control of its officers are intended to ensure that these new objectives are realized.

Despite changes of this kind it remains the fact that full-time officers generally enjoy considerable discretion and freedom from strict supervision. There are several reasons for this. The first is the uncertain nature of officers' work which makes it intrinsically difficult to supervise. The observation research, for instance, indicated that a great deal of officers' time was absorbed in responding to requests from stewards and members and in attending unscheduled meetings. Only 23 per cent of meetings observed were routine, with the remainder being called at fairly short notice by officers themselves, members or employers.

A second support of officer autonomy is the fact that many senior officers do not view the deliberate management of their subordinates as a priority. Instead, many conceive of their position as that of a senior representative, responsible for more important negotiations, servicing key lay committees and presenting the political and public faces of the union to outside agencies. A number of regional officers in the T&GWU did describe their role in terms of coordinating and briefing District Officers in particular industries, but it was made clear that intervention and direction were not particularly intrusive. National officers in the GMB and ASTMS played a similar role, coordinating the work of officers with responsibility for particular industries, but in both cases this was described as a team-building and information-exchanging activity, and in neither case was it founded on hierarchical reporting relationships.

A third support of officer autonomy lay in the system of employment relations, described in chapter 4. In particular, the methods of selection employed by unions ensured the election or appointment of officers with a strong commitment to the goals of their organizations and the task of representation. The requirement for close supervision of officers' work, therefore, was not strong and workforce commitment or self-control obviated the need for imposed, external control (cf. Walton, 1985): 'I do it my way, but that's their way too', was how one T&GWU officer described his relationship with superiors. The importance of selection as a mechanism for ensuring satisfactory work performance is underlined by the fact that union leaders have used changes in selection policy to signal and reinforce changes in union direction. Under Jack Jones, for example, the T&GWU shifted towards the appointment of shop stewards to District Officer posts in order to support the 'de-bureaucratization' of the union and the GMB, in recent years, has tended to recruit Organizers from among its specialist staff to reinforce the union's 'new agenda' of recruiting peripheral workers (cf. Taylor, 1973: 688–9).

A final reason for the relative autonomy of officers has to do with their position as representatives. This is perhaps most apparent in electing unions, like the AEU, where the authority conferred by election provides a counterweight to hierarchical control. One AEU District Secretary, for instance, explained that 'The District is an all powerful base within the union. Almost a union within a union', while a second described the District Secretary as the next most powerful figure to the Executive Councillor, because 'We're elected'. Even in appointing unions, however, the officer's position as representative can act as a prop to independence. A T&GWU District Officer, for example, defended his participation in the campaign for a national minimum wage, although this was counter to his union's policy, on the grounds that this was the only way to advance the interests of his low-paid service sector workers. It was also the case within the T&GWU that Regional Secretaries were very conscious of the need not to erode the representative position of District Officers. Consequently there was an elaborate and customary etiquette governing the Region's intervention in District affairs. A Regional Trade Group Secretary explained that if a steward approached him for advice he would refer him to the District Officer, that he never entered a District without informing the officer and that all copies of correspondence with members were sent to relevant District Officers. The external union, therefore, was conscious of the need to bolster the authority of its officers and avoid compromising them in their relations with employers and members.

Variation in patterns of control and accountability to superiors was found to be associated with a number of factors, with each research instrument highlighting different influences. The head office survey indicated that the use of written job descriptions and performance appraisal were found primarily in unions with bureaucratic employment relations. Thus, unions with job descriptions were more likely to train their officers ($r = 0.48$, $p < 0.01$), while performance appraisal was found exclusively in unions which practised open recruitment ($r = 0.27$, $p < 0.05$). They were also, without exception, white-collar unions ($\chi^2 = 5.98$, $p < 0.05$), with narrow job territories in the public sector or privatized corporations ($\chi^2 < 6.87$, $p < 0.01$), possibly reflecting the spread of appraisal among employees in these industries in recent years or the fact that relatively centralized systems of collective bargaining encourage relatively tight control of officers.

These patterns of association were echoed by the survey of union officers. More frequent contact with superiors, for example, was reported by officers representing public sector workers ($\chi^2 = 18.4$, $p < 0.01$) and those who had been selected through open channels of recruitment ($\chi^2 = 41.6$, $p < 0.001$). As a consequence, such officers tended to be younger ($r = 0.41$, $p < 0.001$), to have been appointed at an earlier age ($r = 0.28$, $p < 0.01$) and to be better educated ($r = 0.31$, $p < 0.01$). Their older, less educated colleagues in closed unions, like the EETPU,

T&GWU and AEU, in contrast, appeared to work more independently of higher-level officers indicating, perhaps, both their greater experience and the importance of representative principles as a check on the emergence of conventional structures of management control within unions (cf. Donaldson and Warner, 1974).

The observation research encountered very few direct references to higher-level officers. References to higher levels of the union restricting officer discretion or the need to refer matters up the hierarchy, however, were related to a number of factors. The most important were the nature and purpose of the meeting observed and the industry in which officers were working. Officers referred to control over their activities at meetings called to discuss union campaigns on privatization and recruitment ($\chi^2 = 48.8$, p $< 0.001$), substantiating the point made earlier that management control of officers becomes more intense when there is a need to mobilize officer resources behind key national objectives. References to control were also made more frequently by officers in the public sector ($\chi^2 = 4.8$, p $< 0.05$), in part because it was these officers who were involved in national campaigns, but also because of the greater centralization of industrial relations, with a consequently greater need to coordinate the work of officers.

### Full-time officers' views on accountability

The preceding sections have provided information on the forms and extent of officer accountability to lay members and superiors. We now want to consider how officers themselves view both forms of accountability and their readiness to accept control from either source. This is an important issue because the theoretical accounts of officer behaviour, outlined above, contain very definite statements on officers' views on accountability. The literature on union bureaucracy, for example, suggests that officers will be anxious to escape lay member control and maximize their own discretion; models of union polyarchy, by contrast, suggest that officers will seek to extend their area of discretion against other representatives, located above and below them in the union hierarchy; while the social action model suggests that officers' views on the legitimacy of different controls over their work will depend on their own values. The aim of the present section, therefore, is to gauge which, if any, of these claims carries greatest weight.

The survey of officers provided strong evidence of a desire to retain discretion and limit control by union members. For example, 74 per cent of officers reported that they preferred members and lay representatives to present them with 'open-ended claims' (e.g. a request for a 'substantial increase') and 75 per cent disagreed with the statement that, 'The full-time officer should always go along with the wishes of his/her members'. These findings indicate that most officers subscribe to a 'leader' conception of their representative role (cf. Batstone *et al.*, 1977: 35). The minority of officers who rejected this definition and who saw themselves as delegates, tended to place themselves on the political left (r = 0.26, p < 0.05). Responses to the questions were thus filtered through officers' ideological frames of reference and a readiness to accept closer lay control over work behaviour appeared to be rooted in the critique of union bureaucracy found on the union left.

Although most officers were keen to preserve their negotiating discretion and escape from close control by members, they readily accepted accountability to members and acknowledged its importance. Table 5.2 indicates that the majority of officers believed it was 'very important' for them to report regularly to lay committees about their work and the observation evidence, presented earlier on member participation in the bargaining process indicates that this belief informed practice. There was a minority of officers, however, who denied that regular reporting to lay representatives was important. These tended to be on the right politically (r = 0.21, p < 0.05), to identify the source of union effectiveness in skilled negotiation (r = 0.20, p < 0.05), rather than member organization and pressure (r = 0.30, p < 0.01), and to have fewer (part-time) convenors in their allocations (r = 0.20, p < 0.05). Officer views on accountability, therefore, were again related to values and orientations to work, though there was also an indication that the sophistication of steward organization in the officer's allocation also exercised some influence.

Table 5.2 also shows that the majority of officers attached importance to regular reporting to their superiors, though for most this form of accountability appeared to carry less significance. More right-wing officers tended to attach least importance to reporting to their superiors (r = 0.18, p < 0.05). While the majority of officers were prepared to acknowledge the need for this kind of accountability, there were examples of resentment and resistance to attempts at greater management control, as the union polyarchy model would suggest. A dairy industry officer in the T&GWU, for example, complained about the additional burden imposed by running leadership and political fund ballots and remarked 'when they're over I'll go back to my priorities'. The same officer also expressed satisfaction at the break up of multi-employer bargaining in his industry, essentially because it would give him greater autonomy: 'I welcomed it in a way because as officers we were then able to get more involved. We were the message boys before; we had no input into those negotiations; we were ignored.' Similarly, a number of officers in

Table 5.2. *Officer views on accountability to lay committees and superiors*

'How important is it for you to report regularly to your superiors and to lay committees about your work?'

|  | Lay committees | | Superiors | |
|---|---|---|---|---|
|  | No. | Per cent | No. | Per cent |
| Very important | 66 | 67.3 | 26 | 26.5 |
| Fairly important | 25 | 25.5 | 47 | 48.0 |
| Fairly unimportant | 7 | 7.2 | 20 | 20.4 |
| Very unimportant | – | – | 5 | 5.1 |
| Totals | 98 | 100 | 98 | 100 |

*Source:* Officers' questionnaire.

ASTMS, GMB and T&GWU expressed discontent over work allocation decisions, which in some cases had led to a withdrawal of cooperation and tacit resistance to change. A GMB officer, for example, with a predominantly brewing and motor industry membership had declined to meet newly allocated members in retailing, leading them to consider a formal complaint to the Regional Secretary.

Although officers were concerned to retain their autonomy and were occasionally resentful at higher-level intervention in their work, the evidence did not provide unambiguous support for the polyarchy model. While conflict between different levels of officer seemed to be fairly common in all unions, its main basis appeared to be ideological and had more to do with the content of policy than the decision-making prerogatives of either side. This was most apparent in the factionalized AEU, where left-wing District Secretaries were scathing in their condemnation of the union's leadership, but also existed in other unions where the lines of ideological division were less clearly drawn. In the T&GWU, for example, we heard both sides of a dispute between a District Officer, committed to organizing low-paid, peripheral workers, and his traditionalist Trade Group Secretary who dismissed such work as 'do-gooding'. This kind of division, between those officers strongly focused on a new union agenda of equal opportunities and recruitment and their colleagues, committed to servicing existing sections of the membership, was encountered in all the unions studied, to a greater or lesser degree (cf. Heery and Kelly, 1989: 201; Kelly and Heery, 1989: 205).

It was also the case that officers' views on the critical issue of collective bargaining structure appeared to reflect values and policy commitments as much as any concern to maximize their bargaining responsibility (cf. Edwards and Heery, 1989: 141). Other dairy industry officers in the T&GWU, for example, were opposed to the break-up of national bargaining and were observed campaigning against it, partly out of loyalty to trade group policy and partly out of a belief that the decentralization of bargaining posed a threat to the union's role in the industry and would generate inequalities in terms of employment inconsistent with union values. Officers' views on bargaining structure and the appropriate relationship between themselves and their superiors, thererefore, did display some concern with defending and extending powers of decision but they were also informed by values and practical assessments of what was good for the union or sections of its membership. This mixture is precisely what one would expect from a professional and committed occupational group, conscious of its own organizational interests but guided as well by normative standards intended to promote the interests of unions and their members.

Perhaps the most significant finding in table 5.2 is that officers accorded greater importance to accountability to lay members compared with superiors. This is the exact opposite of what one would expect from a reading of theorists of union oligarchy, and also suggests that members may exert greater influence over officers' behaviour than do their superiors. The significance of this, in turn, lies in the fact that the goals and priorities of members and leaders diverge. This is demonstrated by table 5.3 which shows officers' reports of the kinds of issues they were encouraged to pursue by members and superiors, and which indicates that the two groups promoted rather different union agendas. Members acted as economic 'insiders' pressing officers for action on basic pay, job security and improved working conditions. Superiors, in contrast, while they shared some of the priorities of members, were primarily concerned with recruitment and equal opportunities. The fact that most union officers ranked higher basic pay (55 per cent) or protecting jobs (39 per cent) as their main priorities, while only 21 per cent cited recruitment and 11 per cent equal opportunities, underlined the importance of lay accountability as a determinant of their activities (cf. Kelly and Heery, 1989: 202).

We believe these findings are very significant because they indicate a barrier unions face in attempting to halt the decline in membership which most have experienced since 1979. Since 1987 the leaders of most large unions in Britain, together with the TUC, have launched high-profile recruitment campaigns designed to attract workers in growing sectors, like services and high-technology manufacturing (cf. Mason and Bain, 1991: 40). In addition, unions have sought to alter their services and collective bargaining agenda in order to make them more attractive to

Table 5.3. *Issues which officers had been encouraged to pursue by superiors and lay members, times mentioned*

| Issue | Encouraged by: | | |
|---|---|---|---|
| | Superiors | Lay members | Superiors and lay members |
| Recruitment | 21 | 5 | 12 |
| Equal opportunities | 11 | 8 | 17 |
| Reduced working time | 8 | 7 | 13 |
| Improved procedures | 5 | 3 | 3 |
| Low pay | 4 | 9 | 17 |
| Protecting jobs | 3 | 10 | 9 |
| Improved working conditions | 2 | 9 | 6 |
| Pensions | 2 | 4 | 5 |
| Higher pay | 0 | 13 | 5 |
| Job control | 0 | 2 | 2 |
| Other | 3 | 5 | 5 |
| Total N (respondents) = 101 | | | |

*Source:* Officers' questionnaire.

new groups of workers (cf. Heery and Kelly, 1988: 502). The GMB, for instance, launched its 'Fair Deal for Women' campaign and has attempted to include greater access to training in its bargaining demands, on the basis of market research which showed that opportunities for training are highly valued by employees.

What all of these initiatives propose is a redirection of union policy and resources away from the existing membership towards groups of unorganized workers, many of whom are also economic 'outsiders' on the periphery of the labour market. Our findings suggest that this redirection will not be easily achieved because the key resource within unions, the full-time officers, remain focused on serving existing members and are primarily responsive to their established interests. The 'radical democratization' of British unions in the 1960s and 1970s, therefore, which forced decision-making down the union hierarchy and strengthened accountability of officers to members, has arguably made it more difficult for the unions to adopt a strategic response to the difficulties of the 1990s (cf. Jary, 1990: 165). What many have identified as the key achievements of the 'new unionism' (Coates and Topham, 1974) of the earlier period have become obstacles in the path of the new unionism of the present decade.

## Full-time officers and the implementation of union policy

Having suggested that the dual system of accountability to which union officers are subject may constrain their participation in centrally-initiated recruitment campaigns, we now want to examine directly the role officers play in the implementation of national union policy. First, however, it is necessary to make the point that union policies assume different forms and have different implications for the work of officers. One distinction lies between policies which impinge on the process of collective bargaining by specifying issues for inclusion or exclusion from negotiations, and those which require officers to assume new tasks beyond the round of bargaining, such as recruitment or public campaigning. The former are generally less disruptive of established patterns of work. Examples of the first kind of policy would be the GMB's attempt to secure collective agreements on training or the T&GWU's attempt to secure the extension of full-time conditions of employment to part-time workers, while examples of the second type would be the recruitment campaigns run by most large unions in recent years or the joint union campaign against water privatization. A second distinction can be drawn between those policies which relate to particular occupational or industrial groups within a union's membership and policies which have implications for the broad mass of members. Examples here would include the engineering campaign for shorter working hours or the attempts by the T&GWU and GMB to boost their membership in the hotel industry, for the first type, and the campaign to retain political funds or tilt the collective bargaining agenda towards the interests of women, for the second.

A Head Office view of the importance of officers' policy role was obtained from the 1991 survey. Respondents were asked to rank ten officer tasks in order of importance, including 'responsibility for implementing national policy'. Of the 38 unions which provided estimates, just under a quarter (23.7 per cent) placed policy implementation among the three most important tasks of union officers. These, without exception, were unions organizing workers in single industries or white-collar occupations, and all but two operated primarily in the public sector or privatized corporations. These findings suggest that policy implementation is a more important aspect of the union officer's job where industrial relations are more centralized and where the existence of a relatively homogeneous membership raises both the need for and salience of centrally-authored policies (cf. Rainbird, 1990: 119). In more heterogeneous unions, by contrast, policy implementation was viewed as less important and for more than a third of unions (36.8 per cent) it was ranked below sixth place in the list of officer functions. In many cases negotiation, supporting workplace trade unionism, building organization and union education were seen as more critical aspects of the officer's job, underlining the point made earlier about the importance of accountability to members rather than to the wider union.

Broadly similar findings were obtained from the survey of union officers. A large minority (44.3 per cent) of officers agreed that the 'implementation of national union policy' was a 'very important' part of their job, while 46.4 per cent said it was 'fairly important' and the remaining 9.2 per cent said it was unimportant. In this case, however, the major sources of variation were not inter-union differences but differences in the characteristics of officers themselves. Those denying policy implementation was important tended to be right-wing ($r = 0.17, p < 0.05$) and to be less interested in politics ($r = 0.17, p < 0.05$), to be older when first appointed ($r = 0.24, p < 0.05$) and to be less supportive of their union's policies ($r = 0.29, p < 0.01$). Given that national policy at the time of the research in at least five of the unions studied (ASTMS, GMB, NALGO, NUPE, T&GWU) was focused on recruitment and equality, it is possible that these findings reflect the unease of more traditional officers with a new union agenda.

The observation research indicated that, while implementing policy could assume central importance for officers, for much of the time it was not a key component of their work. The most frequent reference to the wider union observed at meetings, for example, was the need to act in accordance with policy, but such references were observed at only 29.5 per cent of meetings. These tended to involve public sector officers ($\chi^2 = 6.32, p < 0.05$) and to be concerned with campaigning ($\chi^2 = 6.20, p < 0.05$), providing further evidence of the greater salience of national policy in more centralized, public sector industries.

Turning to the discretion officers have in implementing policy, the officers' survey indicated a wide range of opinion, with 31.6 per cent reporting 'total' or a 'great deal' of discretion in deciding whether or not to implement a particular national policy, 26.5 per cent reporting a 'fair amount' of discretion and 41.8 per cent reporting 'rather little' or 'none at all'. A larger measure of discretion tended to be reported by officers who had been selected through closed procedures ($r = 0.15, p < 0.08$), reinforcing the point made earlier that management controls are more attenuated where there is a strongly representative conception of the officer's role (cf. Undy *et al.*, 1981: 311). Officers reporting more discretion also had distinctive attitudes, in that they were less interested in politics ($r = 0.17, p < 0.05$) and were more likely to agree that their primary loyalty was to the members they serviced rather than the national union ($r = 0.24, p < 0.05$).

Interviews with officers in AEU, ASTMS, GMB and T&GWU also provided a range of opinion. On the one hand an AEU Divisional Organizer explained that he would 'love to agree' to employer proposals that the four year apprenticeship be scrapped in engineering, but that he could be removed from office if he did so, while on the other an ASTMS officer said that he regularly received memoranda from head office asking for progress reports on policy issues, but that, 'I bin [them] if I don't want to reply'. These statements are not contradictory, in that open defiance of national policy may not be possible where it has high salience for senior office-holders within the union, but on the ground, officers may have considerable discretion over the priority they attach to different policies.

This capacity of officers to choose whether they would implement policy with commitment or in token fashion was what stood out from interviews. In both the GMB and T&GWU, for instance, national and regional officers cited variable local officer commitment as a significant constraint on the development of recruitment activity. In the T&GWU's case it was said that officers had responded to the union's Living Wage campaign, designed to attract low-paid workers, in some cases with total commitment and in others with veiled hostility. It was also explained that, while the union could compel recalcitrant officers to participate in the campaign, this type of 'cure might be worse than the illness', as they deliberately disengaged from their normal duties to make a point.

The fact that officers do exercise discretion in the implementation of policy means that their own values and policy preferences influence their behaviour. There were a number of illustrations of this gathered through the observation work. A GMB officer played a central role organizing the campaign against water privatization, to which he was strongly committed, while several of his colleagues were noticeably less energetic in organizing publicity events or briefing shop stewards. In another case a T&GWU officer was deeply involved in attempts to organize hotel and catering workers, in line with national policy, to the extent that he had become involved in campaigns to defend Filipino immigrants, for which he was dubbed 'the community worker' by more traditional colleagues.

Likewise, the main finding of the women officers' survey was that the majority of women bargainers were strongly committed to using unions to advance the interests of women workers and that in a series of policy areas (part-time workers, childcare, maternity leave, sexual harassment and equal pay) they believed they had a stronger commitment than their male colleagues (Heery and Kelly, 1988: 493–5). Moreover, among male officers the officers' survey revealed a significant correlation between left-wing politics and attaching a relatively high priority to equality issues in collective bargaining.

Although officer commitment to policy may be necessary for successful implementation it is unlikely to be sufficient, and for this reason we sought to examine officers' own views on the obstacles they faced in implementing policy. Table 5.4 indicates that most officers saw member disinterest, employer opposition, lack of resources and member opposition as the main obstacles to policy implementation. Member disinterest was reported as a brake on recruitment activity in interviews with officers from both the GMB and T&GWU. Particularly in the latter there had been an attempt to use shop stewards for 'distant' recruitment activity, focused on unorganized workplaces. According to a Regional Organizer this had received a very mixed response, as activists failed to identify with action beyond their own place of work. Employer opposition was also cited as a barrier to recruitment, with examples given of activists being victimized by anti-union employers, though most cases of employer opposition related to policies which impinged on collective bargaining. A number of T&GWU officers, for instance, described the spread of agency labour in road transport, despite the union's attempt to secure agreements outlawing casualization. Numerous examples were also given of members directly opposing or disregarding policies, in areas as diverse as overtime working, acceptance of redundancies, equal opportunities and the spread of performance-related pay. Finally, several officers complained bitterly about lack of resources to implement policy, particularly where policies required them to take on additional duties. Despite the policy commitment of ASTMS, GMB and T&GWU to engage in 'sustained recruitment', officers said that they found it extremely difficult to escape from their routine duties to spend time visiting unorganized workplaces.

The obstacles to national policy reflect the nature of unions as both secondary and voluntary organizations. Unions are secondary organizations in that their members are employees who have been subject to primary organization by their employers. The practical consequences of this are that unions are dependent on employer support, agreement or compliance if they are to achieve many of their objectives, and that failure to secure employer cooperation can mean policy failure as well. Unions are also voluntary organizations in that, despite the *de facto* survival of the closed shop in certain industries, they have to attract employees into membership and then rely on their members' 'willingness to act' (Offe, 1985: 185) if they are to exert pressure on employers and ensure their compliance with policy. In periods of union retreat like the 1980s, securing this 'willingness to act' may be fraught with difficulty. The fact that unions are primarily dependent on subscription income also helps explain the resource problems which bedevil policy implementation. Like most voluntary organizations the majority of unions are strapped for cash,

Table 5.4. *Obstacles to implementation of national union policy*

| Problems encountered in trying to implement union policies | Rank order in importance | | |
| --- | --- | --- | --- |
| | Rank position (percentage) | | |
| | 1–2 | 3–5 | 6–8 |
| Membership disinterest | 69.1 | 23.4 | 7.4 |
| Employer opposition | 57.9 | 36.8 | 17.1 |
| Lack of time and resources | 33.7 | 60.0 | 9.3 |
| Membership opposition | 22.5 | 61.3 | 16.3 |
| Legal obstacles | 14.2 | 55.8 | 29.8 |
| Opposition from other unions | 12.3 | 26.0 | 61.6 |
| Lack of top union commitment | 6.9 | 31.9 | 61.1 |
| Opposition from full-time officers | 1.5 | 18.1 | 80.3 |
| N = between 95 and 66 | | | |

*Source:* Officers' questionnaire.

which imposes a heavy constraint on their ability to invest in new initiatives, such as recruitment campaigns or equality bargaining.

Variation in officers' reports of the obstacles standing in the way of policy was, again, related to a range of structural and personal factors. Overall, and simplifying somewhat, it appeared that those officers on the union and political left tended to rate failings in union commitment ($r = 0.23$, $p < 0.01$) and member disinterest ($r = 0.31$, $p < 0.01$) as more significant barriers to policy, while those on the right tended to identify employers ($r = 0.18$, $p < 0.06$), other unions ($r = 0.18$, $p < 0.06$), the law ($r = 0.17$, $p < 0.09$) and active member opposition ($r = 0.29$, $p < 0.05$). The left, that is, tended to lay the blame at the feet of their own unions and to be less critical of members, while the right tended to blame external forces, beyond the union's immediate control and to be more prepared to describe union members as part of the policy implementation problem.[2]

Officers' ranking of obstacles to policy was not solely a reflection of their own values, but was also related to a number of structural variables, the most significant of which was the main industry in which the officer worked. Officers in well organized parts of the private sector, such as engineering and the docks, were less likely to rank member disinterest as an obstacle to policy ($\chi^2 = 6.0$, $p < 0.05$), but more likely to cite legal pressures ($\chi^2 = 8.0$, p $< 0.05$), suggesting that, while members remain loyal to their unions in such sectors, the presence of more assertive employers, prepared to use legal action, has made it more difficult to translate policy into practice. The collapse of policies on agency labour or apprenticeship provide good examples of this, as employers have used a more favourable economic and legal environment to shake off union constraints on the organization of labour (cf. Metcalf, 1989). For officers working in less organized parts of the private sector, such as services, by contrast, there was a tendency to give a high ranking to lack of top union commitment ($\chi^2 = 11.4$, p $< 0.01$) and opposition from other officers ($\chi^2 = 6.7$, p $< 0.05$). In these industries, therefore, the policy problem basically consisted of a failure of unions themselves to put sufficient weight behind new organizational and representative strategies directed at the peripheral workforce (cf. Mason and Bain, 1991). The findings thus echo those on officer accountability and indicate that, despite the adoption of a radical new policy agenda in several unions in recent years, the forces of institutional inertia have made this difficult to translate into practice.

### Conclusions

Perhaps the central finding of this review of officers' work relations is that in general they are subject to fairly loose forms of managerial control and retain considerable discretion in performing their role. Just as chapter 4 indicated that union officers experience 'professional' employment relations, so this chapter has shown that they enjoy professional autonomy at work. Officers thus exercise judgement in the key task of collective bargaining, despite formal accountability to lay committees and bargaining groups, they are subject to a fairly limited range of line management controls and they exercise discretion in implementing national policy. In some unions, particularly the GMB, there has been movement towards a more managerialist pattern of work relations, in which officers' objectives are specified and their performance monitored from above. At present, however, change in this direction has been limited and union officers have not been subject to the intensification of management control which some other groups of professional workers have experienced in recent years (cf. Starkey, 1989).

The high degree of autonomy enjoyed by union officers, at least *vis-à-vis* the lay representative bodies to which they are formally accountable, provides initial support for the theory of union bureaucracy. Other evidence, however, is not compatible with the theory and leads us to reject its interpretation of the internal functioning of trade unions. For example, although officers may exercise considerable discretion in shaping the agenda of collective bargaining, deciding tactics and bringing negotiations to a close, there are still very real constraints on their activities and members can and do exert real influence over officers (see chapters 8 and 9). This is particularly marked in the key area of selecting bargaining objectives. Second, officers themselves do not generally display a 'bureaucratic' concern to avoid accountability to members and while most are anxious to retain some freedom of manoeuvre in collective bargaining, they also place a high priority on securing the support of, and reporting back to, the members they service. Third, hierarchical relations between officers do not fit the pattern suggested by the model in that line management control is weak and unions generally accord their officers considerable freedom in discharging their role. Fourth, responsiveness and accountability to members is accorded higher priority than responsiveness and accountability to superiors by most officers, which is precisely the opposite of what is suggested by theorists of union bureaucracy.

This last point is particularly important because much recent debate about trade union strategy is based on an implicit belief that unions should act in accordance with the bureaucratic model. Prescriptions of this kind are usually founded on the assumption that union goals should be set at national level and be implemented from the top downwards and occasionally contain an explicit reference to the need to make more effective use of 'human resources' (cf. Hoerr, 1991). There is also often an assumption that the effective control of union activity by existing groups of members should be reduced, particularly where these are white, male and relatively privileged and belong to the 'core' workforce (Willman *et al.*, 1993: 216). The significance of our research is that it demonstrates that unions at present do not fit the bureaucratic model and, whether it is desirable or not that they should do, indicates that there are some potent forces preventing them moving towards it.

The fact that officers are not tightly controlled by their superiors provides initial support for theories of union polyarchy. Further evidence supporting this view was found in the sensitivity of at least some officers to attempts by senior colleagues to encroach on their decision-making prerogatives and their desire to retain autonomy. Again, however, the research yielded counter-evidence. For many officers relations with superiors were not viewed in the competitive terms suggested by the model of polyarchy. Moreover, conflict between officers and their superiors most frequently arose over differences on policy and methods rather than over decision-making prerogatives. This suggests that the basic assumptions of the polyarchy model – that unions essentially consist of competing and self-interested layers of representatives – are too narrow a foundation upon which to build a full account of internal union relations.

Our own model places officers' values and ideologies at the centre of any explanation of their behaviour. In this case there was considerable evidence from a range of sources supporting the key hypotheses of the model. Officers' political and trade union ideologies were correlated with answers to a wide range of questions on their behaviour and relations with lay representatives and superiors. Thus, it was officers who placed themselves on the political and union right who claimed to behave like and espoused the values of the stereotypical 'union bureaucrat', in that they exerted greater control over collective bargaining and denied the importance of regular reporting to lay representatives. Right-wingers were also more likely to display a truculent independence towards their superiors and to question the importance of national policy-making, preferring instead to concentrate on the routines of negotiation and representation in their allocations. Left-wingers, by contrast, appeared more ready to concede influence over their behaviour to lay representatives and accord high priority to democratic accountability, though they were also prepared to play a leadership role in setting the bargaining agenda and were particularly anxious to pursue equality issues. Overall, therefore, there was considerable evidence that officers' values and ideologies count and that the discretion inherent in the job of the union officer is used in different ways by those with different beliefs.

However, officers' values generally accounted for only a proportion of the variation in attitudes and behaviour observed and other influences clearly exercised sway over relations with both lay representatives and superiors. One of these was the pattern of officer organization. In unions with a more extended division of labour formal accountability of local officers to lay representatives was less pronounced, with officers at senior levels holding primary responsibility for reporting to lay committees. A second organizational influence was the method of officer selection. Our findings here broadly echoed those of earlier research (cf. Donaldson and Warner, 1974; Undy *et al.*, 1981) in that elected officers and those appointed through 'closed' procedures were less accountable to superiors, but more accountable to union members.

One important external influence appeared to be the structure of collective bargaining in the main industries in which unions operated. Public sector unions tended to exert greater hierarchical control over their officers, which probably reflects the greater centralization of collective bargaining in much of the public sector, where national agreements continue to be important. A second external factor, the degree of sophistication of workplace trade union organization, appeared primarily to influence relations with lay representatives. Where workplace organization was relatively under-developed, lay representatives were more

dependent on officers and yielded them greater influence over the collective bargaining process. The reverse was true where organization was
more sophisticated, confirming the earlier findings of Boraston *et al.*
(1975).

Finally, it was apparent that lay representatives could exercise more or
less influence over officers depending on the nature of the issue being
negotiated and the degree of importance they attached to it. Similarly,
while senior officers may be content to let bargainers continue with their
activities undisturbed for much of the time, on occasion they insisted on a
more intrusive role and sought greater control. What this indicates is that
work relations between officers and those to whom they are accountable
are not static but fluid. That is, the frontiers of control, both above and
below the union officer, are re-negotiable, and the scope for autonomous
action continually expands and contracts depending on circumstance.

*Part 3*

The full-time officer at work

# 6    Organizing

## Introduction

Organizing workers in trade unions is an aspect of the work of union officers which increased greatly in salience in the 1980s, as a result of the decline in aggregate union membership. Most large unions in Britain have sought to encourage greater officer involvement in recruitment and, accordingly, the first aim of this chapter is to describe the kinds of recruitment activity in which local officers become engaged. An important distinction which has to be drawn in analysing this activity is between *direct recruitment*, where approaches to prospective members are made by officers themselves, and *indirect recruitment*, where officers support and encourage recruitment by lay representatives.

Recruitment, however, is only one part of the organizing responsibilities of officers, and a second concern of the chapter is to describe the work of officers in building, sustaining and shaping organization among existing union members. In part this work can be viewed as directed at raising and maintaining the capacity of trade unions to operate effectively in the workplace. However, it also often involves an attempt to shape union character, in that officers transmit norms of appropriate union behaviour in relations with members, employers and other unions to workplace representatives.

In addition to describing the organizing work of officers, the purpose of the chapter is to test a number of hypotheses about union organizing, derived from theoretical models of officer behaviour. The theory of bureaucracy, for instance, would lead one to expect that officers would be both anxious to limit the autonomy of workplace organization and concerned to offer tutelage to stewards in the norms of 'good industrial relations'. One might also expect a highly pragmatic approach to recruitment in which initiatives are informed by a kind of cost-benefit analysis rather than an ideological imperative to organize the new 'service class'. One might also expect most recruitment to occur through approaches to employers, rather than through attempts to mobilize employees, and for local officers to be primarily involved in the implementation of centrally-authored recruitment policies (cf. Fairbrother and Waddington, 1990).

Theories of polyarchy, in contrast, would lead one to expect variable officer commitment and a tendency to evaluate recruitment initiatives in terms of the extent to which they promote officers' own organizational interests. Officers whose core responsibilities involve servicing established bodies of membership, therefore, may be extremely resistant to national recruitment campaigns directed at new groups of workers, while officers whose responsibilities and careers are linked to servicing such groups will be supportive.

The third theoretical model, which emphasizes officers' values, suggests that there will be a number of sharply divergent approaches to organiza- tion among officers. Among officers on the trade union 'right', for instance, one might expect a desire to limit the autonomy of workplace representa- tives and tightly control steward organization, together with a preference for recruitment through approaches to employers. On the 'left', by con- trast, one might anticipate strong support for independent workplace organization and a preference for recruitment through direct approaches to workers and through demonstrations of union militancy. Finally, among women officers and those belonging to the 'new left' within unions there might be a concern to build organization among previously marginal groups of union members, to encourage activism among female and ethnic minority workers and to target such groups in recruitment campaigns.

Additional sources of variation are suggested by contingency theories of union behaviour. Where officers' allocations cover industries lacking a strong union tradition one would expect that both fields of organizing activity, recruitment and developing organization, would form a relatively large part of officers' total responsibilities (cf. Brown and Lawson, 1973). The structure of collective bargaining might also influence officers' organizing activity, with more decentralized structures leading to greater priority for encouraging independent and effective workplace organi- zation. Finally, union structure might produce differences, with more open unions laying greater emphasis on direct recruitment by officers among new occupational groups and new industries and closed unions relying more on indirect recruitment, with officers directing stewards to recruit around the fringes of existing membership (cf. Kelly and Heery, 1989).

### Direct recruitment

Among unions responding to the 1991 Head Office Survey, recruitment was ranked among the three main functions of full-time officers by 56.4

per cent. Only negotiation and supporting workplace representatives achieved higher average ratings. Among unions responding to the 1986 Head Office Survey only 32.4 per cent placed recruitment among the three most important officer functions, indicating the importance which came to be attached to membership growth by national union leaders in the late 1980s. Information from officers themselves, however, displayed in table 6.1, suggests that recruitment is a central work activity for only a minority of officers. It supports the belief that, notwithstanding declining membership, unions have been unable or unwilling to re-direct their resources towards 'sustained recruitment' (Kelly and Heery, 1989: 197; cf. Beaumont and Harris, 1990; Mason and Bain, 1991). Table 6.1 also indicates, however, that there is considerable support among union officers for a greater shift toward recruitment in that, among officers who expressed a preference, the largest percentage wanted to spend more time on this kind of activity. There was clearly a strong current of support among officers, therefore, for the reorientation of national union policy towards recruitment.

The final part of table 6.1, however, suggests why commitment may not manifest itself in the allocation of a greater proportion of officer time to recruitment. It reveals that although a significant proportion of officers rate increasing union membership as one of the two most important objectives of unions, for the majority raising the pay and protecting the jobs of existing members take precedence. Table 6.1, in other words, bears further testimony to the dilemma facing unions, described in chapter 5: how to promote the organizational interest of unions in building membership at the same time as servicing the interests of existing members, when resources are over-stretched.

More detailed information from the interviews and observation of officers underlined the point that officers' involvement in recruitment was generally limited. None of the officers interviewed or observed were engaged in 'sustained recruitment' (Kelly and Heery, 1989: 197–8). The closest approximation we encountered involved a T&GWU District Officer responsible for hotel, catering and other service industry workers. He claimed that recruitment had been the central component of his job when he was first appointed, when he had only 14 workers covered by a recognition agreement, but that the time devoted to it had declined and been replaced by administration and collective bargaining as organization became established. What this suggests is that 'sustained recruitment', involving generalist union officers, will typically follow a cyclical pattern, with periods of membership growth giving way to periods of consolidation, unless responsibility for newly organized workers can be transferred to other representatives.

Table 6.1. *Officers' involvement in and attitudes towards recruitment*

*Relative time officers spend on recruitment:*

| Rank position of recruitment | No. | Per cent |
|---|---|---|
| 1–3 | 18 | 18.6 |
| 4–6 | 39 | 40.2 |
| 7–9 | 39 | 40.2 |
| 10–14 | 1 | 1.0 |

*Activities upon which officers would like to spend more time:*

| Activity | No. | Per cent |
|---|---|---|
| Recruitment | 34 | 23.1 |
| Guiding lay representatives | 25 | 17.0 |
| Campaigning | 23 | 15.6 |
| Preparing negotiations | 23 | 15.6 |
| Negotiations | 12 | 8.2 |
| Party political work | 9 | 6.1 |
| Branch administration | 8 | 5.4 |
| Office routine | 6 | 4.1 |
| Other | 7 | 4.9 |
| Total | 147 | 100.0 |

*Note:* Responses are to an open-ended question asking officers to list up to three activities on which they would like to spend more time.

*Officers' ranking of trade union objectives:*

| Objective | Times ranked first or second |
|---|---|
| Higher basic pay | 55 |
| Protecting jobs | 39 |
| Help for the low paid | 21 |
| Increasing union membership | 21 |
| Improved working conditions | 19 |
| Help for women and ethnic minorities | 11 |
| Others | 36 |

N (no. of respondents) = 101

*Source:* Officers' questionnaire.

Rather more common was officer involvement in 'intensive recruitment': short, coordinated campaigns targeted at particular groups of employees, such as hotel and catering workers (GMB, T&GWU), retail workers (T&GWU), agricultural workers (T&GWU), taxi-drivers (T&GWU), local government staffs (GMB) and Midland Bank staff (ASTMS). These target groups could be adjacent to or fall within existing job territories, as with the GMB campaign to recruit local government white-collar workers, or they could be 'distant', working in unorganized companies, as with GMB and T&GWU attempts to recruit hotel workers. Work of this kind was typically coordinated by industry or regional officers, who selected targets, briefed and trained local officers, assumed responsibility for planning the campaign and monitored performance. For individual officers such campaigns involved leafleting workplaces, staffing telephone helplines, training lay activists in recruitment techniques, organizing and addressing meetings and attending target workplaces to explain and sell union services and give advice on individual employment problems. The final aim was typically to exert pressure on management and conclude the campaign with a recognition agreement, though this goal appeared to be only rarely attained (cf. Beaumont and Harris, 1990: 275).

A third type of activity was 'passive recruitment', in which recruitment opportunities presented themselves to officers. This could occur through individuals or groups asking to join the union, by activists alerting officers to recruitment opportunities, through routine recruitment of new employees in organized workplaces (e.g. through induction procedures) or through staff associations seeking to transfer engagements. While much of this work was low-key, background activity it could, on occasion, involve officers in substantial campaigns. A T&GWU retail officer, for example, said that developing membership in a previously unorganized warehouse had taken four weeks' intensive work, while a T&GWU building industry officer described recruitment of workers on often short-lived construction sites as a major component of his routine. Work of this kind is not completely reactive, in that officers have discretion over how they will respond to recruitment opportunities and may frequently initiate approaches to employees where pockets of non-membership are discovered within their allocations. A GMB officer, for example, said that he had selected three targets for recruitment activity, home helps working for a county council, a fish packing factory and a brake-linings firm.

### Influences on officer involvement in recruitment activity

Table 6.1 indicates that there is considerable variation among officers in the relative time they spend on recruitment and the priority they attach to it. Four types of influence appeared to determine this pattern: union structure and policy; the nature of the officer's allocation; officers' views on accountability and relations with superiors and lay activists; and officers' own values and the priority they attached to recruitment. By far the most significant influences on the relative time devoted to recruitment were the degree of 'openness' of the officer's union and the extent to which membership growth was a key objective of national policy (cf. Mason and Bain, 1991: 42). Two-thirds of officers citing recruitment as one of their three main activities, for instance, worked for the GMB, reflecting both that union's open structure and the commitment of its leadership to recruiting the 'new service class'. The other two unions with a majority of officers reporting recruitment among their six main activities were the EETPU and T&GWU, which also had policies of extending membership into new areas of employment. In NALGO and NUPE, by contrast, with their relatively closed structures, the vast majority of officers failed to list recruitment among their six most time-consuming activities.

The second influence on officer recruitment, the structure of the officer's allocation, appeared to operate in two ways. First, officers reported less time spent on recruitment where they were responsible for a relatively large allocation of union members ($r = 0.31$, $p < 0.01$). Analysis of the Head Office Survey revealed a similar association, in that unions with relatively large numbers of members per officer placed recruitment lower down their rank order of officer tasks ($r = 0.36$, $p < 0.05$). This is clear evidence of the degree to which officer workloads can restrict involvement in union organizing. Second, there was a weak but significant tendency for officers to report less involvement where they serviced members in established centres of union strength, such as engineering, chemicals, docks or cars ($r = 0.19$, $p < 0.05$). Outside these established centres, however, and particularly where workplace organization was weak, recruitment absorbed more officer time and was regarded a higher priority (cf. Brown and Lawson, 1973).

The third influence was officers' conceptions of their role and the accountabilities within it. A desire to do more recruitment tended to be expressed by officers who disagreed that their primary loyalty was to their members rather than the national union ($r = 0.24$, $p < 0.05$). This suggests that officers with a more bureaucratic and less representative conception of their role may respond more favourably to national union initiatives to raise membership and find space within their work routines to contribute.

Evidence of the final influence, officer values, could be seen in variable commitment to intensive recruitment. A T&GWU Regional Organizer, describing an attempt to recruit Sainsbury's workers, reported that it had been done 'properly with leaflets and meetings' by some officers, while others had 'simply gone through the motions'. Limited commitment appeared to arise in some cases from a lack of sympathy with the groups targeted for recruitment. A T&GWU officer, for example, who described himself as 'king of the brewing industry', was dismissive of attempts to organize hotel and catering workers, while a GMB brewing and car industry officer, who had reacted unfavourably to being given additional responsibility for organizing retail workers, argued that the GMB should remain a manufacturing union and not seek to become 'a second NUPE'. In these cases, therefore, officers reacted unfavourably to intensive recruitment, because they were oriented to representing the interests of established bodies of members in traditional industries, and because the shift in union priorities toward service sector workers posed a threat to their positions as representatives of hitherto central and powerful groups of members. Turning union policy outwards, towards intensive recruitment thus threatened to erode established bases of officer power.

Officer values and orientation to their work, however, could also stimulate involvement in recruitment of either an intensive or a passive kind. An example of the latter was provided through the observation of a woman District Officer in the T&GWU who had made it a priority to recruit part-time women, working as cleaners and caterers, in the heavily unionized engineering plants which comprised the bulk of her allocation. A second example was provided by another T&GWU officer, who had responsibility for hotel, catering and cleaning workers as well as taxi-drivers. Both of these groups were designated recruitment targets but he had devoted most of his time to working with the former, essentially because he had little sympathy with the 'white, male, self-employed and well-paid' cab section.

## The effectiveness of direct recruitment

The final theme which emerged from the research on direct recruitment was that of the ineffectiveness of much activity, and particularly the high-profile 'intensive' campaigns which the TUC and many individual unions initiated in the late 1980s. Much of this criticism emanated from officers with a limited commitment to recruitment, but this was not always the case and the GMB officer who had selected his own personal recruitment targets was scathing about much of the 'cold' recruitment, directed at unorganized workplaces, encouraged by the national union. In his view attempting to recruit without an internal contact was simply 'chasing after moonbeams'. Other criticisms of 'intensive recruitment' referred to the poor planning and management of campaigns, the difficulty of combining work of this kind with servicing a large allocation of members and the problem of retaining new members once recruited, which was particularly acute in seasonal and casualized service industries. These problems were also said to be compounded frequently by the hostility of employers prepared to victimize activists. As a result of these difficulties there was a bias among officers for selecting their own recruitment targets, for following up recruitment leads rather than initiating approaches to workers, for using identifiable grievances as a basis for organizing and for targeting recruitment where management was neutral or supportive of trade unionism. Passive recruitment thus tended to be viewed as more effective than the intensive campaigns promoted by national union leaders, particularly where these were directed at new industries and workers without a trade union tradition.

What this evidence suggests is that many union officers exhibit a 'conservative orientation in recruitment attempts' (Beaumont and Harris, 1990: 281), in which recruitment activity is largely directed at the kinds of workers, workplaces and industries which are already relatively well unionized. To a degree this does appear a rational and cost-effective strategy for unions, particularly given the limited success to date of attempts to recruit newer groups of workers beyond the union heartlands. Metcalf (1991: 22) has pointed out that there are 1.7 million 'free-riders' in unionized workplaces in Britain and that if one-tenth of these could be recruited annually it would more or less offset recent membership losses. However, there are two main dangers associated with a conservative orientation. First, it may stimulate inter-union competition and the recycling of union members from one union to another (cf. Willman, 1989). It was noticeable that the most effective campaign encountered during the research was the GMB's attempt to recruit non-manual workers in local government. But success in this case was partly based on local government workers abandoning increasingly militant NALGO branches in London in favour of the GMB's moderate white-collar section. Second, the long-term effect may be to help produce a form of 'ghetto-unionism' (Freeman, 1990: 305) in Britain, in which union membership is largely confined to mature manufacturing industries and the public sector. This, in turn, may further erode union political and economic influence and cut off the British trade union movement from the kind of broad societal influence acquired by its more 'inclusive' counterparts in Western Europe (Visser, 1990).

### Indirect recruitment

In addition to becoming directly involved in recruitment officers can train, advise and encourage their network of lay activists towards work of this kind. Indirect recruitment of this type is most likely to be relied on in passive recruitment situations, where new employees or pockets of non-membership are absorbed into the membership within already unionized workplaces (cf. Kelly and Heery, 1989: 197; Metcalf, 1991: 28). This is not always the case, however, and shop stewards and other lay representatives may sometimes be used for intensive recruitment targeted at unorganized groups of workers. The T&GWU's Living Wage campaign, designed to recruit low-paid workers, was based on the organization of 'Living Wage teams', comprising full-time officers and lay activists, which targeted unorganized workplaces, new trading estates and large non-union firms for recruitment activity. The campaign was a deliberate attempt to use the union's extensive shop steward network in traditional industries to extend organization to new areas of employment. It expressed the bias within T&GWU policy, since Jack Jones' day, for acting through shop stewards and represented an attempt to update that tradition and demonstrate its relevance in a period of union decline.

Table 6.2 shows the primary uses of shop stewards by full-time officers observed at meetings and the extent of indirect recruitment. It indicates that, although stewards were directed to recruit at about a quarter of meetings, this activity ranked only thirteenth in frequency. This underlines the point made earlier that recruitment is marginal to much of the routine work of officers and that their primary concern is servicing the current membership. Even where indirect recruitment was observed it often arose because of a perception that gaps in membership were compromising the bargaining power of existing groups of members rather than from a concern to extend membership to new groups of workers. An ASTMS officer was observed, for example, advising stewards to recruit in order to maintain bargaining strength in the face of a more assertive management and to maintain membership when the workforce relocated to a less well organized site.

The incidence of indirect recruitment was primarily associated with the strength of workplace trade unionism and was more frequently observed where there was no recognition agreement ($\chi^2 = 11.8$, $p < 0.01$) and where steward organization was less elaborate and sophisticated ($\chi^2 = 11.6$, $p < 0.01$). It tended to be where union organization was less capable of providing a significant counterweight to management, therefore, that officers used often rather skeletal shop steward organization for recruitment. The effectiveness of such action is open to doubt. An examination of the CPSA's recruitment year (Townley et al., 1985) found that recruitment success was positively associated with strong workplace union organization, and this suggests that the isolated, inexperienced and under-resourced stewards, who were most likely to be

Table 6.2. *Main uses of workplace representatives by full-time officers*

| Use of representatives | Percentage of meetings |
| --- | --- |
| Information on members' aspirations | 47.4 |
| Source of bargaining objectives | 47.4 |
| Information on management policy | 39.7 |
| Encourage adoption of more ambitious objectives | 31.4 |
| Encourage use of more militant tactics | 31.2 |
| Develop representative organization | 30.8 |
| Information on the climate of industrial relations | 30.1 |
| Encourage adoption of more moderate objectives | 30.1 |
| Develop strong bargaining relation with management | 28.4 |
| Mobilize members for industrial action or campaign | 28.2 |
| Encourage representatives' independence | 26.9 |
| Develop bargaining awareness | 25.8 |
| Recruitment | 24.5 |
| Encourage broader objectives | 21.8 |
| Communicate collective agreements | 21.8 |
| Information on member militancy/moderation | 21.2 |

N = 156

*Source:* Observation.

urged to recruit by officers, may have had difficulty mounting effective campaigns.

This latter conclusion arguably provides support for the T&GWU's policy of using experienced lay activists for intensive recruitment. The interviews with T&GWU regional and national officers, however, suggested that this policy had not been a success. A Regional Organizer declared that steward responses to the Living Wage campaign had been 'even worse' than those from District Officers, and cited the example of an agriculture officer who had failed to get a single activist to help with the campaign. This he said was 'not uncommon'. What this suggests is that the steward activism, which served the T&GWU and other unions so well in the 1960s and 1970s, cannot be relied upon to resolve problems of membership decline and shrinking job territories in the 1990s. Workplace trade unionism, by its very nature, is directed at servicing existing bodies of members and the very rootedness of stewards in particular workplaces must preclude them from becoming heavily involved in the organization of workers in other establishments.

It has been widely argued in recent years that recruitment activity by unions can not only determine the distribution of members between unions but also increase aggregate union membership (cf. Hartley, 1992;

Kelly and Heery, 1989; Metcalf, 1991; Undy *et al.*, 1981). As a consequence academic attention has been directed towards possible failings of union organizing as a partial explanation for recent membership decline. An influential American study by Goldfield (1987: 217) concluded that falling membership was due partly to the fact that unions had 'neither devoted the resources nor put sufficient effort into new union organizing to counter the employer offensive'. Goldfield (1987: 238) further explained this failing in terms of 'the bureaucratization of U.S. unions', which began in the late 1930s, and which weakened the impulse to recruit and inhibited the kind of militant rank and file action which was necessary to attract workers to unions.

The research findings presented above lead us to reject this interpretation, or at least its capacity to explain failings in union recruitment in Britain over the past decade. First, while Goldfield is right in arguing that militant opposition to management can provide a basis for recruitment, this is not always the case as the recruitment successes of avowedly moderate unions, such as AMMA, PAT and RCN, indicate (Beaumont, 1991: 50). Second, the decentralization of power within British unions, and the growth of workplace organization in the postwar period, have themselves created barriers to sustained or intensive recruitment of new groups of workers. This can be seen in the difficulty officers experience in finding time to recruit, the emphasis they place on accountability to existing groups of members and in the failure of significant numbers of shop stewards to participate in intensive recruitment campaigns. Finally, our research appears to support Goldfield (1987: 210–15) in demonstrating that unions differ in the priority they give to recruitment, and that these differences in policy influence the time officers spend on recruitment. However, in the EETPU, GMB and T&GWU recruitment was initiated by those at the top of the officer hierarchy, was associated with attempts to centralize control over policy and appeared to attract most support from officers with a more 'bureaucratic' conception of their role. Recruitment activity, therefore, appeared to be facilitated by union bureaucracy and was hampered by the dispersal of power within British unions (cf. Freeman, 1990: 318).

### Building workplace organization

In addition to recruitment, union officers have responsibility for building and reproducing workplace organization. The 1991 Head Office Survey revealed that 80 per cent of unions placed support of workplace representatives among the three most important responsibilities of officers, while one-third gave a similar ranking to developing union organization.

Part of this organizational work involves putting the basic building blocks of workplace organization in place. Officers were observed encouraging union members to take on representative positions, directing stewards to training courses, advising stewards on dealing with members and managers, developing steward organization, coordinating the activities of different groups of stewards and coordinating relations with other unions. Much of this work was relatively low-key and occurred in meetings which were not centrally concerned with union organization. Only 8 per cent of meetings observed were called to discuss organizational issues but in 31 per cent an attempt was made by officers to deepen or extend workplace organization. Union organizing, therefore, formed a more or less continual backdrop to the work of many officers.

There was variation, however, in the extent to which officers were involved in organizing. Analysis of observation data indicated that attempts by officers to develop workplace organization were more common where steward organization was relatively recent ($\chi^2 = 16.9$, $p < 0.001$); where there was an absence of shop steward hierarchy ($\chi^2 = 7.7$, $p < 0.05$); and an absence of steward-led bargaining over pay ($\chi^2 = 4.2$, $p < 0.05$). Attempts to build and deepen workplace organization, therefore, tended to occur where existing organization was relatively weak. In addition, however, there was evidence that officers' ideology also exerted an influence. Specific advice to shop stewards to develop their organization tended to be given by those officers we have characterized as 'leaders', who displayed commitment to radical or oppositional values ($\chi^2 = 6.9$, $p < 0.05$). Further evidence of this link was provided by the survey of officers, which revealed a strong association between a commitment to supporting stewards and a belief that 'a well-organized and militant membership is the best guarantee of successful outcomes to negotiations' ($r = 0.32$, $p < 0.01$).

A final influence on officer involvement in organizing was gender, both of officers themselves and of members. Analysis of the Head Office Survey revealed that unions with a high proportion of female members were more likely to report that support for workplace representatives was a central officer function ($r = 0.28$, $p < 0.05$). It can be inferred that female, part-time workers are less able to sustain independent shop steward organization and that therefore officers are required to provide support. Analysis of the individual officer questionnaire also found that women officers were more likely to attach priority to supporting stewards ($\chi^2 = 8.8$, $p < 0.05$). This may reflect the allocations of women officers and the fact that they are often responsible for servicing female members. However, it may also arise from a specific concern among women officers to develop women's organization within trade unions. More than three-quarters

(78.2 per cent) of women completing the women officers' questionnaire stated they were 'more likely to encourage women's participation in the union than male colleagues'. This was particularly true of more recently appointed women, who tended to adhere to a more explicit and radical feminist ideology (cf. Heery and Kelly, 1988: 500). The concern of women officers with organizing, therefore, was a further indication of the importance of officer values in shaping priorities and guiding behaviour.

### Shaping union organization

Attempts by officers to shape workplace organization embraced four types of relationship in which stewards were involved: with the external union, with the rank and file; with management; and with other groups of workers, including those in separate unions. In each of these areas there appeared to be a dominant conception of good practice which motivated the majority of officers observed. While there was also variation in the ways in which officers tried to shape workplace organization, therefore, there was an underlying normative model which influenced the bulk of organizing activity.

#### External union

The themes which guided officers' attempts to shape the steward–union relation were the need for and desirability of shop steward independence. One indicator of this was that at 26.9 per cent of meetings attended officers encouraged stewards to act independently of the external union while at only 6.4 per cent was the reverse advice given. A second indicator was provided by the officers' survey, with more than 90 per cent of officers agreeing with the statement that 'Wherever possible workplace representatives should handle their own collective bargaining'. There was a widespread belief among officers, therefore, that steward organization should be nurtured to the point where routine negotiations and representation could be handled without recourse to external support (cf. IRRR, 1992). This flatly contradicts the claim of theorists of union bureaucracy that officers are concerned to foster membership dependence on their expertise.[1]

One reason for this is logistical, in that the low ratio of officers to members coupled with the fragmented bargaining structure in much of British industry make officers reliant on stewards to service the membership. A second reason was that many officers clearly believed that steward activism was the hallmark of a democratic union. A GMB officer's immediate response to a question on the role of stewards, for instance, was to state 'I've always believed in participation', while a T&GWU officer declared: 'As a Marxist and a socialist, I look at the problem as how can I get people to play a part in society. My job is enabling them. I don't believe in taking problems out of the hands of my stewards.'

Crude notions of aggrandizing bureaucrats anxious to subordinate workplace organization to the external union were not supported by the evidence, therefore, but there were limitations to officer encouragement of workplace independence. Several officers, who said they encouraged stewards to resolve as many problems as they could, also said that they liked to be personally involved in issues with implications for the union's role in the workplace. An ASTMS officer, for example, stated that he liked stewards to involve him in cases of dismissal and a number of officers reported they insisted on being involved in negotiations over redundancy.

Variation in officers' active encouragement of steward independence was primarily related to the structural characteristics of companies, workplaces and workplace trade unionism. Officers tended to encourage independence at smaller firms ($\chi^2 = 17.8$, $p < 0.001$) and establishments ($\chi^2 = 19.6$, $p < 0.001$), where there was an absence of steward hierarchy ($\chi^2 = 13.4$, $p < 0.01$) and steward-led bargaining over pay ($\chi^2 = 12.0$, $p < 0.001$). It seemed that for many officers there was an ideal of a mature and self-sufficient workplace organization towards which less experienced and capable stewards were pushed. In interview, however, several officers commented on the greater difficulty they were encountering in achieving this ideal. Recession, redundancy and more assertive management were said to have eroded steward strength and increased the dependence of workplace organization on external support. A group of NALGO officers interviewed in 1991, for instance, complained of a shortage of stewards and a consequent need for officers to handle disciplinary and other individual cases. 'I'm a shop steward with a car and a mobile phone', was how one described his situation (cf. Millward et al., 1992: 129).

### Union rank and file members

Officers also attempted to shape the relationship between stewards and members. One theme which was promoted was the notion of representativeness and the need for stewards to reflect the makeup and characteristics of the workers they serviced. Typically this involved officers in attempts to increase the number of female and ethnic minority stewards. A GMB officer, for instance, at a meeting of local government stewards called to discuss organization, declared that 'This table does not reflect the membership', and argued strongly for the election of more women stewards and branch officials. This type of concern arose partly from national union policies, but also from a belief that union organization could not function effectively and attract and retain people in membership if stewards were not broadly representative. In the GMB case, for example, it was argued that many women workers were alienated by the union's male profile and that female stewards were necessary, both because they provided a focus for identification and because they shared and were more effective in representing the specific interests of the female membership.

A second theme which was promoted was the need for stewards to keep in touch with and remain accountable to their members. There was a strong emphasis on the need for stewards to consult with members before entering negotiations and to keep them informed of the results of collective bargaining. One of the most frequent pieces of advice officers were observed to give stewards (23 per cent of meetings) was to relay the details of collective agreements back to the shop or office floor. This suggests that officers were concerned lest stewards became isolated from their members, and on a number of occasions officers were observed directly instructing stewards in the need to retain member support. A GMB Regional Organizer, for example, stressed to his local government stewards that they must remain 'cleaner than clean' and not abuse a facilities agreement which provided for full-time release from work for senior representatives. He told a parable of a previous branch secretary who had abused such a system and spent most of his time in the pub, with the result that member confidence in the union and membership levels both dropped.

Although officers stressed the need for stewards to remain accountable there was also an emphasis on the need for leadership. Officers wanted stewards to guide members, mobilize them, shape their objectives and instil discipline, in much the same way as officers did themselves. A T&GWU officer, for example, explained that a good steward has to be able 'to sort the wheat from the chaff, to say on the odd occasion to members, they're not on. Management soon suss out if he's an errand boy.' A second T&GWU officer was highly critical of a bus-section steward for failing to provide leadership and be prepared to risk unpopularity by standing up to members. Specific advice to lead members was given by officers at 15.6 per cent of meetings and there was a slight tendency for it to be observed where union membership was lower ($r = 0.16$, $p < 0.05$) and where steward organization was relatively underdeveloped ($r = 0.15$, $p < 0.05$).

A possible interpretation of this stress on leadership could be that officers were trying to encourage the 'bureaucratization of the rank and file' (Hyman, 1989b: 154), the development of a conservative shop steward tier capable of disciplining dissident groups of members. However, the leadership that stewards were most frequently urged to provide was of the mobilizing rather than the restraining kind, which must cast doubt on any notion that officers were trying to re-create workplace trade unionism in their own 'bureaucratic' image. For example, officers were much more likely to urge stewards to generate membership support for industrial action or a union campaign (28 per cent of meetings) than they were to encourage the demobilization of members (4 per cent of meetings) and the criticism of the bus-section steward, just referred to, was given in the context of a failure to deliver a vote for strike action. There were significant differences, though, between officers and encouragement of mobilization was much more a feature of leader officers' relations with stewards than it was of managerialists ($\chi^2 = 14.9$, $p < 0.001$). It was also a feature of relations with less well organized shop stewards ($\chi^2 = 24.6$, $p < 0.001$). On this dimension of organizing, therefore, both officer values and the sophistication of steward organization were significant influences on attempts to shape workplace unionism.

### Management

Officers also attempted to shape stewards' relations with managers. One theme which stood out was officer encouragement of steward bargaining awareness. At just over a quarter of meetings attended officers encouraged stewards to identify issues which could be raised with management and which might be brought within the span of joint regulation. For example, an ASTMS officer ran through union literature and model agreements on new technology to try and persuade a group of financial services stewards to open negotiations on the use of VDUs, while a GMB officer advised stewards working on a newly privatized NHS cleaning contract to introduce themselves to management and provided them with a list of issues which could be raised in discussions. Not surprisingly, this kind of advice tended to be given where steward organization was less sophisticated ($\chi^2 = 13.5$, $p < 0.01$).

A second way in which officers encouraged bargaining awareness was by urging stewards to use grievance and other procedures to challenge management. Advice of this kind was also given at a quarter of meetings and again tended to be given where steward organization was weak ($\chi^2 = 9.6$, $p < 0.05$). Examples included a T&GWU officer with a hotel membership who told stewards that they must use the non-negotiated staff complaints system in order to raise the profile of the union; a GMB officer with a retail membership who advised contesting disciplinary action for minor infringement of dress regulations for the same reason; and an ASTMS officer who, faced with a management threatening partial derecognition, urged stewards to respond by entering failures to agree. In all of these cases officers were encouraging stewards to use the opportunities afforded by formal procedures to contest and try and control management decision-making. It was notable that a rather different use of procedures, as an alternative to direct action by employees, was recommended by officers in the merest handful (1.9 per cent) of cases. It was also the case, however, that advice to use procedures both to control management and as an alternative to action tended to be given by officers with a managerial orientation ($\chi^2 = 14.1$, p < 0.001; $\chi^2 = 13.1$, p < 0.01), suggesting a stronger procedural bias among officers on the union right.

Another feature of officer attempts to shape steward relations with managers was a quite widespread recommendation that stewards should distrust management and develop an adversarial relationship. Advice of this kind was given at 18.2 per cent of meetings, while at only 6.5 per cent were stewards urged to cooperate with management. In addition, officers' references to and descriptions of management motives and actions were overwhelmingly negative in character (see chapter 9). Officers, therefore, generally promoted a power or conflict model of industrial relations, in which managers were perceived to have opposing interests to workers and effective organization and tight agreements were required to control management behaviour. Further evidence of this was found in the fact that officers were more likely to advise the imposition of sanctions against management (16.9 per cent of meetings) than they were the lifting or avoidance of sanctions (6.5 per cent). Variation on this dimension was again related to officers' orientations to work: leaders were more likely to urge the use of sanctions ($\chi^2 = 4.9$, p = 0.09), while managerialists were more likely to urge restraint ($\chi^2 = 6.9$, p < 0.05).

Within the span of a broadly adversarial relationship, however, officers were keen to promote steward contact and negotiation with managers. It was common for officers to urge stewards to seek meetings with managers (21.4 per cent of meetings) and to offer advice on negotiating behaviour (33.1 per cent). The final theme in officer attempts to shape steward–management relations, therefore, was a desire to encourage 'strong bargaining relations' (Batstone et al., 1977: 155) between stewards and individual managers. Stewards were encouraged to enter such relationships, essentially because they offered a means to influence and exert some control over management decision-making. In this case there was no relationship with officer orientations, though there was a non-linear

Table 6.3. *Officer and steward attempts to influence relations between groups of members and different unions, percentage of meetings*

|  | Officers | Stewards |
| --- | --- | --- |
| Recommend permanent contact with other groups of members | 23.1 | 5.9 |
| Seek support of other groups on particular issues | 21.2 | 6.6 |
| Preference for isolation from other groups | 3.2 | 11.8 |
| Need to develop permanent links with other unions | 7.7 | 5.4 |
| Need to seek support of other unions on particular issues | 18.6 | 0.7 |

N = 156

*Source:* Observation.

relationship with workplace size, such that officers were more likely to urge meetings with management at relatively small and relatively large establishments ($\chi^2 = 8.5$, $p < 0.05$).

### Other workers

A repeated theme in discussion of workplace trade unionism in Britain has been that of sectionalism and the division of workers against themselves (cf. Kelly, 1988: 136–44). A fourth area which was selected for examination, therefore, was officers' attempts to influence relations between groups of workers and between different unions. Table 6.3 indicates, firstly, that attempts by officers to broaden steward organization and develop links across groups of members were relatively common and were encountered much more frequently than advocacy of isolation. A GMB officer, for instance, advised previously warring local authority refuse and highway memberships to sink their differences in a new joint organization, while the ASTMS officer mentioned above, who was faced with derecognition, urged joint meetings of his clerical and engineering stewards to coordinate resistance.

Table 6.3 also indicates that this search for coordination occasionally extended to relations between unions. At nearly a fifth of meetings officers recommended seeking the support of other unions on particular issues, while in a smaller number of cases they recommended establishing permanent cooperation. A GMB officer described how he had met with colleagues from COHSE and NUPE to coordinate activity in the health service and put an end to poaching of each other's members and claimed more time was now spent 'fighting the employer'. Of course inter-union cooperation could break down, and at joint union meetings attended there were often open signs of tension across union boundaries, but the dominant officer orientation was to try and foster cooperation.

The final piece of evidence in table 6.3 is that stewards were more likely to advocate isolation than they were to urge permanent contact with other groups. The refuse and highway stewards referred to above responded to the officer's suggestion by exchanging examples of one failing to support the other, and in the NHS case GMB stewards remained openly competitive in their relations with other unions. What this suggests is that officers may serve as important points of coordination in workplace trade unionism, encouraging groups of stewards and members with fragmented interests to cooperate and pool their collective strength. The relative detachment of stewards from the workplace thus enables them to promote unity between groups of union members. Moreover, unlike other aspects of officers' organizational work, attempts to coordinate union members in this way tended to occur where workplace organization was relatively sophisticated, suggesting that a platform of organization has to be attained before coordination of stewards becomes possible. Recommendations to cooperate with other groups of workers and members of other unions, for example, tended to be given where union density was high ($\chi^2 = 7.0$, p < 0.05; $\chi^2 = 11.3$, p < 0.01).

### Conclusions

It has been alleged by Perkin (1989: 390) that professional workers, including trade union officers, typically 'condescend' to those they service. In an attempt to accumulate power and status for themselves, they foster the subordination and dependence of client groups who rely on their expertise. A similar notion can be discerned in Hyman's (1989b: 158) definition of union bureaucracy as a 'relationship', characterized by 'the dependence of the mass of union membership on the initiative and strategic experience of a relatively small cadre of leadership – both official and unofficial'. The most striking thing about this survey of union organizing is the relative absence of deliberate attempts by officers to foster this kind of dependent relationship. Union officers appear to be enabling rather than 'disabling' professionals, in that at the heart of their work is an attempt to establish vigorous, self-supporting and relatively autonomous workplace trade unionism.

The reasons for this are twofold. First, in a context of decentralized bargaining and limited resources, British unions require lay activists to shoulder much of the burden of day-to-day representation. Second, there is a strong commitment to lay participation and steward activism for their own sake, which has perhaps been strongest in the T&GWU since Jack

Jones' day, but which characterizes other unions as well. This, in turn, is supported by the employment relations within unions, which result in the recruitment of experienced lay activists to officer positions, and by systems of work relations, which emphasize officer accountability to lay committees and shop stewards. It should also be noted that this normative commitment to active participation was an adaptive response on the part of unions to the rise of independent, militant and frequently critical shop steward organization in the period of full employment after the Second World War. The organizing activities of officers described above, therefore, should be seen as historically specific, emerging after a period when official trade unionism was often suspicious of lay activism and anxious to curtail its scope (cf. Beynon, 1984: 64, 267–8; Hyman, 1983: 41–4; Lane, 1974: 145–68).

This point about the historically specific nature of organizing is, we feel, important. Theories of union bureaucracy not only assert that officers tend to foster membership dependence, but also claim that this is a permanent or necessary function of official trade unionism, arising from the pressures to which unions are exposed in capitalist societies. In our view, however, the relationship between union officers and union members cannot be satisfactorily derived in this way, but should instead be seen as contingent and the product of conflict, ideology and different organizational forms. Officer promotion of steward independence at the time of our research, therefore, was the result of a particular combination of influences, including the 'challenge from below' to established union leaderships in the 1960s and 1970s, the spread of an activist conception of union democracy at the same time, changes in union constitutions which empowered shop stewards and the shift in collective bargaining towards the workplace.

While building and supporting workplace organization continues to be central to the organizing work of officers a new organizing agenda has appeared as a result of union membership decline. This is headed by the need to recruit, particularly among sections of the workforce which are expanding and which have low union density. According to Fairbrother and Waddington (1990: 42), recruitment initiatives targeted at such groups 'attest to the pervasiveness of bureaucratic forms of organization'. Our evidence on officer involvement in recruitment provides some support for this view. Officers spent more time on recruitment in unions like the GMB, whose leadership had made it a central priority, and there was also a tendency for officers with a bureaucratic conception of their role, which emphasized loyalty to superiors, to be more heavily involved in recruitment.

In the main, however, our evidence again provided only limited support for theories of union bureaucracy. The interviews, observation and survey research all yielded examples of the limited capacity of unions to direct and coordinate their officers in centralized recruitment campaigns. An important reason for this was the system of work relations, which permitted officers considerable discretion and emphasized accountability to existing members rather than to superiors. In addition, the research revealed a good deal of recruitment activity which did not fit the bureaucratic model. Many officers were engaged in background recruitment, responding to requests for membership from employees, and it was also common for officers to urge stewards to recruit, in order to maintain the collective bargaining strength of existing groups of members. Often there was a clear preference for this kind of 'conservative' or reactive recruitment among officers and an open scepticism of the value of the kinds of high-profile campaign, directed at unorganized workers, which have been initiated by national leaders.

There are also problems with the model of union polyarchy. Officer resistance to centrally-authored recruitment campaigns does accord with the theory, particularly where resistance arises from a perception that a new priority for recruitment involves diminished resources, power and status for those servicing traditional bases of member strength. The basic assumptions of this model, though, remain too narrow to generate a complete understanding of officer behaviour. Much of the organizing behaviour of officers described above was value-driven, rather than instrumental in origin, which is precisely what one would expect from professional employees working for highly ideological voluntary organizations, like trade unions.

There was considerable evidence, therefore, to support the third theoretical model, which lays emphasis on officer values. The observation research revealed a number of differences between militant officers, those we have labelled leaders, and their managerialist colleagues. Leaders displayed greater concern with developing shop steward organization, were more likely to encourage stewards to mobilize member opposition to management and to recommend that stewards adopt a more adversarial posture themselves when dealing with managers. What Hyman (1989b: 159) has termed the 'style and character of leadership' could vary significantly among officers, therefore, with those on the union 'left' demonstrating a greater concern 'to stimulate the collective awareness, activism and control' of union members within the workplace.

A second type of difference, which testified to the importance of officer values, lay between officers committed to a 'new left' ideological agenda, in which gender issues loomed particularly large, and their more traditional colleagues. Support for national recruitment campaigns, targeted at the new 'service class' appeared to be strongest among 'new left' officers. This group were also more likely to encourage women members to take on representative positions in union branches and at the workplace and try and develop steward bargaining awareness on gender issues. Women officers were particularly prominent in this regard and there was evidence that, as a group, they had a higher commitment and devoted more time to organizing than the bulk of their male counterparts. The research, therefore, indicated that the gender of officers 'makes a difference' to organizing behaviour (Heery and Kelly, 1988).

Again, however, an explanation of officers' organizing behaviour which is framed purely in terms of values and orientations to work must be incomplete as there were similarities in approaches to organizing among officers with very different values. Two important structural influences on officers' organizing activities appeared to be union structure and the degree of sophistication of workplace trade unionism. Both the survey and qualitative research indicated that recruitment was a more important component of officers' work in open unions, which had greater need and greater opportunity to extend their job territories into new industries and occupations. Building and supporting workplace organization, in contrast, was heavily influenced by the sophistication of workplace trade unionism. Officers did more of this work and invested more time and effort in trying to develop and shape workplace organization where it was rudimentary and of recent origin and where stewards were isolated, inexperienced and relatively uninfluential in their dealings with management. For many officers there appeared to be an ideal of the self-supporting and effective steward body towards which the more dependent and less effective had to be pushed.

With the decline of traditional centres of union power, however, and the emergence of a less supportive management, this task appeared to be becoming more and more like the labour of Sisyphus. The result was that the two sides to union organizing described in this chapter, recruiting new members and developing organization among existing members, were often experienced as competing pressures by officers. It appeared to be more difficult to attain the goal of vigorous and self-supporting workplace organization, with the result that officers felt constrained in their ability to contribute to recruitment campaigns, even where they had a strong predisposition to do so.

# 7　Bargaining objectives

## Introduction

Collective bargaining with employers is the most time-consuming activity of many trade union officers, and is often their principal point of contact with their unions' membership. Not surprisingly therefore theories of union behaviour have generated a relatively large body of predictions about the bargaining behaviour of officers. For theories of bureaucracy and oligarchy, the union officer acts as a moderating force within the bargaining process, dampening down the unrealistic aspirations of stewards and members, narrowing and accommodating their demands to the economic position of the employers, and avoiding recourse to sanctions proscribed by procedures and statute law. We would consequently expect to find a considerable degree of conflict between stewards and union officers.

The theory of polyarchy suggests that union officers are strongly motivated to retain or enhance their control over the bargaining process. They will consequently prove highly sensitive to any threats to their bargaining rights and will demonstrate a strong preference for procedural objectives (as compared with substantive objectives) and procedural arguments. Contingency theorists have paid particular attention to the structural determinants of officer behaviour, such as workplace size, sophistication of steward organization, collective bargaining structures, trade union policy and bargaining scope. These variables have been used to explain the degree of officer involvement in bargaining and the independence of workplace organization, but they have rarely been used to explain the precise relations between officers and stewards within the bargaining process. Contingency theory therefore directs our attention to a series of structural influences on behaviour but without offering any clear-cut hypotheses about the *direction* of influence.

Our own perspective on officer–steward relations, as outlined and developed in earlier chapters, assigns far more weight than the theories identified so far to the value systems of officers. We argue that the role of the union officer permits considerable discretion in the detailed, day-to-day conduct of bargaining: in the methods of formulating bargaining claims, in the content and ambition of claims, in the arguments used to defend them, in the resort to sanctions, and in the decisions over when to accept an offer. The role itself merely prescribes that officers shall bargain on behalf of their members, but the content and process of bargaining remains indeterminate, to be decided between the officer and his members, hence the scope for the officers' (and the stewards') own value systems. Our typology of officer orientation – managerialist, regulationist and leader – was presented and explained in chapter 2 as a way of trying to capture the key values of officers in their working relations.

In the remainder of this chapter we look at the determination and content of bargaining goals and the criteria used in their formulation. Before addressing these issues we briefly describe three case studies of bargaining in order to give a flavour of the three types of officer (managerialist, regulationist, leader) at work.

### The process of bargaining: ideology at work

*The managerialist*

This case involved a T&GWU District Officer negotiating the annual pay and conditions round in a large, well established retail chain. The union had secured a closed shop agreement in the early 1970s, and by 1986 had built a system of workplace stewards, an annual delegate conference and a national officers' committee. In practice, this seemingly sophisticated organization concealed large variations between stores as well as a low overall level of steward experience and independence. Under a spheres of influence agreement the Southern half of the country was T&GWU territory, the Northern half was USDAW-controlled. Pay and major conditions of employment such as hours, shift patterns and holidays were negotiated nationally each year, with the union side made up of two full-time officers (one T&GWU, one USDAW) and four or five shop stewards. The management side consisted of three members: the Personnel Director, who was the chief negotiator, a Personnel Officer, and a store manager. The main item on the agenda was a demand for a substantial pay rise, and other demands were for extra holidays and for management to investigate abuses of the bonus system. This final point involved a complaint that shop managers were boosting their earnings by illegitimately competing with sales staff for customers and sales commissions. The chief negotiator on the union side was the USDAW official who took this role because of his seniority (he was a national official whilst his T&GWU counterpart was a local officer). Nevertheless, the T&GWU officer played an important role in negotiations and made frequent contributions that were often at odds with those of his USDAW colleague.

At the opening session management responded to the union's claim by agreeing to improvements in holidays which the union side accepted, thus quickly taking this issue out of negotiations. The allegations of 'management selling' were initially rejected, but several bargaining sessions and two months later the management side agreed to 'look into' the issue. That left the annual pay rise as the sole issue in contention. Whilst the USDAW official backed by his stewards pushed for 7 per cent and was willing to hold out for this, the T&GWU managerialist never considered this even remotely achievable. In union side-meetings and pre-meetings he consistently argued the unions' aspirations downwards. Initially he pointed out that the 'going rate' in the private sector was about 5.7–5.8 per cent, and was only 4 per cent in the public sector. He added that commission would add several percentage points to any base rate increase, and that inflation had fallen from 4.5 per cent to about 3 per cent. For all these reasons he believed that management's offer of 5.5–5.8 per cent (varying by grade) was a perfectly reasonable one.

As negotiations continued with no movement on the management side, he then began to invoke management's own arguments against USDAW. He repeated the points that company sales were falling and that profits were needed to fund the major expansion programme decided on several years earlier. Eventually it was agreed that management's offer would be put to a membership ballot but without any recommendation. Although the T&GWU officer would have preferred a recommendation to accept he believed the members would accept the offer in any case and therefore conceded to the USDAW preference for no recommendation. The ballot result was mixed, with T&GWU members voting to accept, but USDAW voting to reject. The USDAW officer insisted that they should make one last attempt to squeeze more out of the company, and the T&GWU officer readily assented, safe in the conviction that management was not going to budge. This proved correct, and after another USDAW ballot, the offer was finally accepted across the country.

The T&GWU managerialist entered negotiations convinced the union would get no more than 5.8 per cent. He accepted management's reasons for refusing to go any higher; he made no attempt to mobilize the membership behind a campaign for a bigger rise and indeed actively worked throughout negotiations to moderate the aspirations of the union side in order to align them with management's objectives.

*The regulationist*

This case involves a T&GWU District Officer negotiating on behalf of a group of mostly female catering staff working on the site of a large multi-national pharmaceutical company. As the catering function was put out to contract some years ago the staff are actually employed by a large catering company. There were 38 employees, working in the canteen (mostly women) and the kitchens (mostly men). There were two stewards, one each for the canteen and kitchens respectively. The female canteen steward was quite experienced and had been in post for over six years, but the male kitchen steward was relatively new with less than two years' experience. The full-time officer had been called in to handle the annual pay negotiations. Employees of the pharmaceutical company had received a 7.5 per cent rise and the catering workers wanted to maintain their long-standing parity and were asking for the same figure. Management's initial offer however was just 5 per cent, on the grounds that inflation was only 4 per cent (in fact the RPI for May 1986 was 2.8 per cent) and this particular group of employees was very well paid because of their historic link with the high-paying pharmaceutical firm. Privately the officer thought the latter argument was a strong one, and moreover as management had tried last year to get rid of parity it was clear they were determined to pursue the issue. In any case she didn't think workers would fight the issue and these considerations very much dictated her strategy.

In the first bargaining session she largely reiterated the arguments put to her by stewards, which stressed the justice of parity, the contributions and commitment of the workers to the company and the fact that the company could afford their claim. After management's rejection of these arguments she returned to the members, calling a mass meeting, and putting to them what management had said. When asked directly what level of settlement she thought the members ought to accept, she evaded the issue, saying it was up to them, but then added that the difference between 5 per cent and 7.5 per cent was very small in real terms. (Privately she said afterwards that 6 per cent had been her calculation all along of what the members were likely to get.) Despite this comment, members voted unanimously to reject 5 per cent. In the second bargaining session the officer reported members' feelings but added, very significantly, that she might be able to recommend an offer between 5 per cent and 7.5 per cent. Management responded to the invitation with an offer of 6 per cent, warning that any higher award would entail cuts in jobs and/or hours. At the second mass meeting of the day the officer merely reported management's offer and viewpoint without comments or criticism. Nor did she advise the members explicitly on how to respond, or suggest any other course of action, or arguments that might persuade them. Although most of the workers who spoke were against the 6 per cent offer, the absence of any lead from the officer largely explained the final vote: 32 for acceptance of the offer, 0 against with 5 abstentions.

This sequence reveals several key features of the regulationist officer in action: the strong sense of pragmatism, the calculation of what is likely to emerge from a balance of power treated as given, the absence of hostility to management, the friendly relations with stewards coupled with the absence of any attempt to lead the stewards or use them to mobilize the membership.

### The leader

This case involves a male ASTMS officer in his early 40s who had been with the union for 14 years. He was a university graduate and even had a postgraduate qualification. A member of the Labour Party, though not especially active, he clearly stood on the left wing of the Party. The firm in question was a medium-sized electronics assembly plant employing 212 people and located in South London. Most of the production workers were women and in the T&GWU and were represented by just two stewards, whilst ASTMS organized the mostly male technical staff as well as some administrative and clerical grades (38 in all). There were two ASTMS stewards one of whom was very experienced and had been in post for four years, whilst the other was relatively new with just 12 months as a steward. Industrial relations in the factory were described by the officer and stewards as fairly good, and most years the ASTMS stewards handled their own negotiations as well as dealing with members' grievances. The works manager was strongly committed to high levels of production and was regarded as firm but fair, and relations between him and the stewards were good. The managing director was another story, as we shall see.

At the time of our research the plant was due to be closed and some of its labour force, equipment and product range transferred to a larger, existing site several miles away. The ASTMS officer (and his T&GWU counterpart) had been called in by stewards following management notification of 49 redundancies. The T&GWU officer (a regulationist) was initially in favour of seeking to negotiate an agreed procedure on redundancy, but the ASTMS leader insisted from the outset on a simple demand of no redundancies at all. He argued forcefully that in the run-up to the relocation, due in 3 months' time, the company was highly dependent on worker cooperation and therefore vulnerable. Consequently he urged stewards to exploit this vulnerability to the full: there was no suggestion that workers and management should cooperate in any common interests. At the outset it was this ambitious, substantive demand that formed the union's opening case and any hints of joint procedures and compromise were pushed aside. The first bargaining session involved both officers, three stewards, the works manager and the managing director (MD) but the ASTMS officer and the MD were the key protagonists. The session was marked by sharp exchanges of views, and the normal inter-group antagonism of the bargaining relationship was overlaid with overt inter-personal hostility.

By the second session the union had shifted ground and was insisting on no *compulsory* redundancies, whilst continuing to press the management for more information about the basis of their figures. The officer attacked both management's competence and their good faith, pointing out to them and to the stewards that whilst they were making existing staff redundant they were simultaneously applying to the Area Manpower Board for young YTS trainees! Moreover whilst their first meeting had agreed to a 30 day consultation period, management had meanwhile begun to interview and select those who were to be made redundant. The officer had now added a series of conditions to the union's demand though management was still refusing to budge on the principle of their right to declare redundancies. At this juncture the officer switched tack, and began to argue that redundancies were neither necessary nor in management interests, arguments that could have been used quite easily by managerialist officers. However when these arguments cut no ice, the officer then announced that he would call a mass meeting to seek support for industrial action, a move previously proposed to, and accepted by, the stewards. The meeting produced an overwhelming vote for industrial action unless management agreed to the union's demands. By this stage the pressure was beginning to split the management side: the works manager informally offered a deal only to find in the formal bargaining session that his MD was still being evasive and was resistant to the union's demands. Faced with the threat of action, a higher-level company manager was brought in at short notice, and after a heated negotiating session, he and the union officer spent one hour in a private, corridor meeting which finally produced a settlement. The union got most of what it wanted: no compulsory redundancies, volunteers to be invited from all departments and relatively generous redundancy terms.

In these negotiating sessions we can see the key elements of the leader officer at work: a commitment to ambitious objectives, a hostile and negative attitude towards the employer, a willingness to encourage industrial action, and the use of shop stewards to promote militancy amongst the membership.

Table 7.1. *Most common method of decision-making about annual pay claims, per cent*

| Stewards and members alone decide | Stewards decide after consultation with officer | Joint decision by stewards and officer | Officer alone decides | Total |
|---|---|---|---|---|
| 48.9 | 23.3 | 26.7 | 1.1 | 100 |

*Source:* Officers' questionnaire.

Having described each of the officer types at work, we now look at the bargaining process in detail, starting with the formulation of objectives.

### Setting bargaining objectives

Union officers frequently have *no* involvement in collective bargaining within their establishments as stewards and members often initiate and conduct their own negotiations (see table 7.1). There are four reasons for this degree of steward and workplace independence, the first of which is simply logistical. As we showed in chapter 3, full-time officers are responsible, on average, for over 3000 union members, and 'front-line' field officers for almost 5000 members organized in 66 establishments (see also IRRR, 1992). Even though negotiation forms one of the most time-consuming parts of the officer's job (see chapter 5, and Kelly and Heery, 1989: 200) there will inevitably be many workplace negotiations that officers are simply unable to attend. Secondly, the presence of sophisticated workplace organizations with full-time stewards and a steward hierarchy (cf. Batstone and Gourlay 1986: 24–6) means there is arguably less need for officers to be involved in their negotiations, and less demand for their services by stewards, compared with less well organized plants (cf. Batstone *et al.*, 1977: 187; Boraston *et al.*, 1975: 78, 92; Frenkel and Coolican, 1984: 236–41). One T&GWU officer was rarely involved in bargaining at a large metals factory in her 'patch' and could go on site only with the stewards' permission. Thirdly, officers themselves have a strong bias in favour of steward independence, as we have already shown (chapter 6 and see also Benson, 1991: 130–1), and finally the nature of the issue is important. Interview data suggested that officers were most likely to become involved in negotiations over complex, major or non-routine issues such as redundancy, dismissals or privatization (to give just three examples), and less likely to be involved in more routine issues, other things being equal.

But there was no simple relation between plant size, steward bargaining independence and the non-involvement of officers. Several officers told us that they enjoyed the bargaining rounds at large multi-plant firms, and the presence of full-time plant convenors was generally associated with *more* officer involvement in bargaining, not less ($r = 0.21$, $p < 0.05$).[1] Observation data confirmed these questionnaire results, showing that officer influence over the initiation of issues on the bargaining agenda was significantly associated with the presence of a shop steward hierarchy within the establishment ($\chi^2 = 19.65$, $p < 0.001$), and with the existence of a joint shop stewards' committee or dominant workplace union branch ($\chi^2 = 0.24$, $p < 0.01$). The high degree of job autonomy exercised by officers (see chapters 3 and 5) permits them to concentrate their bargaining work in large firms, but an additional factor in some industries (such as engineering) are the procedure agreements which govern the involvement of full-time officers at different stages of negotiations.

Where officers were involved in negotiations our data strongly suggests that the bargaining agenda was shaped by *both* officers and stewards (see table 5.1). Whilst 22 per cent of issues were initiated equally by officers and stewards, the latter were more influential in initiating a further 39 per cent (95 issues), the same figure as for officers (39 per cent, 96 issues). The overwhelming majority of issues were discussed in pre-meetings between officers and stewards, and whilst officers frequently succeeded in placing issues on the bargaining agenda stewards enjoyed an almost identical rate of success.

The capacity to control the agenda of meetings corresponds to the second dimension of power identified by Lukes (1974), and a number of studies have documented the ways in which powerful figures prevent contentious items even reaching the agenda of meetings. Our own data suggests that the power balance between officers and stewards is extremely fluid: each of them frequently exercised the capacity to put items onto the agenda, but it was rare for either to succeed in keeping items off the agenda. On the few occasions where officers and stewards strongly disagreed on the wisdom of a particular demand, it almost invariably went through into the bargaining process. Officers' own views of their influence corresponded to this picture, with 88 per cent reporting that stewards 'usually' or 'always' accepted their suggestions for issues to be included in bargaining (see also Benson, 1991: 132–3). One further piece of evidence underlines the influence of stewards and members in the early stages of the collective bargaining process. Where stewards placed issues on the bargaining agenda they often derived from discussions amongst the stewards themselves or amongst the stewards and their members. But the bargaining goals of officers often came from the same sources. In our observations of meetings we classified 27 different ways in which officers made use of stewards. In 73 meetings (47 per cent of the total) they used them to obtain information on members' aspirations, and in 72 meetings (46 per cent of the total) they simply took over the members' objectives as their own. The aspirations of stewards and members therefore entered the bargaining agenda by both direct as well as indirect means.

This evidence suggests a fairly cooperative relationship between officers and stewards, a picture that is consistent with data collected in the 1970s from both case studies (Batstone *et al.*, 1977: 201–11) and from surveys (Boraston *et al.*, 1975). The overwhelming majority of stewards in Batstone *et al.* (1977: 192) reported officer involvement in bargaining to be very or fairly useful. But neither this evidence nor our own implies a completely harmonious relationship between officers and stewards: there was conflict and disagreement between them on 43 per cent of the issues processed at meetings. But whilst officers and stewards were prepared to argue about bargaining goals, each was also prepared to accept the right of the other to nominate issues for negotiation. Any imbalance of power resources between them was hardly ever used to block the inclusion of items for the bargaining agenda, a fact that can be accounted for as follows. First the overwhelming majority of officers came to the job after a period as a shop steward and thus shared a common set of experiences with the stewards they now served (see chapter 4). Second, stewards were unlikely to block officer initiatives because of their belief in the expertise of the officer. The most frequent comments about officers by stewards concerned their competence and negotiating ability, and the most common areas in which they sought advice were bargaining goals (30 meetings), bargaining tactics (29) and bargaining practices (23). And thirdly a minority of issues (36, or 13 per cent) were defended by officers on the grounds that they represented union policy, an argument to which stewards could object only with great difficulty. As for officers, we have already shown that many of them believed strongly in being accountable to and representative of their members (see chapter 5) and this belief would therefore incline them to accept the right of stewards to shape the bargaining agenda.

What types of objectives did officers and stewards pursue, and how did their relative ambitions compare? Table 7.2 shows the issues that were processed at the 156 meetings we observed.

On the whole officers ranked pay and job protection as their top priorities in bargaining (although there was considerable variation among them), a pattern of results that has been found elsewhere (Batstone *et al.*, 1977: 187–91; Dufty, 1979, table 7.3).

Table 7.2. *Issues processed at meetings*

| Issue[a] | No. | (%) |
|---|---|---|
| Pay and pay-related | 100 | 36 |
| Work organization and grading | 55 | 20 |
| Trade union | 47 | 17 |
| Redundancy | 40 | 15 |
| Other | 32 | 12 |
| | 274 | 100 |

*Note:* [a] Details of the issue classification are available from the authors, on request.
*Source:* Observation.

Table 7.3. *Full-time officers' objectives in bargaining, by order of importance*

| Objective | Mean rank | % ranking 1st, 2nd or 3rd |
|---|---|---|
| Higher basic pay | 3.0 | 61 |
| Protecting jobs | 3.6 | 52 |
| Improved working conditions | 4.6 | 37 |
| Help for the low paid | 5.5 | 27 |
| Shorter working time | 5.6 | 24 |
| Increasing union membership | 5.6 | 28 |

*Source:* Officers' questionnaire.

The dominant emphasis on pay and job protection in table 7.3 corresponded very closely to the issues that officers said they were encouraged to pursue by their members and by lay committees. But the issues lower down their agenda, such as recruitment, were the ones being promoted by higher levels of the unions (see table 5.3). Finally if we look at the bargaining issues actually initiated by officers and stewards respectively we find considerable consensus, with pay being the item placed on the agenda most frequently by both officers (31 per cent of issues initiated) and stewards (45 per cent). However officers were more likely to raise trade union matters (26 per cent compared to 13 per cent for stewards), whilst stewards were more likely than officers to initiate questions of work organization (22 per cent compared to 11 per cent for officers). In other words, there was a substantial overlap between the types of objectives pursued by officers and stewards.

Table 7.4. *The bargaining objectives of officers and stewards*

|  | Officers more ambitious than stewards | Officers equal in ambition to stewards | Officers less ambitious than stewards | Total |
|---|---|---|---|---|
| No. of issues | 56 | 122 | 74 | 252[a] |
| (%) | 22 | 48 | 30 | 100 |

*Note:* [a] There were 22 missing values.
*Source:* Observation.

Turning now to the scale of those objectives, we recorded for each issue whether union officers were more, less or equal in ambition to their stewards and members; the results are shown in table 7.4.[2] The evidence shows there was *no* systematic tendency for officers to be less ambitious than stewards, as theorists of bureaucracy and oligarchy would expect. Indeed on one in five issues it was officers who were more ambitious, a result that was corroborated by the questionnaire data based on a larger and more diverse sample, where 35 per cent agreed with the statement that shop steward objectives were often too modest, and 51 per cent disagreed. The advice given to shop stewards in the meetings we observed followed a similar pattern. At 34 meetings stewards were advised to pursue more reasonable objectives, whilst at 31 meetings they were urged to follow more ambitious goals. Officers also used stewards to promote their own goals amongst the membership: at 39 meetings stewards were used to moderate member aspirations, whilst at 49 meetings stewards were urged to escalate the members' aspirations.

One possible defence of the theory of bureaucracy would argue that officers allow stewards and members to promote their demands at the outset of the negotiations, but gradually assert their own, more modest objectives as the bargaining process gets under way. We were able to check this possibility by examining the relative ambition of officers at different stages within a sequence of bargaining sessions on a sub-sample of issues (table 7.5).

Although there was a slight tendency in the direction predicted by theorists of bureaucracy, it was not statistically significant ($\chi^2 = 3.03$, $p = 0.07$) and the most common pattern throughout was equality of objectives between officer and stewards. When we looked at the advice given to stewards about bargaining objectives we again found a small, but insignificant tendency for officers to urge more reasonable as compared with more ambitious objectives as bargaining sessions proceeded ($\chi^2 = 1.57$, $p = 0.3$).

Table 7.5. *Changes in the relative ambition of officers and stewards,*
*% of issues*

| Meeting (position in series) | Officer more ambitious than stewards (%) | Officers equal in ambition to stewards (%) | Officers less ambitious than stewards (%) | Total no. of issues |
|---|---|---|---|---|
| 1st | 29 | 46 | 24 | 51 |
| 2nd and 3rd | 26 | 45 | 29 | 31 |
| 4th and after | 16 | 51 | 33 | 39 |
| | | | | 121 |

*Source:* Observation.

## Sources of variation in bargaining objectives

In looking at structural influences on bargaining goals we followed the
work of Boraston *et al.* (1975) and Batstone and Gourlay (1986), and used
the variables they had identified as possible influences on union power
resources and objectives. The most striking feature of our results was the
insignificance of structural correlates, a theme illustrated in the case of
pressure on stewards to pursue 'reasonable objectives'. Officers urged
such conduct at 34 meetings we attended, and the incidence of such advice
was not significantly associated with any of the following: steward experience or time off for union duties, the level of union density in the
bargaining group, establishment or enterprise, the sophistication of
steward organization within the group, establishment or enterprise, the
presence of steward-led bargaining at establishment or enterprise level,
the size of the bargaining group or enterprise, the pattern of unionism in
the establishment (single, plural, competitive) and the recency of union
organization. We found only one significant association: officers were
more likely to urge goal moderation in smaller establishments ($\chi^2 = 5.31$,
$p < 0.05$). When we looked at the relative ambition of officers and stewards a similar pattern emerged: all but two structural correlates were
insignificant. There was a tendency for officers to be relatively more
ambitious than stewards where density in the bargaining group was low
and where union organization was fairly recent (less than five years old).
But the general finding was that structural properties of union organization and collective bargaining tell us virtually nothing about the
respective ambitions of officers and stewards in collective bargaining.
Why this should be the case is an issue we look at later.

## Inter-union differences

There was considerable evidence of significant differences between unions, with ASTMS officers emerging as consistently more 'militant' than their counterparts in the T&GWU and GMB. ASTMS officers encouraged stewards and members to pursue more ambitious bargaining objectives at 47 per cent of their meetings, compared with 27 per cent for the T&GWU and 24 per cent for the GMB (and the reverse pattern was found for officer attempts to moderate steward objectives: ASTMS – 14 per cent, TGWU – 27 per cent, GMB – 35 per cent, $\chi^2 = 17.3$, p $< 0.001$). Not surprisingly, then, ASTMS officers were less ambitious than their stewards on only 18 per cent of issues, compared with 32 per cent for both the T&GWU and the GMB. On the other hand, there were no differences in the propensity of officers to encourage a broadening of bargaining objectives beyond the core issues of pay, work organization and hours of work. Questionnaire data revealed further evidence of inter-union differences, with ASTMS and EETPU officers showing particularly sharp differences on a wide range of attitude statements. Asked whether union officials should always take the workers' side in disputes, 48 per cent of all respondents agreed that they should. But 71 per cent of ASTMS officers agreed with this statement, compared with only 18 per cent of EETPU officers.

However, our evidence also showed striking differences between officers *within* unions. Within each of the four unions – T&GWU, GMB, ASTMS, AEU – we found officers who were almost invariably more ambitious than their members and stewards, and others who were less ambitious. Within the GMB, for instance, one officer consistently urged stewards to recruit new members by advertising the moderate nature of the union and its opposition to the politically-inspired militancy of NALGO. Yet one of his colleagues in the NHS argued for recruitment into the GMB because it was *more* militant than the other unions in the health service. In other words intra-union differences in goals were as striking as inter-union differences, suggesting that we need to examine other sources of variation.

## The values of union officers

The officers in our observation sample were classified into one of three bargaining orientations, largely on the basis of information about their own objectives and their attitudes towards the objectives of stewards and managers. Table 7.6 shows the results of that classification for a series of measures.

Table 7.6. *The significance of officer bargaining orientation*

| Measures | Managerialist N = 8 | Regulationist N = 13 | Leader N = 6 | $X^2$ |
|---|---|---|---|---|
| Officer goals *more* ambitious than stewards (% issues) | 5 | 22 | 50 | 47.21[b] |
| Officer goals *less* ambitious than stewards (% issues) | 66 | 20 | 4 | |
| Stewards urged to pursue more *reasonable* goals (% meetings) | 59 | 14 | 3 | 33.84[b] |
| Stewards urged to pursue more *ambitious* goals (% meetings) | 3 | 23 | 27 | 5.74,n.s. |
| Stewards urged to *moderate* member goals (% meetings) | 66 | 20 | 3 | 34.18[b] |
| Stewards urged to *stimulate* member goals (% meetings) | 7 | 33 | 50 | 13.18[a] |

*Notes:* [a] $p < 0.01$.
[b] $p < 0.001$.
*Source:* Observation.

Table 7.6 shows two points: first that these dimensions of officer bargaining orientation are powerful discriminators, and point to major and highly significant differences between officers. Second, though orientation is crucial it is not the only factor involved in shaping the objectives of bargaining. There were occasions on which managerialist officers urged stewards to be more ambitious, and others when leader officers tried to curb steward ambitions.

We also looked at the numbers and types of bargaining issue initiated by different sorts of officer (table 7.7[3]). Managerialists were significantly more likely to initiate pay and work organization issues (very much in line with the pattern of issue initiation by stewards) whilst leaders rarely initiated these types of issues, concentrating instead on questions of trade union role and tactics, and equality between different groups of workers (especially men and women) (cf. also Frenkel and Coolican, 1984: 236–41). Regulationists occupied a mid-way position on all five issues, as well as on the number of issues they initiated.

We have classified officers so far on what might we call their *industrial ideologies*, centred on the bargaining relationship, but we can also examine the impact of broader political ideologies using the questionnaire data. Self-reported political positions were highly correlated with officers' own accounts of their most important bargaining objectives. More left-

Table 7.7. *Bargaining issues initiated by different types of officer*

| Issue | No. [a] (per cent) | | |
|---|---|---|---|
| | Managerialist N = 8 | Regulationist N = 13 | Leader N = 6 |
| Pay | 9   (50) | 23   (37) | 1   (4) |
| Work organization | 6   (33) | 6   (10) | 1   (4) |
| Redundancy | 0   (0) | 13   (21) | 6   (23) |
| Trade union | 3   (17) | 17   (27) | 8   (31) |
| Equality/health and safety | 0   (0) | 4   (5) | 10   (38) |
| Total issues | 18   (100) | 63   (100) | 26   (100) |
| Total meetings | 29 | 97 | 30 |
| Issues per meeting | 0.62 | 0.65 | 0.87 |

*Notes:* [a] Main figure is frequency; figure in brackets is per cent.
*Source:* Observation.

Table 7.8 *Bargaining objectives and officers' age seniority and education*[a]

| Variable | Objective | β | t | p < |
|---|---|---|---|---|
| *Older* officers attached | | | | |
| *more* importance to: | | | | |
| | Pensions | 0.25 | 1.92 | 0.06 |
| *less* importance to: | Low pay | 0.29 | 2.21 | 0.03 |
| *More senior* officers attached | | | | |
| *more* importance to: | Procedures | 0.30 | 2.27 | 0.03 |
| *More educated* officers attached | | | | |
| *more* importance to: | Women's issues | 0.22 | 4.29 | 0.03 |
| *less* importance to: | | | | |
| | Pensions | 0.21 | 1.92 | 0.06 |
| | Working conditions | 0.21 | 1.79 | 0.06 |

*Notes:* [a] All other age, education and seniority correlations failed to reach statistical significance.
*Source:* Officers' questionnaire.

wing officers gave significantly higher priority to women's issues ($r = 0.50$, $p < 0.001$) and to low pay ($r = 0.27$, $p < 0.01$), but lower priority to union influence at the workplace ($r = 0.21$, $p < 0.05$) and to recruitment ($r = 0.20$, $p < 0.05$[4]). They were more likely to endorse the ideas that officials should always take the workers' side in disputes ($r = 0.42$, $p < 0.001$) and that officials should always go along with the wishes of their members ($r = 0.26$, $p < 0.05$). And they were more likely to believe that shop steward goals were often too modest ($r = 0.31$, $p < 0.005$). Officers' political views were also linked to age, seniority and education, as chapter 4 showed. Not surprisingly, therefore, age, seniority and education were also related to bargaining goals (table 7.8). Interestingly, officers' income level bore no relation to bargaining objectives, although theorists of bureaucracy might have expected some relationship between income and priority assigned to procedural objectives.

We also have some indirect data on the priorities of male and female officers (reported more fully in Heery and Kelly, 1988). Asked to say whether they were more, less or equally concerned about a range of 'women's' bargaining issues compared with their male counterparts women officers responded as follows. Most felt they were more concerned about childcare and sexual harassment (72 per cent) and maternity leave (65 per cent). But opinion was more divided on part-timers' rights and equal pay where sizeable minorities of women officers (44 per cent and 38 per cent respectively) thought their male counterparts were equally concerned, whilst the clear majority (73 per cent) saw no gender difference in concern over low pay. The data point to significant, perceived gender differences in some areas, but these perceptions were linked to age, education and seniority, and were far more pronounced amongst younger, and better educated women officers new to their jobs.

Two questions remain before we turn to the criteria used in formulating bargaining goals. Firstly, how should we interpret the spectrum of left–right political views in the context of collective bargaining? And second, how can we explain the pattern of results revolving around political views, age, education, gender and seniority? The difficulty in answering the first question is that there are few unambiguous left-wing (or right-wing) bargaining goals. For instance a number of self-defined moderate T&GWU officers were highly critical of members employed by a large dairy because of their near exclusive concern to boost overtime and pay, and they tried unsuccessfully to raise issues of employment and job security as part of a wages–jobs trade-off. But equally we met left-wing District Officers who were just as critical of the wages issue and anxious to pursue ideologically inspired campaigns around the rights of women and ethnic minorities. In the AEU we encountered 'left-wing' officers who regarded the wages struggle as the core of worker militancy against the employer, and the basis on which self-confidence and class consciousness could be developed (see Kelly, 1988 for analyses of the debates around economism and wage militancy). On the other hand several 'right-wing' T&GWU officers confined the bargaining agenda to pay and related issues, and defended this by saying it was all their members wanted. Whilst issues such as pay can be incorporated into a number of quite distinct ideological positions, this is less true of issues such as women's rights and low pay that have recently come to the fore in trade unions. These issues were given low priority not only by more right-wing officers, but also by officers who were older and who had received little or no further education.

### Officers' values: generation or socialization?

The inter-relations between political values, age, seniority and education are open to two possible interpretations. It could be that we have uncovered a *generational* difference between older and younger officers. On this hypothesis, older officers entered the trade union movement in the 1950s and early 1960s at a time when many of the big unions were under strong, right-wing control and they were selected for officer posts in part because of their sympathy for these views. A later generation of officers, who came into post in the 1970s and 1980s, were the shop stewards and branch officers involved in the militancy of those years. They entered the movement with a very different set of values, and continued to evince a strong sympathy for militant, workplace organization and for women's issues. According to the second, *socialization*, hypothesis it could be that most union officers gradually become more 'conservative' in their outlook, regardless of their initial views on entry to the union world. A variety of explanations has been offered for the alleged growth of conservatism (see chapter 2) but the key point in this argument is that it is seniority (i.e. years of service) in the union which is crucial, not the generation (i.e. age group) to which officers belong.

Age and seniority are, of course, highly correlated but as the correlation is far from perfect it is feasible to conduct partial correlation analysis in order to distinguish their separate consequences. In effect this involves holding one variable constant and observing any remaining effects of the other. Table 7.9 shows the results of this exercise.[5]

The top part of table 7.9 shows that when seniority is controlled for, officer age is still highly correlated with a number of bargaining goals. Indeed the removal of seniority makes hardly any difference to the correlations, suggesting that seniority is relatively unimportant but that age is crucial. When age is removed from the correlations in the lower half of table 7.9 two coefficients are both substantially increased but two others disappear almost to zero. This suggests that seniority does have independent though limited effects on bargaining goals: the longer an officer has been with a union the more importance he/she will attach to

Table 7.9. *Age and seniority effects on bargaining objectives*

| Variable | Bargaining objective | Zero-order correlation | First-order partial correlation |
|---|---|---|---|
| | | | *(seniority held constant)* |
| *Age* | Pay | $-0.17$ | $-0.22^a$ |
| | Low pay | $0.35^c$ | $0.30^b$ |
| | Women's issues | $0.25^a$ | $0.22^a$ |
| | Pensions | $-0.37^c$ | $-0.31^b$ |
| | Working conditions | $-0.13$ | $-0.26^a$ |
| | | | *(age held constant)* |
| *Seniority* | Working conditions | $0.15$ | $0.27^a$ |
| | Pensions | $0.22^a$ | $0.02$ |
| | Procedures | $0.16$ | $0.20^a$ |
| | Women's issues | $-0.17$ | $0.02$ |

*Notes:* Correlations not reported in table 7.9 were insignificant, both zero-order and first order partials.
[a] p $<0.05$.
[b] p $<0.01$.
[c] p $<0.001$.
*Source:* Officers' questionnaire.

procedures and to working conditions. Overall, then, the evidence shows support for both age (generational) and seniority (socialization) effects, but the former appear to be more powerful and pervasive.

One of the objections to analysis of individual differences among officers is that their behaviour is likely to be issue-specific. Willman (1980) for instance cited several studies of shop steward bargaining to make this point against Batstone *et al.*'s (1977) leader–populist dichotomy. We therefore examined the nature and scale of officer goals across a range of issues, looking first at attempts to moderate steward goals.

The evidence appears to show that officers were most likely to moderate steward and member aspirations on the issue of pay and work organization, but in fact the difference was not significant. However, when we looked at officer attempts to stimulate members and encourage them to be more ambitious, then a strong issue effect emerged, as table 7.10 shows, particularly on the issue of redundancy and on trade union matters. Evidence on the relative ambition of officers corroborates this point: officers were significantly more ambitious than stewards on redundancy as compared with all other issues. At first sight, then, this data confirms an issue-specific effect, but the appearance is misleading. The redundancy issue was negotiated by just seven of our 27 officers: one was

Table 7.10. *Officer attempts to moderate/stimulate steward–member goals as a function of issue, % issues*

| Issue | N | % attempts at goal moderation | % attempts at goal stimulation |
|---|---|---|---|
| Pay | 100 | 30 | 7 |
| Work organization and grading | 55 | 25 | 15 |
| Redundancy | 40 | 15 | 18 |
| Trade union | 47 | 11 | 21 |
| Other | 32 | 25 | 3 |
| Total | 274 | $X^2 = 8.34$ $p < 0.08$ | $X^2 = 10.16$ $p < 0.05$ |

*Source:* Observation.

Table 7.11. *Officers' criteria for pay claims*

| Criterion | Mean ranking | No. ranking 1st or 2nd |
|---|---|---|
| Cost of living | 3.2 | 41 |
| Members' aspirations | 3.5 | 32 |
| Achievability | 4.0 | 28 |
| Going rate | 4.4 | 19 |
| Union policy | 5.0 | 17 |
| Ability to pay | 5.0 | 14 |

*Source:* Officers' questionnaire.

a leader officer, six were regulationists, but none were managerialists. The apparent toughness of officers over redundancy has less to do with the issue *per se* than with the kinds of officers who negotiated the matter.

### The criteria behind pay claims

In our observation work we collected systematically evidence on the arguments used by officers and stewards to defend or revise bargaining demands, but we did not look systematically at the criteria used to formulate demands in the first place. On that question we have evidence from the officers' questionnaire, but related specifically to pay claims. Two years before the 1989 rise in price inflation our questionnaire data underlined the salience of traditional workers' criteria for pay rises. Asked to rank order a set of possible criteria, officers gave the responses shown in table 7.11.

There was also evidence of inter-union variation since members' aspirations and cost of living dominated the T&GWU and the AEU, and cost of living was reinforced by union policies against low pay in the public sector unions NALGO and NUPE. These four unions therefore revealed the hegemony of workerist, as opposed to managerial, criteria. By contrast officers in the other three unions (ASTMS, EETPU and GMB) often deployed an additional and somewhat different criterion, that of achievability. Differences between officers also emerged clearly in our observation of the early stages of annual pay rounds, when officers had to respond to steward pay targets. Shopworkers, for instance, were chided by a T&GWU District Officer for submitting a hopelessly 'unrealistic' claim of 8–10 per cent that was 'far too high' when inflation was below 5 per cent. An AEU Divisional Officer argued that his job was to act responsibly, taking into account what employers could afford to pay. And a GMB officer told Southern Gas shop stewards that their demand for increased subsistence allowances was unrealistic because the allowances were already 'very high'. By contrast officers who stressed workers' arguments – cost of living, and members' aspirations – rarely made any attempt to moderate members' claims before negotiations. This evidence on pay claim criteria is broadly consistent with evidence from other sources. Daniel (1976) carried out a survey of union negotiators in 98 establishments in 1975, and found that cost of living was the most frequently cited determinant of their most recent pay claim. Data on managers' reports of influence over recent pay settlements showed cost of living on a par with or more important than profitability/productivity throughout the 1980s and up to 1990 (Carruth and Oswald, 1989: 55–60; Ingram, 1991: 102–3; Millward and Stevens, 1986: 246–7; Millward et al., 1992: 238). Both questionnaire and observation data showed that although there were striking inter-union differences, particularly between the EETPU and other unions, and between public and private sector unions, there was also significant intra-union variation. More 'right-wing' officers strongly emphasized what was achievable in formulating pay claims ($r = 0.36$, $p < 0.001$) and downgraded union principles ($r = 0.20$, $p < 0.05$). Older officers gave priority to the protection of differentials ($r = 0.32$, $p < 0.001$) and also downgraded union principles ($r = 0.32$, $p < 0.01$).

However, we need to be careful in the interpretation of bargaining criteria and their relation to political values. The allocation of priority to cost of living was frequently intended to assert workers' interests irrespective of the employer's ability to pay, but cost of living could also be used to support the employers' case. When our observation research began in January 1986 inflation was 5.5 per cent and subsequently fell steadily to 2.4 per cent in July, climbing to 3.9 per cent in January 1987 when our observation work ended. However there was considerable debate about the validity of the RPI, about regional variations in inflation (our research was conducted in and around London), and about future trends. Consequently at any point in time officers could, and did, cite figures for inflation differing by as much as 30 per cent. By taking the lowest estimate in a given month (of about 3.7 per cent) it was possible for one of our T&GWU District Officers to defend a 5.3 per cent pay offer as a reasonably good (1.5 per cent) increase in real terms while his USDAW counterpart was vehemently opposed to such a low offer! The idea of 'the going rate' provided another illustration of the same point. This criterion was sometimes used by regulationists and leader officers to defend ambitious pay claims in the face of an intransigent employer. But it was also used by a group of managerialist T&GWU officers to moderate the aspirations of discontented dairy workers, who were looking for a catching-up claim in double figures. By citing the 'going rate' of about 6 per cent in early 1986, officers managed to defeat the steward claim of 10 per cent at a national delegate meeting.

## Conclusions

The bargaining agenda of the union is shaped by the demands of officers, stewards and members. Each party largely accepted the other's right to put items on the agenda and it was rare for officers or stewards to resist the inclusion of items. We also found there was no systematic tendency for officers to be either more or less ambitious than stewards and members in their bargaining objectives. The substantial variation amongst officers was largely explicable by reference to their value systems. Managerialists were often more moderate than their steward counterparts, whilst leader officers were frequently more ambitious and regulationists fell in between. Interestingly, we found that most structural properties of union organization were not related to officer ambitions. The only exception was in those workplaces with low membership density and fairly recent organization where there was a tendency for officer ambition to exceed that of stewards. There was also significant variation in the criteria used to formulate claims: more moderate officers were more likely to stress figures that were 'achievable' as they saw it, whereas other officers would stress 'workers'' criteria such as the cost of living. Finally we confirmed that the bargaining goals of officers showed a strong generational influence: older officers were more modest in their targets and less concerned with 'newer' issues such as women's rights. There was also a socialization effect in which years of service in the union influenced officers' goals, but this was much weaker than the differences arising from generation.

# 8    The bargaining process

## Introduction

In this chapter we look more closely at the process and outcomes of collective bargaining. We start by examining the general approach to bargaining adopted by officers and, as in chapter 7, proceed to examine the determinants of these approaches, looking in turn at inter-union differences, the nature of the issues involved, the values of officers and the structural properties of unions and companies. We then look more closely at the systems of argument used by officers; at the conditions under which industrial action is threatened; at moves toward final settlement; at the outcomes of bargaining; and finally we consider the power base of the officer in dealing with shop stewards and union members.

## The bargaining process

### Approaches to bargaining

Officers approached collective bargaining in many different ways: some were very friendly and discussed personal matters with their management counterparts both before and after bargaining sessions (see Table 8.1). One managerialist officer even invited two of his management counter-parts back to the union office and proceeded to gossip about a number of their shop stewards. Others (particularly regulationists) adopted a neutral and formal approach, eschewing the 'cosy chats' of their often older and more conservative fellow-officers, and disparaging what they frequently referred to as 'knife and fork' bargaining, conducted over the dinner table. Officers in Watson's (1988) study also criticized those who become over-friendly with the employer, and in very similar terms: 'We all know of officers who go about with a knife and fork in their top pocket' (Watson, 1988: 141).

Watson emphasized the important role of formality in maintaining an appropriate 'distance' between officer and manager and signalling to the

Table 8.1. *Officers' approaches to management, per cent of meetings*

| | |
|---|---|
| Friendly | 25 |
| Formal | 21 |
| Abrasive | 13 |
| Mixed | 41 |
| Total | 100 |

*Source:* Observation.

membership that he has not 'sold out'. This code was frequently adhered to by officers in our study, and sometimes very strictly. A T&GWU regulationist officer was invited to a lunchtime office party during a break in negotiations at a private sector service organization, but turned it down with the comment, 'I thought we were negotiating'. A minority of mostly leader officers were positively abrasive and openly criticized management shortcomings and incompetence in what were often tense and emotionally-charged meetings. Many officers however showed a mixture of approaches between different meetings, and even within the same meeting. An ASTMS leader officer conducted several negotiating sessions with local managers in a very abrasive manner but later on spent over an hour in a private and informal meeting with a senior corporate manager. The fact that officers serviced an average of 66 bargaining units means that they interacted very infrequently with the managers in most of these establishments. Hence the opportunities to establish 'strong bargaining relationships' (Batstone *et al.*, 1977: 168–77) based on high trust and informality were few and far between.

The fact that we were unable to classify officers' behaviour at 41 per cent of the meetings we observed underlines both the complexity of bargaining behaviour, and the pragmatism of many officers. But this variability should not be over-stated, because officers' comments about management, either in negotiations or outside at steward and membership meetings, were almost uniformly hostile and critical. Managements were most frequently described as threatening bargaining rights (on 62 occasions), followed by terms like 'exploitative' (58), 'untrustworthy' (52) and 'devious' (43). Indeed what was remarkable was how infrequently officers found anything good to say about their opposite numbers, and how closely the rank order of their own main comments matched that of their shop stewards ($r = 0.87$, $p < 0.01$).

Turning to the tactics used in bargaining, it is clear these were heavily influenced by officers, far more so than the initial objectives of bargaining or the acceptance of management offers (see table 5.1). Officers exercised more influence than stewards in the objectives of bargaining on just 39 per cent (96) of issues and in the outcomes of bargaining on 64 per cent (165) of issues. But their greater influence over tactics was apparent on no less than 76 per cent (188) of issues processed at meetings.

Officer domination of tactics was reflected in their domination of the bargaining process itself. Almost every bargaining session we attended was led by the full-time officer who made most of the contributions from the union side. A similar picture was revealed by Batstone et al. (1977: 196), even on the shopfloor where steward organization was highly developed. Steward contributions to discussion were far more common in the adjournments to bargaining sessions, a tendency that was particularly noticeable amongst Batstone et al.'s white-collar stewards. We also noted how frequently officers pursued a variety of tactics in negotiations, such as sticking to their position, moderating their goals, offering a *quid pro quo* to the employer, and stressing the shared interests of workers and employers. There were very few differences between unions, except on the question of 'intransigence'. Officers in the T&GWU and GMB retained a hard bargaining position at 23 per cent and 29 per cent of their meetings respectively, but the figure for ASTMS Divisional Officers was 53 per cent.

### Officers' values

The impact of officer values is shown in table 8.2. It confirms striking differences in the incidence of intransigence, militancy and 'moderation', but interestingly shows no differences amongst officers in their willingness to offer *quid pro quo*s or refer to the shared interests of workers and employers. The differences can be illustrated by two examples.

At an electronics firm that was relocating a few miles north, the company was aiming to sack over 200 workers 'surplus to requirements'. The ASTMS leader officer in charge of negotiations insisted on no compulsory redundancies, generous terms for those wishing to leave, and joint union–management control of the redundancy process. He remained intransigent throughout a series of bargaining sessions, and eventually held a mass meeting of his members, securing an overwhelming vote (by show of hands) for industrial action. This forced the intervention of senior personnel from outside the plant and helped secure most of the union's demands. By contrast a T&GWU regulationist officer in a similar situation – an electronics factory relocating from its present site – quickly dropped demands for retention of the present site or acquisition of a nearby site when faced with management opposition. Negotiations then

Table 8.2. *Officer tactics in bargaining as a function of orientation, per cent of meetings*

|  | Managerialist N = 8 | Regulationist N = 13 | Leader N = 6 | $\chi^2$ |
|---|---|---|---|---|
| Hard position: refusal to relax goals | 7 | 39 | 53 | 15.09[b] |
| Moderated demands | 76 | 24 | 22 | 21.67[b] |
| Offered a *quid pro quo* | 28 | 22 | 17 | 0.91, n.s. |
| Stressed shared interests | 38 | 29 | 21 | 1.20, n.s. |
| Threatened industrial action | 22 | 13 | 34 | 7.25[a] |

*Notes:* [a] $p < 0.05$.
[b] $p < 0.001$.
*Source:* Observation.

proceeded swiftly onto the terms of redundancy compensation. Measured by the ambition of their bargaining demands, both of these officers were very militant but this similarity obscured an important difference. Where the leader officer saw managerial intransigence as an obstacle to be overcome by worker mobilization and by threats, the regulationist officer was much more inclined to perceive such intransigence as an immovable constraint to which members had to adapt. Moderation of demands was far more the preserve of managerialist officers, although it still featured in between one-fifth and one-quarter of the meetings led by regulationist and leader officers. On the other hand references to shared interests and the possibility of trading objectives, although less common, were fairly evenly spread amongst different officer orientations.

Theorists of bureaucracy and oligarchy could take comfort from some of these findings. The willingness of all three officer types to offer a *quid pro quo* and to stress shared interests could point to uniformities in the officer role which over-ride their own individual values. And the willingness of all officers to moderate their demands, albeit to varying degrees, is also consistent with theoretical predictions. On the other hand the *differences* amongst officers are far more striking: whilst managerialists normally moderated their demands, leaders and regulationists did so only occasionally. When pressed, leaders frequently refused to relax their objectives, but managerialists rarely refused. But why should officer values apparently influence some aspects of their approach to bargaining but not others? One possibility rests on the distinction between means and ends. Officers might be pragmatic about the means used to achieve their objectives within the bargaining arena, and therefore be willing to deploy any sets of arguments they judge likely to be effective. At the same time they may be less pragmatic and more principled about bargaining objectives, and so personal values could make a significant difference to their willingness (or otherwise) to moderate or adhere to agreed bargaining goals. Frenkel and Coolican (1984: 212) found some differences in broad political objectives between organizers in left- and right-wing building unions, whilst Batstone *et al.* (1977) found different types of shop steward – leader and populist – were concerned with different types of objectives, the former with plant-wide goals, the latter with more sectional goals. Officer values would also be expected to make a difference to threats of industrial action because this is an issue on which we know many officers hold strong views. A number of examples of regulationist officers at work illustrate the variability of arguments across different settings.

A regulationist T&GWU officer was negotiating on behalf of clerical workers in the docks with the Port of London Authority. A small employer had breached the terms of the 1947 Dock Labour Scheme, by using dockers who were not on the PLA's register. Apart from threatening industrial action, the officer also appealed to the vulnerable product market situation of the majority of employers in the PLA. Multi-employer bargaining took wages out of competition, but this situation could be undermined if a 'rogue' employer was allowed to undercut existing pay rates and thus offer a cheaper service to port customers. Employer and workers therefore had a shared interest in defending the Dock Labour Scheme.[1] In another case, an adverse balance of power compelled an ASTMS officer to shift ground in negotiations and resort to 'shared interest' arguments in defence of her claim. She was confronted by an NHS management team operating within strict cash limits and under tight government control. Having failed to achieve any progress by outlining the justice of her members' claim for equal pay, she then switched to 'integrative arguments', stressing the benefits to the employer of a well-paid staff. Finally there were several cases which constituted partial exceptions to the idea of a straightforward conflict between workers and employers. In negotiations for London bus-workers another T&GWU officer frequently defended claims by arguing that they would contribute to a better service for passengers, thereby appealing to management's customer service orientation.

Ideologies which constitute management as an exploitative and untrustworthy opponent of workers' interests have to be 'applied' in concrete settings where particular managers may differ from the stereotypical, or average manager, or where the balance of power inhibits the effective expression of ideological principles. The bargaining process is both a vehicle through which officers' ideologies are expressed, as well as a forum in which particular demands and interests are being pursued. Officers' behaviour is therefore both *expressive* and *instrumental*, and whilst the two modes of action may coincide, the examples quoted earlier illustrate situations where they do not, and where principles are tempered by pragmatism.

### Structural influences

We now consider the structural correlates of officer approaches to bargaining, that is, the properties of union and company organization and of the collective bargaining system. We established that demand moderation, threats of industrial action and intransigence were observed far more frequently with some officers than others, but that references to shared interests and offers of a *quid pro quo* were evenly spread throughout our sample. How would structural contingency theory suggest that the properties of industrial relations systems might influence officer approaches to bargaining? In so far as these properties shape the power resources of the parties, we would expect them to influence the ambition of officer bargaining goals, and hence their willingness to moderate or adhere to their demands. Batstone and Gourlay (1986) combined various facets of shop steward organization into an index measure called 'sophistication', and showed that more sophisticated steward organizations both demanded more say over technical change and also achieved it (1986: 24, 87–8; Batstone *et al.*, 1987). In so far as power resources are crucial in considering industrial action, then threats of action should be heavily influenced by union and employer power resources. However, the types of argument used by officers in negotiations are largely under their own personal control, given their near-monopoly of the exchanges that take place within bargaining, and so there is no particular reason to expect the structural properties of union or company to influence systems of argument.

This is exactly what we found. References in officer arguments to shared interests showed no significant association with any of the following variables: union density at workgroup, establishment or enterprise level; recency of union organization; shop steward hierarchy; joint shop stewards' committee or combine committee; steward-led bargaining at establishment or enterprise level; shop steward experience (in years);

degree of multi-unionism; size of bargaining group, establishment or enterprise; employment sector. The weak predictive power of structural variables was also confirmed when we looked at offers of a *quid pro quo* in bargaining: none of the structural variables listed above showed any association with this approach to bargaining.

It was a different matter when we turned to demand moderation. This was significantly associated with union density, both within the bargaining group ($\chi^2 = 15.1$, $p < 0.001$) and within the establishment ($\chi^2 = 8.2$, $p < 0.05$). The relationship however was curvilinear: demand moderation by officers was most likely to occur where union density was above 50 per cent but below 90 per cent. In other words, it was less likely with either weak unionism (less than 50 per cent density) or very strong unionism (over 90 per cent density). Interpretation of this result is not easy because a large number of other structural factors that might have been associated with density failed to turn out significant. Steward hierarchy, experience and bargaining involvement, as well as establishment and enterprise size showed no relationship whatever to the willingness of officers to moderate their demands in collective bargaining. It may be that with low levels of union density officers have more control over initial bargaining goals, so that subsequent and significant moderation is unnecessary. At high levels of density goal moderation by officers may be impractical because of the power wielded by shop stewards. Threats of industrial action were also highly correlated with structural variables, much as we expected, and were strongly and positively associated with: union density at enterprise level, the presence of sophisticated (i.e. hierarchical) shop steward organization at the level of the bargaining group, establishment and enterprise; and the size of the establishment and the enterprise. However intransigence in negotiations was surprisingly associated with very few structural factors.

In other words, structural properties of the union and company organization influence the power resources of the parties. It is those facets of bargaining which are most susceptible to the distribution of power resource, such as demand moderation by union negotiators and their willingness to threaten action, that are in turn influenced by these structural properties.

## Systems of argument[2]

Officers exercise considerable discretion over bargaining tactics as we have seen, and over the systems of argument that are used to promote members' demands. The three most frequently used types of argument were based on workers' interests: comparisons with other groups within

Table 8.3. *Arguments used by officers and stewards to defend bargaining objectives, no. of times used*

| Argument | Officers (%) | Stewards (%) |
|---|---|---|
| Internal relativity | 70 (14) | 59 (15) |
| Justice | 65 (13) | 49 (13) |
| Rank and file wishes | 59 (12) | 46 (12) |
| Management's interests | 47 (10) | 31 ( 8) |
| Will lead to good industrial relations | 45 ( 9) | 26 ( 7) |
| External relativity | 39 ( 8) | 25 ( 6) |
| Union policy | 36 ( 7) | 18 ( 5) |
| Past precedents | 36 ( 7) | 28 ( 7) |
| Workers' contribution | 35 ( 7) | 52 (13) |
| Standard of living | 24 ( 5) | 30 ( 8) |
| Low cost for the employer | 22 ( 4) | 12 ( 3) |
| Ability to pay | 17 ( 3) | 14 ( 3) |
| Total | 495 (100) | 390 (100) |

*Source:* Observation.

the establishment or firm, the intrinsic justice of the demand, and the fact that it corresponded to the wishes of union members (see table 8.3). These three arguments alone accounted for 194 (39 per cent) of the 495 arguments used by officers in bargaining sessions. If we add to this figure other arguments that refer solely to workers' interests: external relativity (39), union policy (36) and standard of living (24), we end up with a total of 293 out of 495 arguments (59 per cent). Conversely, what might be called 'integrative' or non-zero-sum arguments, following Walton and McKersie (1965) – management's interests, good industrial relations, low cost of the demand and management's ability to pay – comprised just 26 per cent of the officers' and 21 per cent of the stewards' total arguments. Interestingly, union policy was referred to only 36 times, comprising just 7 per cent of officers' (and 5 per cent of stewards') arguments. This is consistent with the arguments of chapter 5 that officers enjoy considerable autonomy from their superior officers within their role as negotiators. As a result of that autonomy, there is less pressure on officers to transmit and implement union policy than might be expected. In any case the core collective bargaining agenda is more likely to be influenced by the demands of stewards and members arising out of their own employment experiences than by the content of national union policy.

Another way of looking at these arguments is in the terms set out by Armstrong *et al.* (1981) who divided workplace arguments into three sets of 'principles' – managerial principles, such as the right to manage; consensual principles, such as relativities, past precedents and justice; and workers' resistance principles, such as rank and file wishes and union policy. It is clear that officers and stewards used all three types of argument, but since Armstrong *et al.* did not quantify their results it is difficult to take comparisons much further.

A number of cases will illustrate the arguments used by officers. An AEU leader officer was negotiating the annual pay rise for a group of staff in the transport industry, known as the tunnel maintenance technicians. These workers had become increasingly skilled over the years and the officer therefore defended a substantial pay claim on the grounds of internal comparability with the more highly-paid skilled, senior traffic officers (STOs). Management rejected the argument, declaring that 'this would give the technicians future pay rises simply because the STOs got them, not because the technicians had earned them'. In a local authority negotiation on disciplinary procedures for manual workers, management wanted the right to deduct pay as one of the penalties for misconduct. The GMB regulationist officer categorically rejected 'fines', saying they were unjust and he simply did not believe in them. Finally, in a private sector housing company, a T&GWU regulationist repeatedly defended a package of demands – on basic pay, overtime rates and paternity leave – by saying they reflected the clear wishes of the membership.

We also found that the same types of argument used to promote workers' demands were also employed to depress them. It was comparatively rare for officers to argue demands downwards, but it did happen: officers used a total of 99 arguments to depress workers' demands with the most frequently used being internal relativity (15 occasions), external relativity (14 occasions) and rank and file wishes (14 occasions). One managerialist T&GWU officer was bargaining for sales workers in a large, national retail chain at a time when inflation was about 3.5 per cent. When stewards suggested going for a pay claim of around 7–8 per cent, he responded with a list of settlements at other stores in the region of 5–5.5 per cent, and urged the stewards to be realistic. But the use of external relativities to deflate member aspirations was not the exclusive preserve of managerialist officers. An ASTMS 'leader' was attempting to resist the introduction of a new bonus scheme on one site of a multi-site oil company. Shortly before the latest bargaining session he learned that workers at one of the company's other refineries had accepted the scheme, against the advice of the local union officer. In the light of this new situation, he felt he had no choice but to moderate the union's bargaining objectives.

What also emerges from table 8.3 is that the arguments used by officers and stewards were remarkably similar. At the aggregate level the two sets

Table 8.4. *Tactical arguments used by officers and stewards, no of times used*

| Argument | Officers (%) | Stewards (%) |
| --- | --- | --- |
| Unity/solidarity | 66 (11) | 31 (10) |
| Moderate goals to engage management | 63 (11) | 20 ( 7) |
| Resist management | 61 (10) | 50 (16) |
| Union's right to participate in decisions | 54 ( 9) | 23 ( 7) |
| Distrust management | 39 ( 7) | 21 ( 7) |
| Officer management a *quid pro quo* | 35 ( 6) | 8 ( 3) |
| Use external agencies | 33 ( 6) | 13 ( 4) |
| Stimulate rank and file militancy | 33 ( 6) | 12 ( 4) |
| Formalize industrial relations | 28 ( 5) | 15 ( 5) |
| Use industrial action | 25 ( 4) | 21 ( 7) |
| Other | 150 (25) | 92 (30) |
| Total | 587 (100) | 306 (100) |

*Source:* Observation.

of arguments follow a very similar rank order ($r = 0.76$, $p < 0.01$). The most substantial differences were both fairly predictable: officers were more likely to refer to union policy, whilst stewards were more likely to cite the workers' contribution to the firm.

In addition to the substantive arguments used to back up bargaining demands, we also looked at tactical arguments. This was a broad category which covered the following: (a) arguments about *how* to pursue a particular issue, e.g. through industrial action, procedures, formalization, etc.; (b) arguments designed to enhance workers' commitment to bargaining goals and to undermine any possible sympathy for management; (3) arguments about the implications or consequences of a particular claim, e.g. for unity, or inter-union relations (table 8.4). In each case we coded officer's comments in bipolar categories, e.g. mistrust management–trust management.

Taken in conjunction with officers' mostly negative comments about managers, this evidence strikingly confirms the adversarial tenor of union–management relations. The injunctions to resist and distrust management; the assertion of the union's right to participate in decision-making through collective bargaining; the emphasis on worker unity and solidarity; and the references to stimulating members' objectives and threatening industrial action: all of these add up to a remarkably coherent picture of an industrial relations system built around low trust and antagonism (cf. Watson, 1988: 164–6 for a rather different view). Examples of these tactical arguments were observed among a wide range of officers in a wide range of industries. In the NHS a GMB regulationist officer had built up a strong bargaining relationship with a District Personnel Manager, but still warned stewards about the dangers of placing too much trust in management. In the gas industry a managerialist GMB officer was pursuing a claim over bonus payments and time allowances to which he was not especially sympathetic. Yet even he insisted on formalizing elements of work allocation to minimize supervisory discretion and avoid managerial ideas about 'flexibility' and 'informality'. In a local authority another GMB officer (a regulationist) urged his stewards to pull out of the Joint Consultative Committee because it was dominated by NALGO reps who had a very 'close relationship' with Council officers. The GMB officer wanted to create an authority-wide GMB shop stewards' committee that would negotiate (not consult) with the Council on a wide range of issues. A T&GWU officer (a leader) at a large chemicals multi-national was highly critical of the shop stewards for their weakness and moderation, and he urged them to be far more independent and critical of management. A fellow officer (a regulationist) was handling negotiations at a London brewery over company plans to introduce changes in working practices. The attitude he conveyed to the shop stewards was a classical expression of a low-trust approach to the wage–effort bargain: try and resist the company's proposals, but if you do have to go along with them, make sure the company pays through the nose! An AEU leader officer, and a supporter of the union's Broad Left, strongly defended militancy at one of the District's quarterly stewards' meetings. He praised a group of workers for refusing to accept training on Computer Numerically Controlled (CNC) machines because they didn't trust the employers to guarantee them work. Another steward was praised for resisting contracting-out of work, even though his members had agreed to go along with it. Finally an ASTMS managerialist who was highly critical of his shop stewards' 'unreasonable demands' in a motoring service organization, and quite sympathetic to the employers' case, also praised members in another branch of the company for going on strike! It was, he said, the only way to shift an employer who was behaving unreasonably.

### Determinants of systems of argument

*Structural factors*

We cross-tabulated officers' bargaining arguments against the full range of structural variables on which we had data: properties of union organization, shop stewards, collective bargaining, management and the organization. Hardly any of these variables showed a significant relationship to the arguments used by officers. This is consistent with the argument made earlier that structural factors should only influence those aspects of the bargaining process that are intimately linked to power resources, such as bargaining objectives. The arguments used to defend those objectives do not depend to anywhere near the same degree on the power resources of the negotiator, and are therefore not closely related to them. Insofar as many of our structural variables are proxies for power resources, then our evidence is consistent with this interpretation.

One consequence of this argument is that structural factors may exert an indirect influence over bargaining arguments by inducing or facilitating a shift in bargaining goals. A T&GWU regulationist officer entered negotiations in a South London electronics plant where union organization was in Batstone and Gourlay's (1986) terms very unsophisticated. There was just a handful of stewards for a factory of 400 workers, there were very few branch meetings, virtually no steward-led bargaining and very little grievance-handling. The factory was scheduled for closure, but the officer tried to push for alternative buyers. When the management team resisted these ideas and insisted on closure and redundancies, the officer had no power resources at her disposal, and was forced to change her objectives and the arguments she used to defend them. Another case was somewhat more complex and involved an ASTMS leader officer and a small but sophisticated union organization at a large Kent metals factory. An experienced and independent group of stewards and members was facing an offensive from a management determined to take its white-collar staff out of the union and out of collective bargaining, and transfer them to individualized appraisal and payment systems without union influence. In this case the union organization was relatively sophisticated in Batstone and Gourlay's terms, but it suffered two problems. First, relations with other plant unions were mixed, and secondly the membership, though organized, was unwilling to act collectively against what they saw as a determined and powerful adversary. Faced with these facts the officer was forced to modify both his bargaining objectives and his system of arguments.

A few structural variables did show significant relationships with officers' systems of argument. In highly formalized systems of bargaining, where meetings were chaired, minutes and agendas circulated, and terms and conditions of employment extensively regulated by collective agreements, union officers made frequent reference to *precedent* and to *union policy*. For example officers negotiating for London bus-workers (T&GWU), London dockers (T&GWU), waterworkers (GMB), gasworkers (GMB) and healthworkers (GMB, ASTMS) were significantly more likely to cite precedent as grounds for pursuing a claim or resisting a management proposal. Union policy was referred to significantly more frequently in negotiations involving dockers and bus-workers. These bargaining sessions were not only formal, but they also took place within highly *centralized* negotiating structures in which policies were often agreed at national level for local application. Union policy thus became a more salient argument for union negotiators, as a way of referring to national negotiations.

Union policy was also cited by officers facing actual or potential dissent from members in order to enhance their own authority and buttress their arguments. An AEU officer (a leader) criticized the unwillingness of a section of members to oppose privatization by telling them they were in breach of union policy. A T&GWU managerialist officer told a group of dairy shop stewards that their concern to boost overtime earnings ran counter to the union's policy of cutting overtime. Two relatively new officers in the T&GWU drew heavily on union policy in dealing with groups of highly experienced members and stewards. Lacking the authority that would stem from experience in these industries, they fell back on the authority vested in them by the union to implement conference policies.

### Inter-union differences

There were small but non-significant differences between unions in the systems of argument used in bargaining. Taking worker arguments to be those stressing rank and file wishes and the justice of the members' case, we found these made up 22.2 per cent of the (63) arguments recorded for GMB officers, 23.9 per cent of the 264 T&GWU arguments and 28.0 per cent of the 168 ASTMS arguments. However, these averages conceal enormous variations within unions and between different meetings attended by the same officer. Within the T&GWU, for instance, there were two officers devoting about one-third of their arguments to depressing workers' demands, but three others who hardly ever argued downwards. Within ASTMS we classified 45 per cent of the arguments of one

officer as 'managerial' (low-cost, ability to pay, in management's interests, will lead to good industrial relations), whereas for one of his colleagues the figure was under 13 per cent. Both the small size of the
inter-union variations coupled with the substantial intra-union variations
led us to conclude there was no statistically significant union effect on
systems of argument.

### Officers' values

Not surprisingly (in the light of what was been said earlier) officers' values
exerted only a limited influence on their systems of argument (table 8.5).
All these results are in the expected direction so that, for instance, leader
officers were more likely than managerialists to defend claims by insisting
they truly reflected members' wishes and that they were intrinsically just.
Nevertheless all but two of these differences failed to reach statistical
significance. The only exceptions centred on the goals of bargaining,
where we found that managerialists were far more likely than other
officers to try and depress workers' expectations by arguing against them;
and were also more likely to use managerial arguments.

These results echo the earlier findings on officers' approaches to bargaining where we showed that officer orientation made a strong difference
to bargaining *objectives*, but had little impact on different sets of *tactics*.
In other words officers are pragmatic in their attitude towards, and use of,
arguments: it is in the sphere of bargaining goals that ideology shows
through and really makes a difference. Correlational analysis confirmed
this point, as shown in figure 8.1. Officers who urged stewards to pursue
'reasonable' objectives were also likely to be less ambitious than stewards
and to resort to arguments depressing steward ambitions. But none of
these facets of bargaining was significantly correlated with the use of
'managerial arguments'.

### Industrial action

We were unfortunate in the course of our research in that we did not
observe a single strike or other form of industrial action, although we did
observe preparations for action in two firms, and threats of action were
issued by officers at 24 of our 156 meetings. There were few overall
differences between officers and stewards, with the latter urging action at
26 meetings. Arguments to restrain action showed a similar pattern:
officers alleged that there would be management retaliation at 18 meetings, stewards at 16; officers claimed that there would be insufficient

Table 8.5. *Types of argument as a function of officer orientation*

| Types of argument | Managerialist N = 8 | Regulationist N = 13 | Leader N = 6 | $\chi^2$ |
|---|---|---|---|---|
| Managerial arguments [a] as per cent of total arguments | 40 | 26 | 21 | 9.14[c] |
| Workers arguments [b] as per cent of total arguments | 22 | 25 | 29 | 0.99 n.s. |
| Arguments to *reduce* worker demands as per cent of total arguments | 40 | 10 | 4 | 78.38[d] |
| Stress shared interests (per cent of meetings) | 38 | 29 | 21 | 1.20 n.s. |
| Offer *quid pro quo* (per cent of meetings) | 28 | 22 | 17 | 0.91 n.s. |

*Notes:* [a] In managerial interests, low cost, ability to pay and good industrial relations.
[b] Rank and file wishes and justice.
[c] $p < 0.05$.
[d] $p < 0.001$.
*Source:* Observation.

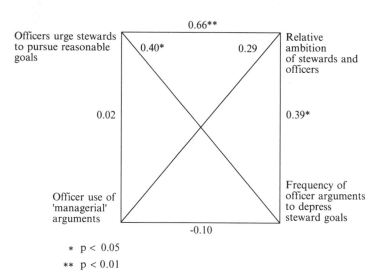

* $p < 0.05$
** $p < 0.01$

Figure 8.1   Spearman correlations between different facets of the bargaining process

Table 8.6. *Officer and steward advocacy of industrial action, nos. of meetings*

|  |  | Officers | | |
|---|---|---|---|---|
|  |  | In favour of action | Not in favour of action | |
| Stewards | In favour of action | 14 | 12 | 26 |
|  | Not in favour of action | 10 | – | 10 |
|  |  | 24 | 12 | 36 |

*Source:* Observation; N = 36 meetings at which industrial action was discussed.

membership support at 22 meetings, stewards at 30. In other words, there was no overall tendency for officers to be either more or less militant than stewards. This finding contrasts with older evidence from the 1960s and 1970s which suggested that full-time officers were less willing to support strike action than shop stewards (McCarthy and Parker, 1968: 91; Parker, 1975, Tables: III, A69, A71), much as theorists of bureaucracy and oligarchy would have expected. Closer examination of these findings shows a more complex pattern, with officers being more militant at some meetings, stewards at others (see table 8.6).

Questionnaire data provided part of the explanation for this variability. Asked to list a number of criteria for supporting strike action in order of importance, officers overwhelmingly chose rank and file wishes and rank and file support (table 8.7). Although we have no questionnaire data on steward criteria for action, the types of argument they used in meetings to support or oppose action were very similar to those of the full-time officers. Differences between officers and stewards were likely to arise, therefore, not because they applied different criteria, but because they were differentially placed to evaluate the same criteria of the wishes of the membership and their willingness to act.

This data should not be taken to mean that officers were merely the civil servants of the membership, willing to implement their every wish in regard to industrial action. 'Members' views' was the most important factor in the thinking of many officers, but it was not the only one. Moreover the wishes of the membership could themselves be shaped by officers. An ASTMS officer, for instance, called a mass meeting to discuss responses to management's continued insistence on compulsory redundancies. At this meeting it was the officer, a leader in our terms, who

Table 8.7. *Officers' criteria for strike support*

| Item | Mean rank | No. ranking 1st or 2nd |
|------|-----------|------------------------|
| Members' wishes | 3.1 | 50 |
| Level of membership support | 3.4 | 32 |
| Nature of the issue | 4.3 | 29 |
| Whether procedure exhausted | 4.3 | 35 |
| Management vulnerability | 4.9 | 13 |
| Management willingness to negotiate | 5.8 | 11 |

*Source:* Officers' questionnaire.

strongly advocated industrial action and responded firmly and vigorously to the doubts of a few waverers. Industrial action was a new experience for many of these members, and it was clear at the meeting that because of their inexperience and uncertainty they looked to the officer for guidance. It was largely because of his advocacy of militancy that the membership voted to act on their grievances.

### Structural correlates of militancy

Threats of industrial action were almost unique facets of the bargaining process in that they displayed a strong association with structural properties of union, establishment and enterprise. Threats of industrial action were significantly associated with shop steward hierarchy at the group and establishment levels, steward-led bargaining at the establishment, and with larger workplaces and medium–large firms. In addition there were weak, but non-significant, associations with trade union density at bargaining unit, establishment and enterprise levels. Our explanation for these associations is that industrial action entails the mobilization of power resources, and these structural variables, in different ways, are a measure of the resources available to the union. In line with our questionnaire data we also found that the nature of the issue made a significant difference to the likelihood of threats (table 8.8).

This evidence is consistent with national trends at the time (1986–87) which shows that pay strikes were few in number compared with levels in the 1970s, and compared with the much higher number of non-pay strikes (*Department of Employment Gazette*, various issues). With pay settlements then running just at or a little above inflation, and earnings increasing faster than inflation, it was argued by several observers that

Table 8.8. *Officer industrial action threats as a function of bargaining issues*

| Issue | Issue frequency | Incidence of action threats, no.(% of issues) |
|---|---|---|
| Redundancy | 40 | 8 (20) |
| Trade union matters | 47 | 6 (13) |
| Work organization | 55 | 7 (13) |
| Equality, health and safety | 32 | 1 (3) |
| Pay and pay related | 100 | 2 (2) |
| Total | 274 | 24 (9) |

*Source:* Observation.

workers had little incentive to strike over pay. Our own evidence confirmed this interpretation. Employers' opening pay offers were almost invariably above inflation, but never below it. Data from eleven separate pay negotiations initiated between February and December 1986 showed that in eight cases the employer's opening offer was above inflation, in one case it was equal to inflation, but in only two cases was it below inflation. In all eleven cases the final settlement was above the current inflation rate. Consequently strike threats were made in conjunction with pay issues at just two out of 100 meetings where pay was discussed. It was redundancy, trade union rights and questions of work organization and grading that provided what few threats we observed. For union officers, it was the ramifications of these issues that drew their fire: redundancies and changes in work organization were likely to prove irreversible whilst attacks on trade union organization could have far-reaching and long-term consequences for a host of issues. In contrast, this year's poor pay settlement could always be made up next year. As one officer said, it was his job to take the longer-term view, and not just concentrate on this year's pay round.

### Inter-union differences

There were no inter-union differences in the incidence of threats of action, though strike criteria did vary significantly. Questionnaire data revealed the preponderance of members' wishes and/or the level of rank and file

Table 8.9. *Officer attitudes to militancy as a function of union affiliation*

| | EETPU (N = 11) | | Other unions (N = 65)[a] | |
| | Strongly agree/ Agree | Strongly disagree/ Disagree | Strongly agree/ Agree | Strongly disagree/ Disagree |
|---|---|---|---|---|
| It can never be right to break an agreement | 9 | 1 | 16 | 49 |
| Strikes represent a breakdown of good industrial relations and should therefore be avoided | 10 | 1 | 24 | 39 |
| A well organized and militant membership is the best guarantee of successful outcomes to negotiations | 2 | 9 | 46 | 18 |

*Note:* [a] T&GWU, GMB, ASTMS, AEU, NUPE, NALGO.
*Source:* Officers' questionnaire.

support in the T&GWU, AEU, ASTMS, NALGO and NUPE. Interestingly the EETPU officers plumped overwhelmingly for 'constitutional criteria': whether procedures had been exhausted (eight out of nine ranked 1st or 2nd), and whether the action was lawful (six out of nine ranked 1st or 2nd). The only other significant difference involved the GMB, where 11 out of 23 officers ranked the procedural criterion 1st or 2nd. This pattern of EETPU exceptionalism was confirmed by attitudinal evidence, as table 8.9 shows.[3] The aggregated data for other unions conceal hardly any inter-union variations, thus underlining the exceptional character of EETPU officer values.

### Officers' values

Although leader officers were somewhat more likely to encourage strikes than their regulationist and managerialist counterparts (on 17 per cent of issues they dealt with as compared with 8 per cent and 6 per cent respectively) this difference proved to be non-significant. Where values did make a difference was in *opposition* to strikes and in the *criteria* used to support them. Managerialist officers opposed strike action or other industrial action by claiming that there was a risk of managerial retaliation

Table 8.10. *Officer's criteria for supporting industrial action as a function of age, seniority and ideology*

| Criterion | Independent variable | | Spearman correlation |
|---|---|---|---|
| Whether action lawful | Age | | $0.46^c$ |
| | | Political views | $0.30^b$ |
| Whether procedure exhausted | Age | | $0.27^b$ |
| | | Political views | $0.28^b$ |
| Attitude of senior officials | Age | | $-0.25^a$ |
| | | Seniority | $-0.24^a$ |

*Notes:* [a] $p < 0.05$.
[b] $p < 0.01$.
[c] $p < 0.001$.
*Source:* Officers' questionnaire.

on 19 per cent of the issues they handled (the figures for regulationists and leaders were both 2 per cent, $\chi^2 = 22.92$, $p < 0.001$), and on 21 per cent of issues they claimed there would be no membership support for such action, a claim made on only 4 per cent of issues by regulationists and 2 per cent of the issues by leaders ($\chi^2 = 19.95$, $p < 0.001$).

What this evidence suggests is that ideological differences between officers cannot be captured by a simple pro-/anti-strike dichotomy. Under the right conditions – strong grievances, membership support for action, management vulnerability – all types of officer will back industrial action. Indeed under these conditions it could well be very difficult to do otherwise. An ASTMS managerialist, for example, fully supported industrial action by members at the Bristol office of a large national road transport organization on the grounds that this was the only way to shift an unreasonable management. Whilst managerialists prefer not to embark on industrial action there are occasions when employer actions will force them into it. Where ideology really shows through is in the efforts officers devote to arguing *against* industrial action.

Officers also varied in the criteria used to decide on industrial action, as table 8.10 shows. The 'constitutional' criteria (legality and procedure) prevalent in the EETPU and to a lesser extent the GMB were strongly associated with older and more right-wing officers (and these results persist even when seniority is partialled out). This points to a 'generational' effect, which we observed in chapter 7 with regard to bargaining objectives, and might explain the results from McCarthy and

Parker (1968) and Parker (1974, 1975) mentioned at the beginning of this section. In other words, an older generation of officers may well have been less militant than shop stewards (in the late 1960s and early 1970s), but the position today is rather different. Moreover with age and experience officers become less sensitive to the attitudes of their superiors, as one would expect. Overall, then, our evidence shows that officers' resort or opposition to strike threats is influenced (1) by the sophistication of union organization, (2) by the nature of the issue, and (3) by their own ideologies. Whilst there are differences between unions, these are best seen as the expression of a strong and distinctive ideology within the EETPU.

### Moving to settlement

The final settlement to negotiations was heavily influenced by full-time officers. On 64 per cent of the issues we observed they wielded more influence than stewards, sharing influence equally on just 17 per cent of issues with the remainder dominated by stewards. Whilst this degree of influence was less than on bargaining tactics (where officer domination was evident on 76 per cent of issues) it was greater than on the construction of the bargaining agenda. Questionnaire data from officers themselves largely corroborated our own observations, with just 22 per cent reporting that they had little influence over the acceptance of pay offers.

The most common arguments used to accept management offers were that the bargaining limit had been reached (38 times), and that management strength (24) and union weakness (21) prohibited any further gains. In addition, officers frequently had recourse to a variety of tactical arguments for drawing negotiations to a close: offers might be withdrawn, satisfactory progress had been secured on key issues, the membership would be unwilling to act in pursuit of their demands. Not surprisingly the arguments for rejecting offers were the mirror image of these: bargaining limits had not yet been reached (63 times), workers' demands had not been met (55), and members would be unhappy with the offer (36). In addition, whilst pragmatic or tactical considerations were frequently deployed by officers to secure acceptance of offers (on 40 issues in all), the opposing idea of 'principles' was appealed to on 48 issues in order to move rejection of employer offers.

Although officers frequently took the initiative and were most influential in moving to settlement, this does not imply that they were convinced by managerial arguments. On the contrary, officers remained fairly sceptical of most of the employers' arguments. On only 9 per cent of issues did they seem to be completely convinced, whilst they showed signs of partial acceptance on a further 38 per cent of issues. On 53 per cent of issues they showed no sign whatever of accepting or internalizing anything the employer had said to them. If collective bargaining is understood primarily as an exchange of concessions (and only secondarily as persuasion), then it is not surprising that union officers rarely accept the employers' arguments. The pattern of arguments used by officers and their response to those of the employer were remarkably similar to those of the stewards who accompanied them on negotiations. The rank order of steward arguments for accepting management offers correlated ($r = 0.62$, $p < 0.05$) with that of the officers, whilst the pattern of arguments for rejection was an almost perfect match with those used by officers ($r = 0.89$, $p < 0.01$). Likewise stewards completely rejected employer's arguments on 59 per cent of issues, and completely accepted them on only 6 per cent of issues, a pattern very similar to the officers. This evidence, as with much else in this chapter, reinforced the idea of the officer–steward relationship as one of close cooperation founded on similar objectives.

The degree of officer influence over settlements bore little relation to any of the key structural variables looked at throughout this chapter: the recency of organization, union density at group, establishment or enterprise levels, steward hierarchy and the sophistication of workplace union organization. Nor was there any association between the patterns of argument used by officers and these same structural variables. We did however, find some inter-union differences, but the results were mixed. ASTMS officers reported significantly more influence over settlements than their counterparts in other unions, but observation data failed to corroborate this claim. ASTMS officers also claimed that they were often against accepting offers of which their members were in favour, and observation data indirectly confirmed this point. Whilst T&GWU officers accepted managerial arguments 'completely or partially' on 56 per cent of issues (and GMB officers on 41 per cent of issues) the same was true of ASTMS officers on only 36 per cent of issues. However, there are strong grounds for thinking that these apparent inter-union differences actually conceal significant intra-union variation, and that in fact they are better understood as ideological differences between officers that are partly, though weakly, associated with union. We found that managerialist officers used significantly more arguments in favour of accepting offers than their regulationist or leader counterparts (see table 8.11).

Leader officers were most prone to urge rejection of offers, followed by regulationists and then by managerialists. These differences emerged significantly on four types of argument: whether the limits of bargaining had been reached, whether management was weak and could be pushed

Table 8.11. *Officer arguments to reject and accept management offers*

| | Managerialist N = 8 | Regulationist N = 13 | Leader N = 6 |
|---|---|---|---|
| Number of arguments to *reject* offers | 41 | 195 | 93 |
| Number of arguments to *accept* offers | 82 | 84 | 7 |
| Arguments to *reject* offers as per cent of total arguments | 33 | 70 | 93 |
| $\chi^2 = 91.63$, p < 0.001 | | | |

*Source:* Observation.

further and whether there were issues of legality or principle at stake. Conversely, there were differences in the opposite direction in the use of arguments for acceptance, above all on the limits of bargaining, on management strength and union weakness. All these differences were highly significant, with most reaching the 0.001 level. In other words, managerialists were much more readily convinced that the balance of power in the bargaining relationship constrained the union and made it futile to continue insisting on demands being met. Leaders, by contrast, rarely evinced such a view, believing that the actions of the members and their representatives could secure their objectives. Nonetheless our evidence suggested that leaders were only marginally more influential than other officers in influencing the outcome of negotiations when compared with stewards. Whilst leaders wielded more influence than their stewards on 70 per cent of issues, the figure for regulationists was 66 per cent and for managerialists 56 per cent, a difference well short of statistical significance.

The political views of officers had a major effect on their attitude to settlements. The more right-wing the officer (according to their own categorization), the more likely they were to favour settlements that their stewards thought inadequate ($\chi^2 = 6.89$, p < 0.01). Older and more senior officers who believed in close relationships with management and who thought it wrong to break agreements were also more likely to find themselves espousing offers that their stewards were against. But whilst more senior officers (i.e. those with more years of service in the union) were likely to succeed in influencing stewards (r = 0.26, p < 0.01), age *per se* gave officers no such advantage. Not surprisingly, then, it was more senior officers who were prone to disagree with stewards over acceptance of offers ($r = 0.22$, $p < 0.05$).

### The power base of the full-time officer

In chapter 2 we set out a framework for looking at the power resources of unions in relation to employers, derived from Edwards and Heery (1989). Many of these resources are available to full-time officers in their dealings with shop stewards, and are frequently cited in arguments – e.g. procedure agreements, the willingness of the membership to act, the provisions of the law and relations with management. But these resources are not the exclusive preserve of the officer, and indeed most (if not all) are just as available to shop stewards. Consequently they do not in themselves explain the power base of the full-time officer within the officer–steward relationship. We have shown throughout this and previous chapters that the officer wields considerable influence over shop stewards, that this influence is largely accepted, if not actually requested, by the stewards themselves, and that the officer–steward relationship remains nonetheless fairly cooperative.

An alternative way of looking at power resources that may prove helpful was provided by French and Raven (1959), who identified several types of power resource that can be wielded by power-holders: *reward* power is based on the officer's control of salient rewards and sanctions, such as access to stewards' training courses, or the power to remove stewards' credentials. *Expert* power is based on the officers' expertise and *referent* power on the identification of stewards with their officers. To what extent do these resources explain the pervasive influence of officers within the bargaining process? *Reward* power were rarely used by officers, and rewards such as access to training courses were rarely requested by stewards. Several officers did tell us of occasions when they had withdrawn stewards' credentials, and the power to do this was written into the AEU rule book. Batstone *et al.* (1977: 204) also noted the withdrawal of credentials as one element in the AEU officer's power base.

On the other hand, several officers also told us of stewards who had complained about them to senior officers, and it was generally believed that such complaints were taken very seriously. In other words *both* officers and stewards had the capacity to reward and punish each other, and it was not obvious that the balance of resources favoured the officers. Although the frequency with which a resource is used is an unreliable guide to its potency (indeed the sanction that is rarely deployed is often extremely powerful) our impression was that control of rewards and punishments did not play a significant role in explaining officer influence.

By contrast, the expertise of full-time officers appeared to be crucial. This was revealed first of all in the fact that they dominated decision-making on bargaining tactics, far more than on objectives and outcomes. It also emerged in the kinds of assistance requested by stewards: negotiating goals (help requested at 30 meetings), negotiating tactics (29), explanation of agreements (24) and negotiating practice (23) (cf. also Batstone *et al.*, 1977: 206). By contrast issues outside the immediate bargaining process, such as relations with members and personal problems, were raised less frequently by stewards. Thirdly, of the five comments most frequently made by stewards about their officers, three revolved around their expertise as negotiators: competence (28 times, ranked 1st, 10 per cent of all comments), negotiating ability (23 times, ranked 3rd, 8 per cent) and the quality of their settlements (18 times, ranked 4th, 7 per cent).[4] This pattern of requests and comments was mirrored by the unsolicited advice offered to stewards. Top of the list was advice on negotiating practice, offered at 50 (32 per cent) of the meetings we observed, followed by injunctions to moderate bargaining goals (39 meetings), use procedures against management (37), help with interpretation of agreements (35) and advice to meet management (34). Only one other piece of advice ranked as high, and that concerned cooperation with other groups of workers (40).

This evidence clearly underlines the expertise of the full-time officer in collective bargaining, an expertise readily acknowledged by stewards themselves. Batstone *et al.* (1977: 192) reported that 67 per cent of their white-collar stewards (but only 25 per cent of manual stewards) felt that the full-time officer's involvement was useful because of this expertise. But this was not the only power resource of the officer, and we found that leader officers in particular (and regulationists to a lesser degree) were able to influence stewards because of the close identification between them. By contrast, managerialist officers could rarely mobilize this resource. One strong piece of evidence in support of this argument comes from the incidence of dissent between officers and stewards. We observed such dissent on 67 per cent of the issues processed by managerialist officers, compared with just 32 per cent for regulationists and 35 per cent for leaders, an enormously significant difference ($\chi^2 = 24.62$, p < 0.001). (Batstone *et al.*, 1977: 199, found that officer–steward conflict in bargaining and adjournments accounted for just 25 per cent of all disagreements, and that conflict between officers was far more common.) The explanation for this pattern of dissent rests largely with goal differences amongst officers: managerialists were far more likely to opt for modest bargaining objectives, and to urge their stewards to do likewise, than other types of officer. The greater degree of goal consensus between the non-managerialist officers and their stewards would provide such officers

Table 8.12. *The fruits of negotiation: percentage pay rises for different groups of workers as a function of officer orientation*

|  | Managerialists | Regulationists and leaders |
|---|---|---|
|  | 5.75 | 6.0 |
|  | 5.50 | 7.0 |
|  | 5.65 | 6.0 |
|  | 5.25 | 6.7 |
|  |  | 6.4 |
|  |  | 6.0 |
|  | ——— | ——— |
| Mean | 5.54 | 6.35 |

*Source:* Observation.

with an additional power resource – that of steward identification – over and above their expertise.

### The outcomes of bargaining

In *Shop Stewards in Action* Batstone *et al.* (1977) attempted to measure the effectiveness of different types of steward (leader and populist) by looking at wages and earnings in different sections of a factory, and they claimed that leader stewards secured higher earnings for their members than did populists. In our own case, comparisons between different types of officer are rendered almost impossible because of the many other determinants of pay rises, such as industrial sector. In addition, officers bargained about a wide range of non-pay issues and we cannot be confident that outcomes on the two sets of issues would be similar for any given officer type. For what it is worth, we were able to record increases in basic rates of pay negotiated for ten groups of workers by seven officers and the results showed that regulationist and leader officers secured significantly higher rises than managerialist officers (table 8.12). Whilst the pay data is suggestive, and consistent with officer objectives and orientations to bargaining, it falls short of being conclusive because of other influences on pay settlements.

### Conclusions

One of the main findings in chapters 7 and 8 is that officers and stewards display some striking similarities in their collective bargaining behaviour.

They deployed similar types of argument to defend their claims, they were equally averse to accepting management's arguments, and they showed an equal propensity to threaten industrial action. In their objectives we found officers and stewards in agreement on roughly half the issues we looked at, whilst the rest divided fairly evenly between those where officer ambition exceeded that of stewards and vice-versa. In other words, on only about one-quarter of the 274 issues we looked at did steward ambition exceed that of full-time officers, contrary to the prediction of bureaucracy theory. Moreover, officer pressures on stewards to raise and broaden their objectives were about as frequent as pressures the other way (to depress and narrow their aims).

Within the bargaining process officers showed a wide range of approaches to management, including hostility, formality and friendliness. Nevertheless there was near ubiquitous insistence by officers that managers were not to be trusted and stewards were urged to act accordingly. Officers wielded considerable influence over collective bargaining, above all over bargaining tactics, where they dominated proceedings on 76 per cent of the issues we looked at, with stewards wielding more influence on just 13 per cent of issues. Officer dominance was somewhat less on bargaining outcomes (they exercised more influence than stewards on 64 per cent of issues) and least of all on setting the bargaining agenda, where steward influence matched that of officers. In other words, whilst the bargaining agenda was a joint creation, officers then 'took over' and exerted significant influence over tactics and outcomes. But this influence was largely accepted by stewards and was based both on the officer's proven expertise and (in some cases) on a close identification of goals and values. In turn, the officers depended on stewards for information about membership aspirations and managements' actions, and they used the stewards to mobilize members behind bargaining claims and (on occasion) to build support for industrial action. The officer–steward relationship was therefore built on a large measure of consensus and a high degree of interdependence (cf. Batstone et al., 1977).

There were, however, striking differences between officers which significantly alter the general picture of uniformity. Officers divided into three basic orientations towards collective bargaining, managerialist, regulationist and leader, based on their goal ambitions, willingness to use sanctions, hostility to management and use of stewards to mobilize members. In turn, these three types of officer varied significantly in the criteria they used to formulate claims and to judge the suitability of industrial action, in their willingness to moderate steward ambitions, and in the frequency of conflict with stewards. The managerialist was the archetypal officer of bureaucracy theory, but just eight of 27 officers fell in this category. The regulationist was above all pragmatic, adjusting readily to the balance of power, whilst the leader officer displayed a strong desire to enhance and broaden the outlook and ambition of members as part of a more political approach to trade union work. The significance of officers' own values systems in explaining key facets of their behaviour was corroborated by questionnaire data, and strikingly confirms the analytical power of a theoretical orientation based on systems of values.

However officer behaviour cannot be seen simply as expressive of values, but was also instrumental in character and designed to secure certain objectives. This point leads to three qualifications to the value orientation approach. First, virtually all officers were in favour of greater shop steward independence (albeit for different reasons), and virtually all were highly sensitive to threats against procedural rights. Regardless of orientation officers generally believed that stewards should handle more of their own bargaining, and that the right to bargain was the *sine qua non* of effective trade unionism. Second, officers were highly pragmatic in the types of argument they used to defend their claims, essentially using whatever arguments they thought likely to be effective regardless of their ideological connotations. Finally, officer behaviour did vary across situations, partly as a function of the different constraints between companies, and partly as a function of the issues they were handling. Managerialist officers, for instance, did occasionally threaten industrial action and leader officers did occasionally try to moderate the ambitions of their members. The point is that officers' own values systems have to be translated into concrete actions in particular situations.

We also looked at the role of structural factors – properties of unions, union–management relations and establishments – and found, contrary to Boraston et al. (1975), that these rarely made any difference to a wide range of dependent variables centred around bargaining goals, tactics and outcomes. There were, however, three exceptions to this pattern of negative results. First, officer attempts to moderate steward goals were most pronounced at moderate levels of union density, presumably because such moderation was unnecessary at low density (because of steward weakness) and difficult at high density (because of steward strength). Second, in highly formalized systems of industrial relations, e.g. London buses and docks, officers relied strongly on arguments about precedent, union policy and management interests. Third, threats of industrial action were strongly associated with sophisticated workplace organization (Batstone and Gourlay, 1986), i.e. where there was high density, steward hierarchy and steward time off for union duties.

Inter-union differences were frequently found, but often turned out to be reflections of officers' orientations to bargaining, described above.

Moreover there was considerable intra-union variation amongst officers, as one would expect of British trade unions since officers exercise a high degree of job autonomy and operate in unions which rarely espouse a strong, clear and coherent ideology. An officer's union therefore makes a strong difference to his/her behaviour only where these conditions are absent, i.e. where power in the union is highly centralized and where the national leadership espouses and diffuses a strong ideology. Hence the only substantial union effect on officer behaviour was found in the EETPU.

Finally, we found evidence for strong generation and socialization effects on officers' bargaining behaviour. Managerialist officers were the old guard of the trade unions, often in their 50s or 60s, and had first become active in trade unionism during the era of right-wing, Cold War domination (from the late 1940s to the late 1950s). This was reflected in their sympathy for management, disagreements with shop stewards and hostility to strikes. By contrast, the leader officers were often younger, the products of the 1960s and 1970s, and therefore of a very different political era. By and large the values developed by officers in their early years of activity carry through into their later activities as full-time negotiators and representatives. This strong generational effect does not preclude the effects of role socialization. But we found that years of experience in the union had fewer and weaker effects on officers' attitudes and behaviours than generation. More senior officers, for instance, appeared more able to influence stewards, presumably because of their accumulated knowledge and expertise. But overall it was the generational differences between officers that stood out, not the socialization effects of union occupancy.

# 9 Dealing with managers

## Management in the 1980s

The 1980s presented managers with an enormous array of changes in their social environment: economic recession, new labour laws, mass unemployment, a strongly anti-union government, a dramatic decline in trade union membership and a favourable shift in the balance of power. As managers responded to these changes and began to exploit them so the academic debates got under way. It soon became clear that there was no single, dominant management strategy, and that the widely-discussed revival of 'macho' management was specific to particular firms and sectors of the economy (cf. Edwardes, 1983 on BL; MacGregor, 1986 and Edwards and Heery, 1989 on British Coal; and more generally Batstone, 1988, chapter 5; Edwards, 1987, chapter 5). Another argument suggests that personnel issues have become increasingly central to competitiveness and hence the rise of the personnel manager under the new label of 'human resource manager'. Human resource management seeks both to motivate employees and to secure their commitment to the objectives of the company. In some accounts, it tries to replace traditional, or adversarial industrial relations with a new, more cooperative employee relations policy, very much akin to the high-trust unitarism described by Fox (1966; see Guest, 1989; Keenoy, 1990; Marchington and Parker, 1990; Storey, 1989, 1992). Despite pluralist-inspired academic attacks on 'unitarism', it was clear from national surveys of managers that the majority of British managers in the late 1970s and early 1980s strongly endorsed some key unitarist propositions (e.g. Poole *et al.*, 1981). They were strongly committed to the idea of a harmony of interests between worker and employer and hostile to industrial democracy and to trade union power. According to Poole and Mansfield (1993) there was little change in these attitudes between 1980 and 1990.

How would these attitudes be reflected within the collective bargaining process? In Walton and McKersie's (1965) terms, we would expect attempts by managers to pursue an 'integrative' bargaining strategy in

173

which they emphasized common interests and downplayed or tried to avoid conflict. Such a strategy could involve placing new non-conflictual issues, such as training, on the agenda, but could also involve the use of 'integrative arguments' to defend management's position on traditional issues such as pay and productivity. This prediction, however, does have to be qualified on two counts: first, it has been argued that integrative bargaining is most likely to take place where there is high trust and friendliness between the negotiators, an open flow of information, some scope for concessions and a rough balance of power (Peterson and Tracy, 1977; Beaumont, 1990). Doubts about the prevalence of the last two conditions in Britain in the 1980s dictate caution in predicting a wide-spread move to integrative bargaining. Secondly, management strategies and arguments in bargaining will also depend on the perceived strategies and arguments of their union opponents. The persistence of 'adversarial arguments' by union negotiators would provide no reinforcement for integrative strategies by managers, and would thus inhibit or negate any moves in that direction (Grzelak, 1988).

Although the present study was not designed to investigate arguments about management bargaining strategies we do nevertheless have data which can shed some light on them. First, in so far as employers seek to promote closer relations with unions and to link the fortunes of workers to those of their firms, we can examine how far these objectives are reflected in the views and comments of officers about management. We can also examine more specifically the advice offered to stewards and members on how to deal with management. And finally, under this heading, we can examine the corollaries of union officers' attitudes to management. Second, we have a considerable amount of data on the arguments used by managers to justify their own claims and to resist union demands, and we can therefore consider how far management negotiators actually used arguments stressing common interests between themselves and their workers. Third, we can examine the similarities and differences between the arguments used by both sides in negotiations. We established in previous chapters that there is relatively little variation amongst officers in their systems of argument, because many are fairly pragmatic and used whatever argument they judged likely to be effective. Nevertheless it is of interest to see how far their own systems of argument reflect those of management. Finally we consider what little evidence there is on recent changes in patterns of argument, drawing on earlier studies of management and negotiation.

Theories of bureaucracy, oligarchy and polyarchy would all suggest (albeit for different reasons) that officers are likely to develop close relations with management based on a high degree of trust. In Batstone *et al.*'s (1977) terms this could approximate to a 'strong bargaining relationship':

A strong bargaining relationship (W. A. Brown, 1973: 134–5) involves the development of a relationship between steward and manager which goes beyond the minimum formal relationship which necessarily exists between them. At the minimum, this relationship is specific in terms of goals, affectively neutral, and universalistic ... A strong bargaining relationship exists where the negotiating relationship becomes particularistic and affectively positive ... The basic opposition of interests which exists within negotiation is therefore mediated by personal relationships which facilitate the constructive resolution of problems (Batstone *et al.*, 1977: 168–9).

Strong bargaining relations between stewards and managers are based on a balance of power, on a considerable degree of contact and on the possession by each side of resources, such as information, valuable to the other side. Officers, however, occupy a somewhat different position. As employees of the union they are less dependent on a particular management than shop stewards who need management support for such things as facilities. Because of their allocations and workloads officers will have relatively little contact with most of their management counterparts most of the time, and will therefore have little opportunity to build close and strong bargaining relationships. Any such relationships are likely to be built only with the small number of managers with whom an officer has regular contact.

Of the 156 meetings we observed, 66 included managers (as well as union officers and/or stewards and members) and 58 of these were negotiations, although five were consultative meetings. 35 meetings were at establishment level whilst 31 were multi-establishment (either divisional or company) level. None were multi-employer. 29 companies or organizations were involved in these meetings and there was a good spread of public (12 organizations, 20 meetings) and private (17 companies, 46 meetings), industry (14 companies, 29 meetings) and services (15 companies, 37 meetings). All but three of these meetings involved teams of 2–3 managers, normally comprising both personnel and line managers. The chief negotiator was either a divisional or company personnel manager (29 meetings) or a division/company executive (28 meetings). Even where divisional or corporate personnel did not take the lead in negotiations they were almost invariably members of the team. Side-meetings were not uncommon, being observed at one in six of the 66 meetings we attended.

### Officers' views of management

We reported in chapter 8 that the overwhelming majority of the comments made by officers about management were negative; table 9.1 sets

Table 9.1. *Officers' and stewards' comments about management*

|  | Officers | Stewards |
|---|---|---|
| Threatening bargaining rights | 62 | 40 |
| Exploitative | 58 | 59 |
| Untrustworthy | 52 | 45 |
| Devious | 43 | 30 |
| Able to make concessions | 38 | 21 |
| Likely to make concessions | 37 | 6 |
| Breaking agreements | 37 | 24 |
| Inefficient | 33 | 21 |
| Strong | 32 | 13 |
| Controlled from above | 32 | 9 |
| Other | 268 | 155 |
| Total | 692 | 423 |

*Source:* Observation.

out the detail. This was the case whether management was present or not. There were positive comments made about management's trustworthiness, fairness, competence and the like, but even on the broadest definition such positive remarks comprised just 29.3 per cent (203) of the 692 comments we recorded about management (see also IRRR, 1992: 10–11). We also reported that the rank order of main comments made by officers was almost identical to that of the shop stewards ($r = 0.87$, $p < 0.01$), underlining the close affinity between officers and stewards that we have already documented.

Comments about management can be made in many different contexts, and we therefore cannot assume that critical remarks about management will have the same impact in a formal negotiating session as compared with an informal post-negotiation talk with stewards. We therefore need to look more specifically at any advice given by officers in respect of management and at specific arguments in negotiations. Officers frequently encouraged stewards and members to meet with management (32 meetings, 21 per cent of the total) and to pursue grievances through existing procedures (35 meetings, 22 per cent of the total). But these injunctions need to be understood in the context of the negative attitudes held by officers about management. Stewards were not being restrained from militant actions they might otherwise have pursued, but were being urged to act independently on behalf of their members and pursue legitimate grievances against managements that could not be trusted. This evidence, taken as a whole, shows little sign of the positive feelings

Table 9.2. *Correlates of officer attitudes to management*

Those *agreeing* that 'a close relationship with management is a great asset for a negotiator', will:

|  |  | $r$ |
|---|---|---|
| – | have more right-wing political views | $0.42^c$ |
| – | be older | $0.33^b$ |
| – | be keen to maintain/restore differentials | $0.28^b$ |
| – | be keen to increase union membership, | $0.37^c$ |
|   | improve working conditions | $0.21^a$ |
|   | and protect jobs | $0.27^c$ |
| – | be less interested in women's rights | $0.47^c$ |
| – | give a low priority to rank and file wishes in deciding on strike action | $0.20^a$ |
| – | give a high priority to legal issues in deciding on strike action | $0.35^b$ |
| – | be more likely to accept offers, which stewards want to reject | $\chi^2 = 6.02^a$ |
| – | see strikes as a breakdown of industrial relations | $0.52^c$ |
| – | be opposed to breaking agreements | $0.26^b$ |

*Notes:*
[a] $p < 0.05$.
[b] $p < 0.01$.
[c] $p < 0.001$.

*Source:* Officers' questionnaire.

towards management that were described by Batstone *et al.* (1977) as one of the hallmarks of a strong bargaining relationship. Evidence on formality in bargaining reveals a similar picture. Officers attempted to maintain or enhance formality in the bargaining process at 36 meetings (out of 156) but tried to avoid formality at just ten meetings, and the bias towards formality is again inconsistent with the development of a strong bargaining relationship.

Though managerialist officers did not promote mistrust as frequently as regulationists and leaders, the differences were not significant. This is consistent with the findings in previous chapters that patterns of argument were fairly similar between union officers, despite differences in orientation, as it is on bargaining goals and tactics that orientation makes a difference. Consequently it was leader officers who were most likely to urge stewards to resist management arguments against their demands (on 48 per cent of the 46 issues they processed at meetings), compared with regulationists (21 per cent of 161 issues) and managerialists (7 per cent of 68 issues, $\chi^2 = 26.3$, $p < 0.001$).

*The correlates of officer attitudes to management*

Officer orientations to bargaining were defined in terms of several key dimensions of the bargaining process, one of which was 'sympathy for managerial goals and arguments'. We can now look in more detail at attitudes to management in order to establish just how central they are to officers' actions and attitudes within the bargaining process. One item in the officers' questionnaire survey asked for agreement or disagreement with the statement 'A close relationship with management is a great asset for a negotiator'. Table 9.2 sets out the main correlates of responses to this statement, and confirms the centrality of attitudes to management.

What emerges from table 9.2 is that officer attitudes to management are strongly related to many other views and attitudes pertaining to collective bargaining. They relate to bargaining objectives, to the criteria used in strike decision-making, to the likelihood of accepting management offers, and are associated with attitudes towards strikes and procedures. All of these relationships are statistically significant and some are highly significant. These results therefore strongly reinforce the significance of one of the dimensions used in the construction of officer orientations.

## Managements' negotiating arguments[1]

We used the same categories to describe managements' negotiating arguments that we had used for union officers and stewards in order to facilitate comparison. In some cases this was fairly straightforward and involved no difficulty, e.g. references to internal or external relativity, ability to pay. In other cases it was merely a question of inverting union arguments, e.g. 'high cost' instead of 'low cost'. Other arguments were more difficult to translate: 'worth of workers' contribution' on the union side became 'worth of workers' current rewards' on the management side. Finally some managerial arguments had no obvious union counterpart: managements would sometimes say they were constrained by Head Office, whereas it was almost unknown for union officers to admit to any limits on their discretion. (Independent evidence suggests that references to Head Office constraints over local pay negotiations are likely to be genuine. Marginson *et al.*, 1988: 163, found that high-level company managers were 'extensively involved' in pay negotiations at establishment level, particularly in companies with a low degree of product diversification.) Bearing these points in mind, table 9.3 sets out the rank order of managements' negotiating arguments across our whole sample.

The most frequently used arguments tried to show that management's offer was really in the best interests of workers and that in any case the

Table 9.3. *Managements' negotiating arguments*

|                                              | (Times mentioned) |
| -------------------------------------------- | ----------------- |
| Management offer is in workers' interests    | 59                |
| High cost of union demands                   | 36                |
| Workers' current rewards are good            | 33                |
| Management policy/prerogative                | 31                |
| Internal relativity                          | 22                |
| Claim not just/must be *quid pro quo*        | 20                |
| Precedent                                    | 19                |
| Workers don't support union claims           | 18                |
| External relativity                          | 17                |
| Industrial relations/morale effects          | 17                |
| Top management constraints                   | 17                |
| Ability to pay                               | 16                |
| Cost of living                               | 5                 |
| Total                                        | 310               |

*Source:* Observation; 137 issues at 58 meetings.

terms and conditions currently enjoyed by workers were fairly good. Sometimes these claims would be supported by references to other company employees (internal relativity) or to other workers elsewhere, usually in the same industry (external relativity). On other occasions, negotiators would simply assert that their offer was 'just' or 'fair'. These five arguments comprised just under half (49 per cent, 151) of all managements' arguments, and were far more common than arguments focused on the costs of union demands. For example, managers in a national transport service organization were attempting to introduce a series of new work practices which would entail, *inter alia*, longer shifts and some redundancies. Their main arguments emphasized the benefits of more skilled work and more promotion prospects for those employees who remained. In annual pay negotiations at a national housing company the union had insisted on pay rises equal to those given in the main funding body, a local authority. Company managers repeatedly challenged the relevance of the comparison (although they finally conceded after months of negotiation). In redundancy negotiations at a South London electronics factory the company forcefully asserted that their package of compensation was fair and generous because it exceeded the statutory minimum.

Management negotiators certainly tried to show that union claims would be costly in the very near future, or that they would create a potentially costly precedent, and they also disputed union claims about the damage that would be done to worker morale or industrial relations if a reasonable offer was not forthcoming. Interestingly, however, complaints about inability to pay were comparatively rare. These four cost-based arguments accounted for just 28 per cent (88) of managements' arguments. For instance, in a manufacturing plant scheduled for closure the management negotiators laid great emphasis on the cost of meeting the union's redundancy pay claim and simply ruled it out of court. In annual pay negotiations for port shipping clerks the employer rejected union claims that his low offer would cause problems of poor morale and labour turnover. He maintained they already had several hundred staff 'surplus to requirements' and that in any case dockers could quite easily carry out the clerks' duties. One of the few settings in which ability to pay featured prominently was the NHS. In annual pay negotiations for a specialist professional group the union presented a long and detailed justification for a substantial pay rise based on parity with fellow NHS professionals. The high-powered management team listened to all this and then simply said they could only afford 6 per cent and that was that.

In a number of organizations management insisted firmly on their prerogatives, particularly when faced with leader officers determined to defend their members' interests. At a large metals factory management had decided to take white-collar staff out of collective pay bargaining and transfer them to annual appraisal and merit pay. In the face of vigorous union opposition managers simply insisted on their right to manage and to introduce changes in the interests of the business. At an electronics factory the management team was clearly taken aback by the union's rejection of their redundancy package and their claim that it was in the workers' best interests. Consequently they fell back on straightforward assertions of managerial prerogative (which, needless to say, were counterproductive).

Overall, then, what emerged was a strong emphasis on the rewards that would accrue to workers from accepting management's offer, with much less emphasis on the costs that might arise from rejecting it. In Walton and McKersie's (1965) terms, managements were far more likely to use *integrative* arguments, stressing rewards and common interests than *distributive* arguments based on costs and competing interests.

So far, we have talked about management in general, irrespective of their negotiating opponent. But it seems reasonable to argue that there would be variation amongst managers in the arguments they would use, not least because of the orientation of their opposite numbers on the union side, and it is to this issue that we now turn. Of the 58 negotiating sessions we observed, 38 involved regulationist officers and ten each

Table 9.4. *Inter-correlations between management arguments as a function of officer orientation*

|                 | Leader  | Regulationist |
|-----------------|---------|---------------|
| Managerialist   | 0.66[a] | 0.51[a]       |
| Regulationist   | 0.57[a] |               |

*Note:*
[a] $p < 0.05$.

*Source:* Observation.

involved leaders and managerialists. Of the 137 issues processed at these meetings, 77 were handled by regulationists, 40 by managerialists and 20 by leaders. Although there is not quite as much information on leader officers as we would like, there is nevertheless sufficient to allow meaningful comparisons. We therefore divided the negotiating sessions according to union officer orientation, calculated the rank order of management arguments separately for each one and then computed the correlations (table 9.4).

The rank order of management arguments was fairly similar irrespective of officer orientation. For instance, arguments based on worker rewards (offer in workers' interest, or fair, current rewards, internal and external relativity) comprised 52 per cent (44) of the arguments put to managerialist officers, 42 per cent (71) of those put to regulationist officers and 62 per cent (36) of those put to leaders. There are clearly differences here, but they are not statistically significant. Likewise, the four arguments based on cost showed no significant variation, with the figures being 27 per cent, 32 per cent and 21 per cent for managerialists, regulationists and leaders respectively.

### Union and management arguments compared

We noted in chapter 8 the main arguments used by union officers to promote their own claims and resist those of management. Internal relativities, the justice of their own claims and the wishes of rank and file members were used most frequently. Officers also tried to maintain that their claims would serve managements' interests as well as those of their own members. If we look at the rank order of arguments used by officers and managers respectively we find a modest, but not significant, degree of similarity ($r = 0.33$, n.s.). (We also tested for differences in the rank order of arguments and found none: $U = 65.6$, n.s.) A similar result obtained

Table 9.5. *Relationships between management and union officer arguments in negotiations as a function of officer orientation*

|  | Managers and managerialist officers | Managers and regulationist officers | Managers and leader officers | Managers and all officers |
|---|---|---|---|---|
| r | 0.80[a] | 0.31 | −0.17 | 0.33 |
| No. of management arguments | 84 | 168 | 58 | 310 |
| No. of officer arguments | 80 | 293 | 93 | 466 |
| No. of meetings | 10 | 38 | 10 | 58 |

*Note:*
[a] $p < 0.01$.

*Source:* Observation.

when we looked at the arguments of managers and shop stewards ($r = 0.31$, n.s.). Officers and managers each tried to show that their own demands would also serve their opponents' interests, and that their demands really did reflect the wishes of union members. Conversely, neither side resorted very often to arguments about the cost of living or the employer's ability to pay. However these four similarities were balanced by some striking differences in systems of argument: management's frequent emphasis on the high cost of the union's claims was rarely matched by union attempts to disprove such assertions.

Given the significance of officer orientations in collective bargaining it makes sense to take this analysis one step further and look at the relations between managerial and officer arguments for each type of union officer in turn. Table 9.5 shows the results. The rank order of arguments used by managers and managerialist officers was strikingly similar, thus validating the use of the term 'managerialist' to designate this category of officer. For the other two types of officer there was no significant association between officer and management arguments, although interestingly the negative correlation for leader officers showed that they had a slight tendency to make frequent use of arguments hardly used by their management opposite numbers, and vice-versa.

If we compare the three sets of officers and managers, it is the managerialists who stand out. The parallels (r = 0.80) between the arguments of managerialist officers and their management counterparts were significantly closer than either the regulationist officers and their managers (z = 1.65, p < 0.05, one tail) or the leader officers and their managers (z = 1.97, p < 0.025, one tail). In other words, managerialist officers were close to their management counterparts, not only in the modesty of their bargaining goals (as we saw in previous chapters), but also in the systems of argument they were inclined to use. These affinities clearly differentiated the managerialist officers from their leader and regulationist counterparts.

### Trends in managements' systems of argument

One further issue of interest is whether the types of argument used by managers changed significantly after the onset of recession in 1979–80. There are several grounds for making such a prediction. First, the 1970s was dominated by explicit and comprehensive incomes policies which could have distorted both the outcomes and the processes of pay bargaining, whereas the 1980s was a time of 'free collective bargaining' in the private sector coupled with an implicit and selective incomes policy in the public sector (Daniel, 1976; Willman, 1982). Second, there has been growing interest in human resource management and associated attempts to enhance workers' commitment to their firms through schemes such as quality circles and the like (Storey, 1989, 1992). The emphasis on the joint interests of workers and employers may have filtered through into collective bargaining, as it has done in joint consultative committees (Cressey et al., 1985). Third, the balance of power has shifted in favour of employers (Kelly, 1990). However it is unclear whether this should lead to a rise in 'integrative' arguments (because unions are weak and may therefore be more receptive to them), or to the decline of such arguments (because managers can push through changes without having to justify them). Finally, the profitability of British companies was significantly higher in the mid- and late 1980s compared with the 1970s, whilst inflation was somewhat lower. Hence arguments about ability to pay and cost of living might have been expected to be less prominent in the 1980s than in the preceding decade.

Although there is no directly comparable data set from the 1970s, there is some evidence which allows us to make tentative comparisons. Daniel (1976) conducted a study of management (and union) negotiators in late 1975, and asked them about the arguments used to resist union claims in annual pay bargaining. His sample consisted of 148 managers from manufacturing industry. In order to produce evidence that was approximately

Table 9.6. *Principal management arguments in annual pay negotiations, 1975, 1986–87, times cited and rank*

| Argument (1975) | 1975 Frequency (rank) | 1986–87 Frequency (rank) | Argument (1986–87) |
|---|---|---|---|
| Financial position of firm/ability to pay | 48   (1) | 10   (5) | Ability to pay |
| Already had big increases/challenged validity of cost of living figures | 31   (2) | 21   (2) | Workers' current rewards |
| Effect on prices/ competitive position/ future trading prospects | 26   (3) | 15   (3) | High cost |
| Productivity quid pro quo/threat to jobs | 15   (4) | 12   (4) | Claim not just/ must be *quid pro quo* |
| Comparison with other groups | 11   (5) | 26   (1) | Internal relativity/ external relativity |
| No. of managers | 148 | 23 | No. of meetings |

*Sources:* 1975: Calculated from Daniel (1976), table VIII.3: 90; 1986–87: Observation.

comparable we first extracted annual pay negotiations from our full set of data on negotiating sessions, and re-counted the main arguments used by managers in rebutting union claims. By combining some of Daniel's (1976) categories and some of our own, it was possible to compare the rank order of five sets of arguments (table 9.6).

Clearly these comparisons have to be treated with extreme caution, and they can obviously be no more than suggestive. Nevertheless they show remarkable similarities and equally striking differences in the *relative* frequency of managements' arguments. In 1975 it was the firm's ability to pay that dominated management argument, whilst comparisons with other groups were far less salient. In 1986–87 the position was reversed. Ability to pay was cited fairly infrequently, whilst arguments about relativities were used far more often (relatively speaking) than in the past. The declining salience of ability to pay is probably a reflection of growing profitability which simply makes it a weaker argument for management to deploy. The (relatively) greater salience of arguments about relativities (assuming that this is a real change) could reflect managements' determination to differentiate pay rates and pay criteria for different groups of employees as part of the trend towards greater management control of pay. For instance, in a large retail chain organized by the T&GWU, the union's chief negotiator was attempting to reduce the growing pay disparity between workers in the older high street stores and those in new edge-of-town stores. But the company negotiators were adamant that the pay discrepancies would remain and were wholly justified, and they simply refused to concede uniform pay rises for all groups of employees. In national negotiations at a large dairy chain the employers used external relativities to keep the annual pay settlement down. With settlements elsewhere in the industry running at 5.6 per cent, the union's claim of 8 per cent (when inflation was at 4 per cent) foundered on the company's insistence on sticking to 'the going rate'.

## Conclusions

Officer views about management were overwhelmingly negative. Their comments in stewards' meetings and in negotiations, the arguments they used and the advice they proffered, all reinforced the message that management was untrustworthy and devious and would act against workers' interests. Officers frequently urged stewards to meet with management and use grievance procedures against them, but this reflected a commitment to adversarial bargaining, not faith in management. For their part, management negotiators sought to challenge this view by stressing the benefits that would accrue to workers from acceptance of management offers. In other words, their most frequently used arguments reflected an ideology of common interest, against that of the unions' more adversarial approach. There was some evidence to suggest that managerial arguments may have shifted over the past 20 years. The recovery of profitability and the intense competition of the 1980s probably led to a decline in the salience of 'inability to pay'.

Managers' patterns of argument were much the same irrespective of their union opponents. These patterns in turn were neither very similar to nor highly dissimilar from those used by union negotiators, as indicated by modest, though non-significant, correlations. Some of the dissimilarities derived from the organizational differences between unions and businesses. Union negotiators were far more likely to stress the wishes of their members, an expression of the democratic character of union organization; and to refer to the intrinsic justice of their claim by appeals to broader notions of fairness or equality. Finally, we established that the

patterns of argument used by managerialist officers and their management counterparts were remarkably similar, a relationship that did not
hold for either leader or regulationist officers. These results once again
confirmed the utility of officer orientations as an analytical tool.

*Part 4*

# Conclusions

# 10    Working for the union

In this final chapter we first review the main findings of our research, looking in turn at officer organization and officer behaviour. In each case we also set out our conclusions on the strengths and weaknesses of the different theoretical approaches examined throughout the book. The second half of the chapter then draws out some of the implications of our work for several areas of debate: the politics of trade unionism, the prospects for trade unions in the years ahead and the characteristics of union organization.

### Review of findings: officer organization

British trade unionists are serviced by a remarkably small workforce of approximately 3000. Although there are fewer full-time officers today than ten years ago their numbers have declined more slowly than union membership as a whole. Average officer–member ratios therefore improved during the 1980s from approximately 1:4500 in 1980 to about 1:3500 in 1991, but this trend has been offset by the continued decentralization of collective bargaining and the consequent proliferation of bargaining units. There were two other striking trends in the 1980s: first the increased spatial dispersal of officers around the country as unions adapted to the decline of national bargaining and its geographical decentralization; and second the increased number and variety of specialist officers, particularly in areas of strong policy commitments such as women's rights and membership recruitment. Both trends underline the capacity of unions to respond to changes in their environment with organizational adaptations.

The officers of the trade union movement have a complex relationship with the bodies that employ them. On the one hand, there are bureaucratic or professional elements in the form of salaried appointments, job security, open recruitment, selection on merit and considerable job autonomy. On the other, there is relatively little training, a weakly developed career structure, and (in some unions) a strong ethos of accountability to lay members and recruitment and selection from a narrow stratum of the union's own activists. These latter elements are consistent with a representative, rather than a bureaucratic, conception of the officer's role, in which emphasis is placed on the officers' proximity to and similarity with the members they represent rather than on the formal expertise that can be deployed on their behalf. These differing conceptions of the officer's role vary across unions, with white-collar unions more likely to be influenced by a bureaucratic and manual unions by a representative conception. But this is only a tendency, albeit a significant one, and in practice most unions will display elements of both. Policies towards officers are therefore likely to reflect tensions between these differing conceptions and can be seen clearly in debates over officer salaries: should officers be paid 'the rate for the job' in line with other professional negotiators (bureaucratic conception), or should they be paid a salary similar to that of the members for whom they work (representative conception)? In the area of recruitment and selection the representative conception is likely to produce a gendered officer workforce that reflects the predominantly male activists, whilst a more bureaucratic selection procedure has facilitated the entry of women into the officer ranks.

Within the union officers were generally subject to rather loose managerial controls and exercised a high degree of job autonomy sufficient in some cases to thwart or impede the implementation of national policies in areas such as recruitment. This combination of loose controls and job autonomy reflects the uncertain and unpredictable character of the local officer's work, the values of both local officers and some of their superiors, and the fact that officers have been selected or appointed, *inter alia*, for their commitment to union goals, thus obviating the need for close supervision.

Much of the variation in officer organization between unions can be accounted for by the structural factors of the size of union membership and the levels of bargaining in the union's main job territories. The numbers of officers employed, the ratio of officers to members, and the degrees of dispersal, specialization, hierarchy and formal controls were all strongly associated with size and bargaining structure. The balance of power between officers and stewards was also strongly influenced by structural factors, with decentralized bargaining and sophisticated workplace organization favouring greater steward influence *vis-à-vis* officers.

## Officers in action

The majority of officers were primarily oriented to organizing and servicing their existing memberships. Any recruitment activity was generally confined to the margins of existing job territories and bargaining units, and was mainly reactive rather than proactive. Officers serviced their members through collective bargaining and individual casework, and the preparation and conduct of negotiations were their most time-consuming activities (office administration followed closely behind). In carrying out their duties most officers worked very closely with shop stewards, and their relations with stewards were often characterized by a high degree of cooperation, a wide measure of consensus on bargaining goals and basic union values and a considerable degree of interdependence. Officers and stewards often worked together in the formulation of bargaining objectives and once bargaining was under way stewards were, for the most part, content to leave the conduct of negotiations in the hands of the officer. This trust largely reflected the great overlap in bargaining priorities, systems of argument and resistance to management views.

Whilst disagreement between officers and stewards was not uncommon (and was certainly more frequent than disagreements amongst stewards or amongst officers) it did not generally correspond to the pattern predicted by bureaucracy theorists of conservative officers attempting to moderate membership aspirations. Whilst some officers in some situations did behave this way, other officers were just as likely to be raising or broadening the aspirations of their members. On bargaining goals, the priorities of officers and stewards largely coincided around the substantive goals of pay and job security, although it is also true that the officers were more sensitive than stewards to employer threats against the union's bargaining rights. This cooperative and consensual relationship was underpinned and reinforced by interdependence. Officers relied on stewards for their close knowledge of the membership's aspirations and of management's intentions. Conversely, stewards relied on officers both to conduct negotiations and to advise them on bargaining tactics and union organization. Most officers were keen to promote strong, independent workplace organization and advised stewards to this effect, emphasizing the importance of maintaining good links with the membership and keeping them informed of agreements. In similar vein officers encouraged a low-trust, adversarial approach to management and the negative tone of their comments about management was striking. This dominant officer–steward relationship was reinforced by several aspects of the work and employment relations we have already documented. Most current union officers are themselves former shop stewards and thus come from similar industrial backgrounds to the stewards with whom they now work. Many officers stressed the importance of accountability to lay representatives and the membership, an attitude that was generally facilitated by the high degree of job autonomy and encouraged (in some cases) by union policy (as in the T&GWU).

Overall, then, most officers stressed the importance of steward independence from and distrust of management, strong workplace organization and the need to protect the union's procedural rights. But on this common substrate of officer values and actions there emerged striking degrees of variation amongst officers on a series of key issues: their willingness to moderate or enhance steward and membership goals, the ambitiousness of their own demands, the degree and nature of their conflicts with stewards, their respect for procedures and for the law, the criteria used to formulate and settle bargaining demands, their willingness to mobilize the membership and threaten industrial action and their sympathy for managerial goals and arguments. On all these questions we found substantial variation amongst officers.

Some of the variation in officer actions can be accounted for by structural factors. Threats of industrial action were more common in workplaces with high density and sophisticated stewards' organization, presumably because industrial action requires the mobilization of power resources and density and organization are conventional (if crude) proxy measures of union power. But otherwise structural factors were largely irrelevant in accounting for variations in officer behaviour. Far more important were the officers' own values, which we conceptualized at two levels of abstraction. First, there were general political orientations assessed in left–right terms. These correlated highly with officer support for (or antipathy to) the 'new agenda' of women's issues, part-timers' rights and recruitment amongst the unorganized.

Second, there were more specific industrial relations orientations, which were defined as clusters of attitudes – to shop stewards, to bargaining goals, to industrial action and to management – which helped to make sense of officers' actions and variations between officers. We isolated three industrial relations orientations which we labelled *managerialist*, *regulationist* and *leader*. Managerialists were the classical officers of bureaucracy theory, modest in their ambitions, willing to try and control shop stewards, hostile to industrial action and with some sympathy for managerial arguments. Leaders, by contrast, were ambitious in their objectives, identified closely with shop stewards, far more willing to threaten industrial action and markedly unsympathetic to managerial arguments. Regulationist officers fell somewhere between these two extreme types, and their actions were characterized by a considerable degree of pragmatism as they sought to maintain the fabric of joint regulation with the employers. Officers' orientations were strongly associated with age and through statistical analysis we were able to show that this was a generational rather than a socialization effect. In other words, officers import into the job a set of orientations acquired through their experiences as lay activists in a given historical period. Once in post, these values undergo relatively little modification, although there is a weak socialization effect as officers are influenced by their new milieu.

### Theoretical implications

There are several general points we can make about theories of officer organization and action before we evaluate each in more detail. First, theories of bureaucracy and polyarchy seriously understate the degree of variation in officer organization and action both between and within unions. The scale of variation is so widespread that we are justified in heavily criticizing, if not rejecting, any theory which cannot account for it. Second there is indirect evidence of historical change in officer–steward relations. Managerialists and more right-wing officers were likely to be older than their leader and left-wing colleagues, and as they gradually retire from the trade union movement this implies (other things being equal) that the officer workforce is becoming somewhat more left-wing and more pro-shop steward in orientation. Theories which either deny the existence of such shifts over time or prove unable to account for them (as is the case with some versions of bureaucracy theory) are inadequate. There are versions of bureaucracy theory which do recognize historical fluctuations in officer–steward relations and attribute them to the level of worker militancy and mobilization (Bramble, 1992; Callinicos, 1982). During periods of heightened mobilization bureaucratic (or what we have called managerialist) tendencies amongst officers will be kept in check by workplace and/or factional organization. But during periods of labour quiescence such as the 1980s managerialist tendencies amongst union officers should have been much more pronounced. The TUC's 'new realism' and the signing of so-called 'no-strike deals' by a wide range of unions could be cited as evidence of a pronounced bureaucratic shift amongst Britain's union officers. Our own research suggests that if anything the opposite is the case and that managerialist values are on the wane as the older, more right-wing officers gradually retire and are replaced by more left-wing successors. However there is an important caveat that needs to be added to our argument and that concerns vertical differentiation amongst the officer workforce. Our research focused primarily on the *local* full-time officers who are in day-to-day contact with shop stewards and branch officers, but said little about the national officers who are somewhat more distant from collective bargaining. There is some evidence from our research that the priorities of these two groups may differ and that analyses which apply to one group may not hold for the other. In chapter 5 we showed that many local officers had been encouraged by their superiors to pursue recruitment and equal opportunities more frequently than any other issues. Yet their own bargaining priorities – pay and job security – largely coincided with the demands of their members. In line with these findings many officers believed that their accountability to lay committees was more important than accountability to their superiors. This evidence points to a distinct differentiation within the union hierarchy as local officers struggle to balance competing demands from above and below, and end up leaning below, towards the stewards and members.

We can now return to the competing arguments about bureaucratic (or managerialist) tendencies amongst union officers in the 1980s and early 1990s and suggest the following resolution, drawing partly on Crouch (1982: 178). National and local officers may be subject to somewhat different pressures because the former are more involved in national union organization and policy-making, whilst the latter are more involved in collective bargaining with shop stewards. Declining political influence is felt much more acutely by national officers, who therefore have more incentive to adjust union policies in order to restore their influence as well as their finances, and hence the top-down promotion of 'new realism' in its various forms. Local officers, on the other hand, remain subject to pressures very similar to those felt by shop stewards and, where union organization and collective bargaining have been preserved, have less sense of a crisis of trade unionism that requires strategic re-thinking. Hence throughout the 1980s it is quite plausible to argue that whilst some national officers became more managerialist in their outlook (in the sense we have used the term so far), local officers, as a body, may have shifted in the opposite direction as right-wing local officers were gradually replaced.

Let us now look at each of the theories in turn, starting with the theory of union *bureaucracy*. It is undoubtedly true that the employment and work relations of union officers contain bureaucratic elements, notably specialization of function, hierarchy, and control systems. Second, there is a section of the officer workforce, the managerialists, whose actions do conform to the predictions of bureaucracy theory. Third, most full-time officers *do* seek autonomy for themselves (or value their existing autonomy), and finally they do exercise considerable influence over the bargaining process and over the outcomes of negotiation.

But the key problems with the theory in the light of our research are that it over-generalizes from limited evidence and exaggerates the uniformities in officer organization and activity at the expense of variation. Many of the bureaucratic elements of officer organization are only weakly present in the actual organizational practices of unions. For instance, the content of the officer's job is very diffuse and union control systems fairly rudimentary. Moreover, there is an important countervailing force in the form of a representative conception of the officer's role. Officer activity is rarely motivated by notions of personal aggrandizement or material self-interest, but is heavily influenced by ideological conceptions of the aims and values of trade unionism and collective bargaining. Part of this general outlook, shared by many officers, is the ethos of accountability to the membership. It was clear from our observation work that this was not mere rhetoric or self-serving ideology, but was an important officer value that actually influenced officers' day-to-day actions. The diffuse content of the officer's role, coupled with the weakness of organizational controls, means that officers enjoy a high degree of discretion in the performance of their job and under these conditions their own values will shape their behaviour. Officers do exercise power inside the union but with the possible exception of managerialist officers, this power is generally exercised on the members' behalf and often at their behest. The failing of bureaucracy theory is to confuse the contingent activities of an historically specific (and conservative) section of union officers with the inevitable actions of all union officers everywhere (unless kept in check by worker militancy). There *are* conservative officers but there are also pragmatic officers and leader officers whose politics are very different and whose numbers are almost certainly in the ascendancy within the lower reaches of the trade union movement. On officer organization the theory of bureaucracy is guilty of treating too seriously and uncritically the formal properties of union organization. Unions may well *look* like bureaucracies and have the trappings of bureaucracy, but closer examination reveals a very different picture comprising weak and uneven bureaucratic development alongside representative conceptions of the officer's role that stress the importance of value-driven behaviour and accountability to the membership.

*Polyarchy* theory therefore appears somewhat more realistic in its appreciation of multiple cleavages within trade unions, such as the three-fold division between national leaders, local activists and membership (Banks, 1974: 92, Crouch, 1982: 176–9) although in principle there could be numerous lines of division inside unions as James (1984: 5–9) has argued. Our own research has certainly pointed to divisions between local and national officers, between male and female officers, and to divisions associated with generation and ideology. Many of our findings could therefore be accommodated within polyarchy theory, but whether they can be accounted for, or explained, by the theory is a question that highlights the central difficulty. There is no agreement amongst writers in this tradition about the motives of the different actors inside the union. Crouch's distinction between the procedural orientation of officers and the substantive orientation of the members is a clear-cut (and conventional) distinction, but it does not fit our data. Whilst it is true that officers were highly sensitive to procedural rights, such as changes in bargaining arrangements, they were equally, if not more, concerned with the creation and improvement of independent workplace organization. The conventional distinction between procedural issues, which depend on employer recognition, and the substantive goals of the membership is used to generate the notion of a dilemma for the officer. Preservation of procedural rights requires good relations with the employer who may press for substantive concessions on wages and/or jobs as a *quid pro quo*. On the other hand, firm pursuit of the members' substantive interests may threaten employer profitability and prerogatives and lead to the withdrawal or curtailment of procedural rights. Hence the officer is sometimes portrayed as an intermediary figure who has to balance these competing demands. What this account leaves out is the critical activity of officers in promoting and strengthening workplace organization so that union members are better able to act for themselves and make their own decisions about goal priorities. To the degree that officers succeed in promoting sophisticated workplace organization they will shift some of the dilemmas of bargaining onto the stewards and their members.

Another motivational base for polyarchy theory is James' (1984) notion that activists compete for control over decision-making inside the union, but this concept is equally unsatisfactory. Conflicts over decision-making certainly did take place: several officers welcomed the decline of national bargaining in their industry because it would provide them with greater involvement in the increased volume of local bargaining. Likewise many local officers placed a high value on the autonomy they exercised in their job and were reluctant to be controlled more closely by their superiors. But it would be wrong to infer that competition amongst activists was therefore a pervasive and central feature of their relations. On the contrary, we have already documented the extensive cooperation between officers and stewards in the bargaining process and in other areas of union activity, such as campaigning. Moreover the clear majority of officers were keen to offload bargaining responsibilities to shop stewards rather than retain control for themselves.

Banks' (1974: 94) contention that activists dispute the purposes of trade unionism is true, as seen in the divisions between managerialist, regulationist and leader officers. But where Banks' ideas remained vague and ill-defined we have tried to formulate the bases of division more precisely and to map some of their correlates, such as generation, age and gender. To conclude, then, polyarchy theory is right to stress the possibility of multiple cleavages inside unions and take us beyond the over-simplistic bureaucracy vs. rank and file division. But its weakness lies in the specification of the roots of division, as the various formulations on offer are either inadequate, narrow or vague.

*Structural contingency theory* has been influential in studies of union organization, in particular those by Boraston *et al.* (1975) and Clegg (1976). But our research suggests that while the theory does indeed offer valuable insights, too much has been claimed for it. In the early chapters of this book we showed that a number of structural properties of officer organization were strongly associated with structural variables such as union size, collective bargaining structure in the union's job territories and the sophistication of workplace organization amongst the union's members. The theory also performed reasonably well in accounting for patterns of behaviour closely tied to structural variables. For instance, threats of industrial action and patterns of officer control inside unions, both of which entail the acquisition and mobilization of power resources, were both associated with the structural factors mentioned above: size, bargaining level and sophistication of workplace organization. But once we move away from patterns of organization and towards officer actions then the utility of structural explanations rapidly diminishes. In other words, as we shifted our attention to areas of activity in which officers exercised considerable discretion then their own values played an increasingly important role in accounting for their actions. So, to recapitulate, we found that officers differed significantly in the ambitiousness of their demands, their willingness to moderate steward demands, the degree of conflict they experienced with stewards, the criteria they used in formulating demands, their willingness to mobilize union members for industrial action, their sympathy for managerial arguments, their respect for constitutional and legal arguments, and their judgement of what was achievable in negotiations. Officer actions in all these areas were expressions of distinct sets of values, or orientations, themselves related to generation.

Having suggested that structural variables (such as union size) are better at explaining other structural variables (such as hierarchy or specialization), and officer values are more important where officers exercise discretion, we now need to qualify this argument in two ways. First, structural factors are not independent of officer values. The degree to which power is centralized inside trade unions or devolved to shop stewards and branches is in part a reflection of the values of key national officers. In support of this claim we can cite the fact that turnover of national officers can result in major changes in union policy and organization, as in the T&GWU from 1968 or the EETPU from the early 1960s. Secondly, officer values have to be applied in particular settings where officers may be subject to particular constraints. Consequently they may, and do, sometimes act in ways that are discrepant from their own values. Nonetheless this observation only reinforces the point made earlier that the impact of officer values on their behaviour is most likely to be observed in situations where officers exercise considerable discretion. Neither bureaucracy, polyarchy or structural contingency theory were particularly useful in accounting for union officer actions under these circumstances, whereas our emphasis on officers' values was far more illuminating.

We now turn to consider some of the implications of our findings and arguments, beginning with union politics.

### Union politics and generational change

One of the advantages of our emphasis on officer values is that we are able to offer some insights into the mechanisms of political change inside trade unions. Bureaucracy theory portrays the dynamics of trade unionism in one of two unsatisfactory ways: first, they are the expression of an historically invariant logic of struggle between a 'bureaucracy' and a 'rank and file' whose interests and aspirations are known in advance. Although the composition of these social categories changes over time their interests and inter-relations are historical constants. Alternatively, the actions of 'the bureaucracy' are seen to be determined primarily by their own structural interests but secondarily by the degree of worker mobilization. This generates countervailing pressures on the bureaucracy to take some account of workers' interests as distinct from those of other social groups. Our own research suggests that the 'politics of the union bureaucracy' are differentiated in at least two important respects: there is vertical differentiation at any point in time between national and local officers in part because of their differing proximity and accountability to shop stewards and to other significant pressure groups. Second there is differentiation over time as the politics of 'the bureaucracy' as a whole shift because of changes in the composition of the officer workforce. In particular, we have noted that the stereotypical, managerialist officers are significantly older than their more left-wing, regulationist or leader counterparts, a difference indicative of the steady replacement of one generation of officers by another.

Turnover of key national officers is a theme discussed by the most far-reaching study of change in trade unions, the book of that title by Undy and his colleagues (1981). *Change in Trade Unions* combines a wealth of information on the most important changes in the major British unions between 1960 and 1980. Union government, collective bargaining, job territories, growth, mergers and internal power were all discussed and extensively documented. As a source book of data, *Change in Trade Unions* is excellent, but as a source of theory it is very much weaker. The authors presented a 'model' in which change emerged from the actions of change agents acting through or around existing national leaderships and union decision-making structures (Undy *et al.*, 1981: 28). The term 'change agents', however, was used very loosely to refer to internal or external agents, where the latter included 'developments in the labour market, technology, government economic and industrial relations policies, employer organizations and other unions, including the TUC' (1981: 29). Moreover Undy *et al.* did not intend their model to be used as an abstract analytical device, but rather 'as a device for structuring the discussion of the processes of change' (1981: 27). Although data was presented and discussed under the headings contained in the model these were more akin to chapter sub-headings than to theoretical constructs.

Having said this, Undy *et al.* are clearly right to argue that unions are influenced by external forces, but in the light of our emphasis on officer values there are two aspects of this influence that we would highlight. First, unions are large employing and membership organizations that are subject to many of the same pressures and influences as other organizations in society. The impact of the women's movement and of feminist ideas about gender equality, discrimination, childcare and ways of organizing has been felt inside the trade union movement as much as anywhere else. The women's officers of large private corporations have their counterparts in the trade union movement; debates about quotas of women (and ethnic minorities) on selection panels, shortlists and decision-making committees can be found in local authorities and political parties as well as in trade unions. A second and perhaps less tangible example is the decline in deference to authority. In the 1960s and 1970s this expressed itself in a variety of forms such as the movement for industrial democracy, the growth of single-issue social and political campaigns, the emergence of 'anti-statist' welfare claimants' groups and the alleged breakdown of order and discipline in schools and colleges. Underpinning these diverse patterns of behaviour and organization was an increased willingness to question authority and an insistence by individuals and groups on organizing and acting for themselves. Again this movement had its reflection inside the trade unions, with the postwar period witnessing a devolution of power to shop stewards at the workplace, and more recently the emergence of special interest sections inside unions, such as gays and lesbians, ethnic minorities and women.

One of the ways in which changing social values impact on trade unions is through changes in the composition of the officer workforce, itself a product of wider political changes. Schematically therefore we can suggest the following account of the recent evolution of the officer workforce. The trade union movement of the immediate postwar period was dominated by figures such as Arthur Deakin of the T&GWU, Tom Williamson (GMWU) and Will Lawther (NUM) (Hyman, 1983: 58–9). Writing of a slightly later period (though his comments apply equally to the 1950s), Lane observed that:

Most of the national leaders of the sixties had their formative years in the 1920s and 30s – a period in which shop stewards ... were ... often associated with rank and file communist organisations ... few leaders would have had a great deal of personal experience of shop stewards in factories ... [and] stewards would tend to be looked upon as actual or potential disrupters of the union organisation (Lane, 1974: 216–17).

Not only were their attitudes formed in a certain political climate, there was also an important economic dimension. Brown (1986: 164–5) argued that workers' current expectations are shaped by material circumstances at the time they entered the labour market, so that the union leaders of the immediate postwar period would have acquired modest ambitions because of their harsh socialization in the long inter-war Depression. By contrast the postwar generations had less and less memory of these years, and had known only full employment and rising living standards. Hence the scene was set for inter-generational conflict within unions, sometimes taking the form of factional struggles (as in the AEU and NUM, for instance). Brown's ideas were picked up by Cronin (1979: 64–6), who used them to argue that generational change within unions was an important link between changing economic circumstances and changes in union behaviour such as strike activity.

By the time of Clegg et al.'s (1961) study shop stewards were beginning to enter the ranks of the full-time officer workforce with 35 per cent of their sample having a background as stewards. The rise of the shop steward movement, the 'challenge from below' as Flanders (1970) called it, coincided with the gradual exhaustion of the postwar economic boom and the upsurge of industrial militancy in the 1968–74 strike wave. This strike wave had implications for governments and employers, both expressing and reinforcing a shift in the postwar balance of power between workers and employers. But it also set in train a gradual shift in the composition of the union officer workforce. Through the 1970s and 1980s many of the activists from that period became full-time union officers, carrying with them the values they had acquired, and given expression to, during the days when union power was in the ascendancy. Their entry into full-time union work was made possible by key changes in national leadership as the right-wing old guard (Deakin, Williamson,

Carron and others) was replaced by officers far more sympathetic to shop steward organization and union militancy. Jones in the T&GWU (from 1968) and Scanlon in the AUEW (from 1967) are the examples normally cited, but more militant leaders were emerging in other large unions, too, such as UCATT, NUPE and ASTMS. Under these leaders and their successors a record of shop steward activity was looked upon far more favourably than in the past, so that by the time of our officers' surveys in 1987 approximately 90 per cent of male and female officers then in post had previously served as shop stewards (Heery and Kelly, 1989: 196). This new generation of officers has therefore come into post in the 1980s with sets of values acquired in the 1970s and late 1960s. Hence the character-istic pattern of strong support for workplace organization, a belief in steward independence, encouragement for ambitious bargaining goals, a willingness to sanction industrial action and a deep mistrust of manage-ment. In short, such officers have sought to reproduce in the 1980s the strong workplace organization and low-trust adversarial industrial rela-tions that were so prominent in the 1970s.

If this account is correct (or at least contains a strong element of truth), then it has an interesting and important implication for trade unionism in the 1990s. Insofar as local full-time officers (particularly regulationists and leaders) successfully transmit their own industrial relations values to the shop stewards in their bargaining units, then they act as a potentially criti-cal obstacle to the success of employer communications designed to engen-der cooperation and high trust. Since our evidence suggests that officers and stewards have many attitudes in common, then officers are likely to be perceived by stewards as credible and trustworthy sources whose state-ments about industrial relations will therefore reinforce existing steward values. We should consequently not be surprised at the persistence of 'them and us' attitudes in industrial relations (Kelly and Kelly, 1991).

There are, however, a number of countervailing forces that make it difficult to produce any straightforward predictions about the future. First, as we have already said, unions are organizationally differentiated between national and local officers, with the former more heavily involved in union policy-making than in collective bargaining. As national officers they are more likely to identify with the union as a whole (rather than with particular bargaining units) and therefore to be more concerned than local officers about declining membership, poor finances and loss of national influence, and some of the evidence we presented in chapter 5 is consistent with this account. Some national union leader-ships, in the GMB, AEU and EETPU, for instance (the two latter now merged as the AEEU), have responded to these national problems by trying to 'soften' their union's militant image, downplaying their support for strikes and, in some cases, entering into 'new style recognition agreements' with employers. These agreements have included, *inter alia*, so-called 'no-strike' clauses, as well as various flexibility measures to improve productivity, in line with the 'new realist' thinking of the TUC and other unions from 1984 onwards. These and other policy initiatives from national union leaders may well negate or erode the rather different, and more traditional, messages being purveyed by local officers.

Second, local officers themselves undergo a degree of socialization inside unions as they come under the influence of fellow officers, both at their own and at national level. Our evidence suggests, however, that the scale of organizational socialization is somewhat limited. In part this is because the process of officer selection will filter out those who hold values highly discrepant with those of the current national leadership, and in part because the pattern of work and employment relations inside trade unions inhibits the close supervision that could otherwise provide a channel for top-down influence.

Third, local officers are subject to some of the same pressures exerted on shop stewards from the external environment, and in particular the general political climate, the legal restrictions placed on union activity throughout the 1980s and early 1990s and the adverse economic circumstances in both the private and public sectors. Highly militant leader officers will be forced to take some account of these external pressures even if their basic values undergo little change. But these sorts of pressures can be easily exaggerated, and it is worth reiterating that much of our data on officer values was collected in the mid- and late 1980s after the longest recession since the 1930s and the longest period of Conservative rule since the 1950s. That data threw up little evidence of the impact of such pressures on officer values. Finally the composition of the officer workforce will continue to change as current post-holders retire or resign, though the pace of change will be slower than in previous years because of the overall decline in the number of officer posts. With average appointment ages in the 30s the big unions will be starting now to select officers whose entire experience of the labour market will be confined to the post-1979 period. Will such officers display the values transmitted to them by an earlier generation of militant officers? Or will they reflect the adverse economic and political circumstances of the 1980s and display a lower propensity to militancy and a greater willingness to cooperate with employers as compared with that older generation? Sectoral differences may be critical here, since it is mainly private sector employers who have sought union cooperation in productivity and flexibility agreements, and where the frequency of strike action has declined sharply. In the public sector, on the other hand, employer militancy under financial constraints has helped maintain a relatively high level of strike activity, which may find its reflection in the attitudes and values of stewards and new full-time officers.

It is difficult to assess the balance between these competing pressures, towards a traditional, low-trust, adversarial model of industrial relations and towards a more cooperative (or compliant) model. What we can say is that many of the officers now in post constitute an important (and neglected) bulwark of traditional, adversarial industrial relations.

One factor that will influence the balance between competing value systems is the structure of unions as organizations and their mode of operation, so it is to this area that we now turn.

## Unions as organizations

Union dynamics are often described and analyzed in terms of a tension or contradiction between democracy and bureaucracy, and within the ambit of bureaucracy theory these twin poles are often equated with the interests of the membership and the leadership respectively. Fairbrother and Waddington (1990) portray union dynamics in exactly these terms, and are highly critical of centralized, bureaucratically effective forms of trade unionism because they believe 'union renewal' is likely to come about from collective, participative activity at the workplace. Such activity is in 'tension' with centralized, bureaucratic activity, but paradoxically is also its bedrock since unions must continue to rely on lay activists to conduct local negotiations and administer branch activity.

There clearly are tensions between different levels of union activity, and in chapter 6, for example, we discussed at length the problems faced by the large general unions in attempting to mobilize their officer workforces and shop stewards for major recruitment drives in unorganized establishments. Whilst national officers were, and are, anxious to arrest membership decline, local officers remain for the most part primarily oriented to servicing the unions' existing membership through collective bargaining and individual casework. The ineffectiveness of some of the well publicized union and TUC recruitment campaigns underlines the degree to which unions are *not* centralized bureaucracies whose leaders exert control over their own human resources. But whilst Fairbrother and Waddington (1990) are right to portray the tension between national and local initiatives as critical in union dynamics they are on shakier ground in implying that union renewal will come through the triumph of workplace activity at the expense of the bureaucratic mode of operation. In criticizing 'bureaucratic' unionism they rightly point to the danger of building trade unionism on the basis of 'individually based recruitment strategies, membership services and surveys' (1990: 42), which is that members recruited in these ways will have only a weak sense of collectivist values and fail to appreciate the need for collective organization and action. Conversely, they are right to stress that public sector unions faced with a rapid decentralization of bargaining units and a proliferation of bargaining activity must quickly develop strong workplace organization to function alongside national campaigns.

But workplace trade unionism has its weaknesses and 'bureaucratic' trade unionism has certain strengths which Fairbrother and Waddington downplay or ignore. Many writers, from Flanders (1970) onwards, argued that the postwar devolution of power inside unions to workplace organizations was both inevitable and, on the whole, desirable. One indirect piece of evidence on the effectiveness for union members of workplace organization was the strong desire of several governments and many employers to curb it (see, for instance, Strinati, 1982), whilst more direct evidence can be found in Batstone *et al.* (1977, 1978) and in Terry and Edwards (1988). But the effectiveness of workplace organization was dependent on a series of conditions that were progressively eroded throughout the 1970s: full employment, corporate profitability, government support for trade unionism and a permissive legal climate. In the different conditions of the 1980s workplace bargaining began to display weaknesses hitherto shrouded from view (see Terry, 1989, for a full discussion). The multiform threats to trade unionism during the past decade arguably required a coordinated response since no individual union possessed the resources to meet them (as the miners discovered in 1984–85). Such coordination entails a degree of centralization of power within individual unions (and within the TUC) if resources are to be conserved, mobilized and targeted on priority issues such as membership recruitment or campaigns over women's rights. Yet the very decentralization set in train during earlier decades and which equipped the movement so well at that time only served to inhibit the centralization required in the very different conditions of the 1980s and 1990s. The process of decentralization locked local full-time officers into the close relations with shop stewards that we have documented throughout this book and which have arguably contributed to the resilience of trade unionism in organized establishments. But the other side of the coin is that national leaders have experienced considerable difficulty in shifting the priorities of local officers and stewards away from the existing membership and outwards towards unorganized workers in unorganized establishments. In this respect one of the problems for unions has been too little centralization of power, not too much (*pace* Fairbrother and Waddington, 1990). We also showed, in chapter 4, that the entry of more women into the ranks of union officers has been facilitated by centralized control over selection procedures as against more representative systems of officer selection which have tended to reproduce a male-dominated officer workforce.

On the other hand, we should not under-estimate the difficulties of implementing change, even in highly centralized organizations. Ahlstrand (1990) has graphically documented the 25 year history of productivity programmes at Esso's Fawley refinery, in the wake of its pioneering agreement made famous by Flanders (1964). One of Ahlstrand's conclusions was that despite all the internal and external resources available to the management of this multi-national firm, the substantive results were disappointing and by 1985 the firm was 'still locked into roughly the same kind of "low-pay/low effort" strategy that Allen had identified in 1958' (Ahlstrand, 1990: 231). Ahlstrand's case study carefully documented many of the problems that continually beset Fawley's management and prevented them transforming the 'organizational culture' in the way that Flanders (1964) had anticipated and hoped for. As Guest (1991: 170) has argued, enduring change in organizational culture is much more likely to come about through changes in the composition of its personnel, a process that often takes time, but which can be speeded up given centralized control of selection procedures in the hands of key national officers. Precisely this strategy was used by Jack Jones when he assumed the General Secretaryship of the T&GWU in 1968 and wished to accelerate the ongoing devolution of power to shop stewards. One leading national official was forced to resign and Jones' deputy general secretary attended all interviewing panels for the union's full-time officers in order to influence the outcomes (Maksymiw et al., 1990: 334; Undy et al., 1981: 94–5, 270). Likewise after John Edmonds assumed the General Secretaryship of the GMB in 1985 he encouraged a number of existing officers to take early retirement in order to create the opportunity to appoint replacements more sympathetic to his own views about the importance of membership recruitment and women's rights.

These observations take us directly to a second theme that flows from our findings, which is the changing conceptions within the trade union movement of the 'officer' and the 'membership'. According to Undy and his colleagues it was common practice in the 1950s particularly in the two big general unions (GMWU, T&GWU) for collective bargaining to be conducted by officers and settlements reached without the presence or agreement of shop stewards and members. The officer acted paternalistically on behalf of the members, both determining and satisfying their interests. Throughout the 1960s this conception increasingly gave way to the notion of the officer as a partner who worked alongside shop stewards and, where necessary, encouraged workplace organization. Hence the largely cooperative relationship between local officers and stewards reported in this book, as well as in the earlier study by Boraston *et al.* (1975). More recently, however, as we noted in chapters 4 and 5, unions have made increasing use of questionnaire surveys in order to establish the objectives and interests of their membership and have devoted increasing resources to officer training. This twin set of practices is arguably related to, and indicative of, a conception of the membership as consumers and the full-time officer as an expert provider of services. The fear amongst some commentators is that this conception will encourage a view of the membership as passive recipients of union services and will discourage the idea that they can and should be mobilized for collective action (cf. Fairbrother and Waddington, 1990: 42; Hyman, 1989a: 230–2).

Three factors are likely to militate against such a development and prevent the collectivist ethos of unions withering away with the spread of individual services. First, shop steward organization is now widespread in unionized settings and where there are 'leader' stewards in place (Batstone *et al.*, 1977) then collectivist values will be diffused throughout the union's membership. Second, as we have shown earlier, many of the full-time officers now in post are committed to the creation of independent workplace organization with strong ties to the membership. Last, and by no means least, pressure from employers on jobs, wages, payment systems, working practices and the terms and conditions of employment is likely to reinforce the perception amongst employees that strong unions are necessary to protect their interests. Whilst this perception will not necessarily translate into the belief that collective action is necessary, we would argue that it does entail the basic idea of collective organization, namely that it is necessary for employees to 'stick together' for mutual protection. It is also worth noting that the tension between individualist and collectivist values can be over-stated and the threat posed by the former to the latter can be exaggerated. Unions have always supplied workers with both collective and individual goods and services. Even in the best organized workplaces stewards and officers will spend a considerable amount of time helping individuals with grievances or preparing individual claims to medical or other tribunals. Union journals regularly boast of the millions of pounds recovered in compensation for sick or injured members through the casework of officers and stewards. The coexistence of individual casework and collective organization and action in unionized settings should caution against the simple-minded idea that more 'individualism' necessarily entails less 'collectivism'.

In this book we have tried to assess systematically the strengths and weaknesses of a number of existing theories of union organization and activity. Whilst structural explanations of union organization have much to commend them it is officers' values that are central to the explanation of their day-to-day activity. Our focus on values allowed us to explore differences amongst the officer workforce and to suggest the importance of generational change in the analysis of union dynamics.

# Appendix
## Research methods

The research fell into three parts. First, there were pilot interviews with 41 full-time officers carried out between August and December 1985. Second, there was observation work, conducted between January 1986 and January 1987, and finally there was questionnaire distribution, covering the period January 1986–October 1987 with a follow-up in Summer 1991. The pilot interviews were unstructured as their principal purpose was to familiarize us with the work of the full-time officers. The interviews proved to be particularly illuminating and the local officers in the unions we contacted were extremely helpful. We therefore used the interviews as an occasion to negotiate access for the observation stage of our research. We did speak to some shop stewards, but only on an informal and *ad hoc* basis, because it soon became clear that selecting a representative sample of stewards who worked with our target officials would be an enormous and complicated undertaking. Our target officials serviced an average of 66 separate bargaining units, containing anywhere from one to 50 shop stewards. Although a separate study of shop steward perceptions of union officials would have been desirable, we decided to rest content with our observation of officer–steward interactions in the meetings we attended.

Our observation work focused on 27 officers (the original plan was '25–30') from four unions (rather than '2–3'). Access to the T&GWU and AEU gave us a contrast between appointed and elected officials, but we could not obtain access to the two big public sector unions, NALGO and NUPE. We therefore obtained cooperation from the GMB, partly to give us another general union whose reputation and image contrasted with that of the TGWU and whose officer–steward relations might therefore be expected to differ. But the GMB also gave us access to public sector unionism, in the utilities, local government and NHS. Finally we obtained access to ASTMS so that we could study a white-collar union with a highly qualified group of officers.

Our choice of officers for observation was initially shaped by the numbers willing to volunteer. Within that group we tried to maximize variation on the criteria of age, gender (hardly possible given that most officers are male), industries covered, seniority, and a loose assessment of their own political ideology from pilot interviews. This sample design allowed us to assess the effects of such differences, and to compare and contrast them with the uniformities in the officer role often pointed out by theorists of trade unions. In particular, it allowed us to test the utility of a 'social action' approach to the study of officer behaviour, which emphasizes the values and orientations they bring to their work.

We decided for each officer to take one or two issues, preferably one wage and one non-wage issue, and follow the issue through from the earliest possible stage of decision-making to completion. This allowed us to observe officer-steward interactions in a range of different meetings (policy formation, bargaining, adjournments, report back to members) across different phases of the bargaining process. However we obtained unequal numbers of observations from our officers, making inter-individual comparisons (though not inter-union comparisons) rather difficult. We also experienced difficulty in getting commitments from AUEW officers and ended up with very few observations in that union, which seriously restricts what we can say about the differences between elected and appointed officers.

The observation work presented a considerable challenge since we had to devise a recording schedule that would be detailed enough to capture all the information of interest, but not so detailed as to be unwieldy and too time-consuming to complete. After considerable experimentation, we devised a general meeting schedule and an issue schedule, both of which were completed from our field notes after each meeting was over. In the meeting schedule we recorded: the participants and their status; the occupations and experience of lay representatives; history and details of shop steward organization; company organization (size, sector, ownership); venue, date, duration and type of meeting; indices of formality; FTO comments on lay reps (positive/negative), and vice-versa; FTO instructions/advice to reps and other attempts at influence; FTO references to the wider union and to management (positive/negative); FTO conduct towards management; lay requests for FTO advice.

An issue schedule was completed for each separate issue at the meeting (an average of 2–3 per meeting) and recorded the following: nature, level and initiator of issue; initial goals of all parties present; final outcome; relative importance of issue to officer and stewards; relative influence over initiation, tactics and outcome of officer and stewards; dissent within the union side and its basis; arguments advanced by FTO, lay reps, members, and management respectively; degree of acceptance/rejection of management case by officers, stewards and members.

The aim of these schedules was to permit the recording of systematic data relevant to our theoretical concerns. Hence we were concerned with the goals of officers and stewards, with the way these shifted over one or a series of meetings and with the nature and direction of influence exercised by the officers. We also attempted to record the bases on which officers successfully exercised authority by noting the arguments advanced in support of positions and the stewards' responses. By recording the arguments of all those present at a series of meetings we were also able to make statements about the ideologies of officers, and to buttress this data with other information such as officer references to management and advice to stewards.

One further point about the research concerns the range of meetings we observed. Originally we had intended to observe bargaining and non-bargaining sessions, processing both individual and collective issues. Through pilot work we found that individual casework was not particularly pertinent to our research questions and all such meetings were therefore dropped. As most of the officer's remaining workload revolved around collective bargaining then this inevitably showed up in the types of meeting we observed.

At the end of our twelve month observation period, we had attended and recorded 156 meetings. We had a good spread of 274 issues, both wage and non-wage; of workplace sizes, industries, and occupational groups. Our sample included many types of manager, both line and personnel, and stewards with a wide range of experience. The weaknesses in the sample were too few multi-union bargaining units, too few foreign-owned establishments, and too few meetings with AUEW officers. Nevertheless, we collected a very large quantity of extremely rich data.

Once the observation work was completed we developed a very detailed coding frame so that, to take one example, the FTO comments on management could be coded under any one of 28 separate headings. The reliability of the recording schedules and the coding frame were checked by having the two researchers jointly attend six meetings in the early stages of research and independently complete recording schedules. Likewise, both researchers independently coded schedules from these meetings later in the research, and after ironing out some minor differences, we found a high level of agreement on both the recording schedules and the coding frame. Almost all meetings thereafter were attended by only one of the researchers, and we were able to ensure that half the officers in our sample of 27 were observed at some time by both researchers as a further reliability check.

The third part of our research consisted of three questionnaire surveys. The first was a postal questionnaire which was mailed in 1987 to a population of 273 full-time union officers in our four core unions, plus three other unions (NALGO, NUPE, EETPU). We decided to distribute most of them in the South and South East of England where we had conducted our observations, because we thought it unlikely we could collect enough data to carry out regional comparisons. In addition, the questionnaire allowed us to ask many of the same questions we had pursued through observation, in order to test the method-sensitivity of our observation data, and to give us more confidence in findings that held up across different methods. We obtained 101 usable responses, making a response rate of 37 per cent.

The second survey was a postal questionnaire-cum-telephone interview of the Head Offices of all the TUC unions with membership above 3000, in order to collect basic data on numbers of officers and members, officer remuneration, specialization, selection and training. We distributed 69 questionnaires in 1986 and obtained 63 usable replies, yielding a very high response rate of 91 per cent. This survey was repeated in the Summer of 1991, but with the addition of a small number of the more substantial non-TUC unions (including the EETPU). We posted out 67 question-naires and obtained 55 usable replies, a response rate of 82 per cent. The final survey was a postal questionnaire to all known women union officers in Britain (a total of 170 in November 1986), which produced 87 replies (a 60 per cent response rate), and is the only study of its kind in this field. Copies of all the schedules and questionnaires are available from the authors on request.

# Notes

### 3 FULL-TIME OFFICER ORGANIZATION

1 It must be emphasized that this estimate is confined to officers with a substantial collective bargaining function and does not include specialists, such as research officers. It also excludes employees of the TUC and other union confederations.
2 In this and a number of other tables Maksymiw *et al.*'s *The British Trade Union Directory* (1990) has been used to fill gaps in the 1991 Union Head Office Survey.
3 This figure includes a small proportion of officers who have local responsibilities but work from central union headquarters.
4 This was computed by dividing the total number of officers in the most junior grade by the total number of officers in more senior grades.

### 4 EMPLOYMENT RELATIONS

1 Practice within the GMB deserves special comment, for although the union practises open recruitment, appointed officers are required to submit to a confirmatory election in which they may be subject to challenge from existing members. In the analysis which follows the GMB has been grouped with unions which appoint from beyond their own membership, because this aspect of the union's selection procedure appears dominant.
2 Trade unions are excluded from the provisions of the Employment Act 1990, intended to outlaw the pre-entry closed shop, which make it unlawful to refuse employment on the grounds of union membership or non-membership. It should also be noted that this discussion does not refer to General Secretaries or other national officers with seats on trade union executives. As a result of the Trade Union Act 1984 and the Employment Act 1988, such officers are required to be elected and re-elected once every five years through a secret ballot of the membership. At this level of organization, therefore, the differences in procedure between unions have diminished as a result of legislation and are much less marked than those which are found at lower levels (Steele, 1990: 66–8).
3 62 unions, employing a total of 2564 officers, provided a gender breakdown.
4 The openness of union selection procedures was directly associated with officers' political affiliations ($\chi^2 = 12.7$, $p < 0.05$), but not with membership of a political group, like CND.
5 Although very few officers receive direct incentive payments, it could be argued that an indirect incentive exists for a larger proportion because, in unions

representing discrete bodies of members, it is common to base the officer pay structure on that of members. In EIS, for example, officers are paid on teachers' pay scales plus 10 per cent. The 1986 Head Office Survey found this kind of link in 40 per cent of, mainly public sector, unions.

6 This second group of unions is also distinguished by its preparedness to accept independent trade union representation for its officers. The 1986 Head Office Survey found this in 41 per cent of unions, 91 per cent of which primarily represented white-collar workers. In these unions the position of the officer as a salaried expert provides the basis for pluralist employee relations within unions. In unions with a representative conception of the officer's role, by contrast, employment relations are structured on unitarist lines and union membership is viewed as inappropriate for employees expected to display a high degree of loyalty to their organizations.

## 5 WORK RELATIONS

1 Unlike other regions of the T&GWU, Region 1, where we carried out our research, does not have a District Committee Structure.

2 It was particularly noticeable that officers in the EETPU stressed opposition from other unions as an obstacle to policy. Although at the start of our research the EETPU had not been suspended from the TUC, its aggressive hunt for recognition agreements and its stridently competitive ideology had led to a deterioration in its relations with other unions (cf. Bassett, 1986: 80–3).

## 6 ORGANIZING

1 Although the vast majority of officers believed stewards should handle their own collective bargaining, there was some variation. A tendency to agree strongly with the statement, for example, was associated with a relatively high number of convenors in the officer's allocation ($r = 0.24$, $p < 0.05$), suggesting that officer endorsement of steward independence depends to a degree on the sophistication of steward organization and capacity to bargain effectively. There were also associations with a number of officer characteristics, with older ($r = 0.31$, $p < 0.01$) and less educated officers ($r = 0.21$, $p < 0.05$) and those with steward ($r = 0.26$, $p < 0.05$) and senior steward ($r = 0.20$, $p < 0.05$) experience being more enthusiastic about steward independence. This suggests that officers' socialization, and the route through which union work is entered, can influence attempts to shape workplace organization. Steward independence thus appeared to be particularly valued by those who had served a lay apprenticeship and acquired their skills in the 1960s and 1970s, the decades of shop steward growth.

## 7 BARGAINING OBJECTIVES

1 r is Pearson's product-moment correlation. Significance tests are two-tailed unless stated otherwise. p values greater than 0.05 are considered non-significant.

2 The total number of issues observed was N = 274. Because of missing values the Ns will vary from table to table.
3 The N for this table is 107 compared with an N of 96 for table 5.1 and the discrepancy is due to the use of different measures of officer influence. Table 5.1 is based on an assessment of officer influence *relative* to stewards, whilst table 7.7 is based on a measure of *who* initiated an issue on the bargaining agenda.
4 These relationships all remained significant in multiple regression analyses using age, education, seniority and political views as independent variables.
5 The zero-order correlation coefficients are different in magnitude from the coefficients in table 7.8 as the latter are standardized regression coefficients.

## 8 THE BARGAINING PROCESS

1 Employer acceptance of this argument in 1986 did not last long. The Port of London Authority was in the vanguard of employer militancy during the 1989 strike over the abolition of the Dock Labour Scheme (see Turnbull *et al.*, 1991).
2 The concept of a 'system of argument' has been taken directly from Batstone *et al.*, (1977: 6–7).
3 Response totals vary question by question because some respondents failed to complete the whole questionnaire.
4 The other most frequent comments revolved around the officer's helpfulness (mentioned 17 times), communication skills and relations with the rank and file (each mentioned 15 times).

## 9 DEALING WITH MANAGERS

1 Reliable data on managers' arguments was available from 58 of the 66 meetings we attended and all subsequent analyses in this chapter use a meeting N of 58.

# Bibliography

Abbott, P. and Wallace, C. (1990). 'The sociology of the caring professions: an introduction', in Abbott, P. and Wallace, C. (eds.), *The Sociology of the Caring Professions*, Basingstoke: Falmer

Ahlstrand, B. (1990). *The Quest for Productivity*, Cambridge: Cambridge University Press

Albrow, M. (1970). *Bureaucracy*, London: Macmillan

Allen, V. L. (1954). *Power in Trade Unions*, London: Longmans
  (1957). *Trade Union Leadership*, London: Longmans

Applebaum, L. and Blaine, R. (1975). 'Compensation and turnover of union officers', *Industrial Relations* 14(2): 156–7

Armstrong, P. J., Goodman, J. F. B. and Hyman, J. D. (1981). *Ideology and Shopfloor Industrial Relations*, London: Croom Helm

Bamber, G. (1986). *Militant Managers? Managerial unionism and industrial relations*, Aldershot: Gower

Banks, J. A. (1974). *Trade Unionism*, London: Collier-Macmillan

Bassett, P. (1986). *Strike Free: new industrial relations in Britain*, London: Macmillan

Batstone, E. (1988). *The Reform of Workplace Industrial Relations in Britain*, Oxford: Clarendon

Batstone, E. and Gourlay, S. (1986). *Unions, Unemployment and Innovation*, Oxford: Blackwell

Batstone, E., Boraston, I. and Frenkel, S. (1977). *Shop Stewards in Action*, Oxford: Blackwell
  (1978). *The Social Organisation of Strikes*, Oxford: Blackwell

Batstone, E., Gourlay, S., Levie, H. and Moore, R. (1987). *New Technology and the Process of Labour Regulation*, Oxford: Clarendon

Beaumont, P. B. (1990). *Change in Industrial Relations*, London: Routledge
  (1992). *Public Sector Industrial Relations*, London: Routledge

Beaumont, P. B. and Harris, R. I. D. (1990). 'Union recruitment and organising attempts in Britain in the 1980s', *Industrial Relations Journal* 21: 274–86

Benson, H. (1986). 'The fight for union democracy', in Lipset, S. (ed.), *Unions in Transition*, San Francisco: ICS Press

Benson, J. (1991). *Unions at the Workplace: shop steward leadership and ideology*, Melbourne: Oxford University Press

Beynon, H. (1984). *Working for Ford*, 2nd edn., Harmondsworth: Penguin

Blumler, J. and Ewbank, A. J. (1970). 'Trade unionists, the mass media and unofficial strikes', *British Journal of Industrial Relations* 8: 32–54

Boraston, I., Clegg, H. A. and Rimmer, M. (1975). *Workplace and Union*, London: Heinemann

Bramble, T. (1991). *The Conservatism of the Trade Union Officialdom. A Review of the Literature*, Department of Economics, La Trobe University, Australia, unpublished ms

　(1992). *Driving a Hard Bargain? The role of the full-time officials in the vehicle builders employees' federation, 1963–1991*, proceedings of the AIRANNZ conference, Coolangatta, Australia

Brown, H. P. (1986). *The Origins of Trade Union Power*, Oxford: Oxford University Press

Brown, W. (1989). 'Managing remuneration', in Sisson, K. (ed.), *Personnel Management in Britain*, Oxford: Blackwell

Brown, W. and Lawson, M. (1973). 'The training of trade union officers', *British Journal of Industrial Relations* 11(3): 431–48

Brown, W. and Wadhwani, S. (1990). 'The economic effects of industrial relations legislation since 1979', *National Institute Economic Review* 131: 57–69

Callinicos, A. (1982). 'The rank and file movement today', *International Socialism* 2:17: 1–38

Callus, R. (1986). 'Employment characteristics of full-time trade union officials in New South Wales', *Journal of Industrial Relations* 28(3): 410–27

Carew, A. (1976). *Democracy and Government in European Trade Unions*, London: Allen & Unwin

Carruth, A. A. and Oswald, A. J. (1989). *Pay Determination and Industrial Prosperity*, Oxford: Clarendon

Certification Officer, *Annual Reports* (various years)

Chaison, G. N. and Rose, J. B. (1977). 'Turnover among Presidents of Canadian national unions', *Industrial Relations* 16(2): 199–204

Child, J. (1984). *Organization: a guide to problems and practice*, 2nd edn., London: Harper & Row

Child, J., Warner, M. and Loveridge, R. (1973). 'Towards an organisational study of trade unions', *Sociology* 7(1): 71–91

Clegg, H. A. (1976). *Trade Unionism Under Collective Bargaining*, Oxford: Blackwell

　(1979). *The Changing System of Industrial Relations in Great Britain*, Oxford: Blackwell

　(1985). *A History of British Trade Unions Since 1989. Volume 2 1911–1933*, Oxford: Clarendon

Clegg, H. A., Killick, A. J. and Adams, R. (1961). *Trade Union Officers*, Oxford: Blackwell

Clegg, S. and Dunkerley, D. (1980). *Organisation, Class and Control*, London: Routledge & Kegan Paul

Cliff, T. (1971). 'The bureaucracy today', *International Socialism* 1:48: 31–3

Clinton, A. (1984). *Post Office Workers. A trade union and social history*, London: Allen & Unwin

Coates, K. and Topham, T. (1974). *The New Unionism*, Harmondsworth: Penguin

　(1988). *Trade Unions in Britain*, 3rd edn., London: Fontana

　(1991). *The History of the Transport & General Workers' Union. Volume 1 The*

*Making of the Transport and General Workers' Union. Part 1 1870–1911*, Oxford: Blackwell

Colling, T. and Dickens, L. (1989). *Equality Bargaining: Why Not?*, London: HMSO

Cressey, P., Eldridge, J. E. T. and MacInnes, J. (1985). *Just Managing: authority and democracy in industry*, Milton Keynes: Open University Press

Crompton, R. (1990). 'Professions in the current context', *Work, Employment and Society*, Special Issue, May: 147–66

Cronin, J. E. (1979). *Industrial Conflict in Modern Britain*, London: Croom Helm

Crouch, C. (1982). *Trade Unions: the logic of collective action*, London: Fontana

Cupper, L. (1983). 'A profile of white-collar union officials', in Ford, B. and Plowman, D. (eds.), *Australian Trade Unions*, Sydney: Macmillan

Daniel, W. W. (1976). *Wage Determination in Industry*, London: Political and Economic Planning Report 563

Daniel, W. W. and Millward, N. (1983). *Workplace Industrial Relations in Britain*, London: Heinemann

Department of Employment (1983). *Democracy in Trade Unions*, Cmnd 8778, London: Department of Employment

Donaldson, L. and Warner, M. (1974). 'Bureaucratic and electoral control in occupational interest associations', *Sociology* 8(1): 47–57

Dufty, N. (1979). 'The characteristics and attitudes of full-time union officials in Western Australia', *British Journal of Industrial Relations* 17(2): 173–86

Edelstein, J. D. and Warner, M. (1979). *Comparative Union Democracy*, revised edn., New Brunswick, NJ: Transaction Books

Edwardes, M. (1983). *Back from the Brink*, London: Collins

Edwards, C. and Heery, E. (1989). *Management Control and Union Power: a study of labour relations in coal mining*, Oxford: Clarendon

Edwards, P. K. (1987). *Managing the Factory*, Oxford: Blackwell

England, J. (1979). 'How UCATT revised its rules: an anatomy of organizational change', *British Journal of Industrial Relations* 17(1): 1–18

  (1981). 'Shop stewards in Transport House', *Industrial Relations Journal* 12(5): 16–29

Fairbrother, P. and Waddington, J. (1990). 'The politics of trade unionism: evidence, policy and theory', *Capital and Class* 41: 15–56

Fisher, J. and Holland, D. (1990). *Training for Full-time Officers of Trade Unions*, London: Further Education Unit

Flanders, A. (1964). *The Fawley Productivity Agreement*, London: Faber

  (1970). *Management and Unions*, London: Faber

Fosh, P. and Cohen, S. (1990). 'Local trade unionists in action: patterns of union democracy', in Fosh, P. and Heery, E. (eds.), *Trade Unions and their Members*, London: Macmillan

Fox, A. (1966). *Industrial Sociology and Industrial Relations*, Research Paper 3, London: Royal Commission on Trade Unions and Employers' Associations

  (1974). *Beyond Contract: work, power and trust relations*, London: Faber & Faber

  (1985). *Man Mismanagement*, 2nd edn., London: Hutchinson

Freeman, R. B. (1990). 'On the divergence of unionism among developed countries', in Brunetta, R. and Del'Aringa, C. (eds.), *Labour Relations and Economic Performance*, London: Macmillan

French, J. and Raven, B. (1959). 'The bases of social power', in Cartwright, D. and Zander, A. (eds.), *Group Dynamics: research and theory*, 3rd edn., London: Tavistock

Frenkel, S. and Coolican, A. (1984). *Unions Against Capitalism? a Sociological comparison of the Australian building and metal workers' unions*, Sydney: Allen & Unwin

Fuller, K. (1985). *Radical Aristocrats: London busworkers from the 1880s to the 1980s*, London: Lawrence & Wishart

Goldfield, M. (1987). *The Decline of Organized Labor in the United States*, Chicago: University of Chicago Press

Goldthorpe, J. H. (1982). 'On the service class, its formation and future', in Giddens, A. and MacKenzie, G. (eds.), *Social Class and the Division of Labour*, Cambridge: Cambridge University Press

Gouldner, A. (1955). 'Metaphysical pathos and the theory of bureaucracy', *American Political Science Review* 49(2): 496–507

Grzelak, J. (1988). 'Conflict and cooperation', in Hewstone, M. *et al.* (eds.), *Introduction to Social Psychology*, Oxford: Blackwell

Guest, D. (1989). 'Human resource management: its implications for industrial relations and trade unions', in Storey, J. (ed.), *New Perspectives on Human Resource Management*, London: Routledge

   (1991). 'Personnel management: the end of orthodoxy?', *British Journal of Industrial Relations* 29(2): 149–75

Harris, M. (1990). 'Review article: working in the UK voluntary sector', *Work, Employment and Society* 4(1): 125–40

Hartley, J. (1992). 'Joining a trade union', in Hartley, J. and Stephenson, G. M. (eds.), *Employment Relations: the psychology of influence and control at work*, Oxford: Blackwell

Heery, E. and Fosh, P. (1990). 'Introduction: Whose union? power and bureaucracy in the labour movement', in Fosh, P. and Heery, E. (eds.), *Trade Unions and their Members*, London: Macmillan

Heery, E. and Kelly, J. (1988). 'Do female representatives make a difference? Women full-time officials and trade union work', *Work, Employment and Society* 2(4): 487–505

   (1989). '"A cracking job for a woman" – a profile of women trade union officers', *Industrial Relations Journal* 20(3): 192–202

   (1990). 'Full-time trade union officers and the shop steward network', in Fosh, P. and Heery, E. (eds.), *Trade Unions and their Members*, London: Macmillan

Hemingway, J. (1978). *Conflict and Democracy: Studies in trade union government*, Oxford: Oxford University Press

Hinton, J. (1973). *The First Shop Stewards' Movement*, London: Allen & Unwin

   (1983). *Labour and Socialism*, Brighton: Wheatsheaf

Hoerr, J. (1991). 'What should unions do?', *Harvard Business Review*, May–June: 30–45

Howells, J. M. and Alexander, A. E. (1970). 'The ability of managers and trade union officers to predict workers' preferences', *British Journal of Industrial Relations* 8(2): 237–51

Hyman, R. (1983). 'Trade unions: structure, policies, and politics', in Bain, G. (ed.), *Industrial Relations in Britain*, Oxford: Blackwell

(1989a). 'Dualism and division in labour strategies', in Hyman, R., *The Political Economy of Industrial Relations*, London: Macmillan

(1989b). 'The politics of workplace trade unionism: recent tendencies and some problems for theory', in Hyman, R., *The Political Economy of Industrial Relations*, London: Macmillan

(1989c). 'The sickness of British trade unionism: is there a cure?', in Hyman, R., *The Political Economy of Industrial Relations*, London: Macmillan

IDS (1984). 'Trade union leaders' pay', *Incomes Data Services Top Pay Unit*, August: 20–21

Ingram, P. (1991). 'Ten years of manufacturing wage settlements: 1979–89', *Oxford Review of Economic Policy* 7(1): 93–106

IRRR (1992). 'The changing role of trade union officers I: the devolution of pay bargaining', *Industrial Relations Review and Report* 526: 5–12

(1993). 'The changing role of trade union officers II', *Industrial Relations Review and Report* 527: 3–11

James, L. (1984). *Power in a Trade Union*, Cambridge: Cambridge University Press

Jary, S. (1990). *Trade Union Organisation and New Technology Bargaining*, University of Southampton, unpublished Ph.D. thesis

Keenoy, T. (1990). 'HRM: a case of the wolf in sheep's clothing?', *Personnel Review* 19(2): 3–9

Kelly, J. (1988). *Trade Unions and Socialist Politics*, London: Verso

(1990). 'British trade unionism 1979–89: Change, continuity and contradictions', *Work, Employment and Society, Special Issue*: 29–65

Kelly, J. and Heery, E. (1987). *The Role of Full-Time Officials in Trade Union Recruitment*, paper for the TUC Special Review Body

(1989). 'Full time officers and trade union recruitment', *British Journal of Industrial Relations* 27(2): 196–213

Kelly, J. and Kelly, C. (1991). '"Them and us": social psychology and the "new industrial relations"', *British Journal of Industrial Relations* 29(1): 25–48

Kessler, S. and Bayliss, F. (1992). *Contemporary British Industrial Relations*. London: Macmillan

LACSAB (1991). *Performance Related Pay in Practice: a national survey of local government*, London: Local Authorities' Conditions of Service Advisory Board

Lane, T. (1974). *The Union Makes Us Strong*, London: Arrow

(1986). 'Economic democracy: are the trade unions equipped?', *Industrial Relations Journal* 17(4): 321–8

Lester, R. A. (1958). *As Unions Mature*, Princeton, NJ: Princeton University Press

Littler, C. (1982). *The Development of the Labour Process in Capitalist Societies*, London: Heinemann

Lukes, S. (1974). *Power: a radical view*, London: Macmillan

MacGregor, I. (1986). *The Enemies Within*, London: Collins

Maksymiw, W., Eaton, J. and Gill, C. (1990). *The British Trade Union Directory*, Harlow: Longman

Marchington, M. and Parker, P. (1990). *Changing Patterns of Employee Relations*, Hemel Hempstead: Harvester Wheatsheaf

Marginson, P. *et al.* (1988). *Beyond the Workplace*, Oxford: Blackwell

Martin, R. (1992). *Bargaining Power*, Oxford: Clarendon

Mason, B. and Bain, P. (1991). 'Trade union recruitment strategies: facing the 1990s', *Industrial Relations Journal* 22(1): 36–45

McCarthy, W. and Parker, S. R. (1968). *Shop Stewards and Workshop Relations, Research Paper* 10, London: Royal Commission on Trade Unions and Employers' Associations

Metcalf, D. (1989). 'Water notes dry up: the impact of the Donovan reform proposals and Thatcherism at work on labour productivity', *British Journal of Industrial Relations* 27(1): 1–32

(1991). 'British unions: dissolution or resurgence?', *Oxford Review of Economic Policy* 7(1): 18–32

Michels, R. W. (1915). *Political Parties*, 2nd edn., New York: Free Press

Miller, D. (1988). *Stress and the Trade Unionist*, Newcastle: Newcastle upon Tyne Polytechnic, Trade Union Studies Section

Mills, C. W. (1948). *The New Men of Power: America's labor leaders*, New York: Harcourt Brace

Millward, N. and Stevens, M. (1986). *British Workplace Industrial Relations 1980–1984*, Aldershot: Gower

Millward, N., Stevens, M., Smart, D. and Hawes, W. R. (1992). *Workplace Industrial Relations in Transition*, Aldershot: Dartmouth

Mitchell, O. J. B., Lewin, D. and Lawler, E. E. (1990). 'Alternative pay systems, firm performance and productivity', in Blinder, A. S. (ed.), *Paying for Productivity*, Washington, DC: Brookings Institution

Morris, T. (1986). 'Trade union mergers and competition in British banking', *Industrial Relations Journal* 17(2): 129–40

Offe, C. (1985). *Disorganised Capitalism*, Oxford: Polity Press

Offe, C. and Wiesenthal, H. (1980). 'Two logics of collective action'; reprinted in Offe, C., *Disorganised Capitalism*, Oxford: Polity Press

Ogden, S. (1991). 'The trade union campaign against water privatization', *Industrial Relations Journal* 22(1): 20–35

O'Toole, B. (1989). *Private Gain and Public Service. The Association of First Division Civil Servants*, London: Routledge

Parker, S. R. (1974). *Workplace Industrial Relations 1972*, London: HMSO

(1975). *Workplace Industrial Relations 1973*, London: HMSO

Pearce, B. (1959). 'Some past rank and file movements', *Labour Review* 4(1); reprinted (1975) in Woodhouse, M. and Pearce, B., *Essays on the History of Communism in Britain*, London: New Park

Pelling, H. A. (1987). *A History of British Trade Union Unionism*, 4th edn., Harmondsworth: Penguin

Perkin, H. (1989). *The Rise of Professional Society. England since 1880*, London: Routledge

Peterson, R. B. and Tracy, L. N. (1977). 'Testing a behavioral theory of labor relations', *Industrial Relations* 16: 35–50

Poole, M., Blyton, P. and Frost, P. E. (1981). *Managers in Focus*, Aldershot: Gower

Poole, M. and Mansfield, R. (1993). 'Patterns of continuity and change in managerial attitudes and behaviour in industrial relations, 1980–1990', *British Journal of Industrial Relations* 31(1): 11–35

Purcell, J. and Sisson, K. (1983). 'Strategies and practice in the management of industrial relations', in Bain, G. (ed.), *Industrial Relations in Britain*, Oxford: Blackwell

Rainbird, H. (1990). *Training Matters: union perspectives on industrial restructuring and training*, Oxford: Blackwell

Rees, T. (1990). 'Gender, power and trade union democracy', in Fosh, P. and Heery, E. (eds.), *Trade Unions and their Members*, London: Macmillan

Roberts, B. C. (1956). *Trade Union Government and Administration in Great Britain*, London: Bell & Sons

Robertson, N. and Sams, K. (1976). 'The role of the full-time union officer', *Economic and Social Review* 8(1): 23–42

(1978). 'Research note: on the work pattern of union officers', *Industrial Relations Journal* 9(1): 61–4

Sandver, M. H. (1978). 'Determinants of pay for large local union officers', *Industrial Relations* 17(1): 108–11

SERTUC (1992). *A Step Closer to Equality*, London: SERTUC

Sisson, K. (1989). 'Personnel management in perspective', in Sisson, K. (ed.), *Personnel Management in Britain*, Oxford: Blackwell

Smith, C. (1989). *Incentive Schemes: people and profits*, London: Croner

Starkey, K. (1989). 'Time and professionalism: disputes concerning the nature of professionalism', *British Journal of Industrial Relations* 27(3): 375–95

Steele, M. (1990). 'Changing the rules: pressures on trade union constitutions', in Fosh, P. and Heery, E. (eds.), *Trade Unions and their Members*, London: Macmillan

Storey, J. (1992). *Developments in the Management of Human Resources*, Oxford: Blackwell

Storey, J. (ed.) (1989). *New Perspectives on Human Resource Management*, London: Routledge

Strinati, D. (1982). *Capitalism, the State and Industrial Relations*, London: Croom Helm

Swabe, A. I. R. and Price, P. (1984). 'Building a permanent association: the development of staff associations in the Building Societies', *British Journal of Industrial Relations* 22(2): 195–204

Taylor, R. (1973). 'Officer class', *New Society*, 29 March

Terry, M. (1989). 'Recontextualising shopfloor industrial relations: some case study evidence', in Tailby, S. and Whitston, C. (eds.), *Manufacturing Change: industrial relations and restructuring*, Oxford: Blackwell

Terry, M. and Edwards, P. K. (eds.) (1988). *Shopfloor Politics and Job Controls*, Oxford: Blackwell

T&GWU (1992). *One Union*, London: Transport & General Workers' Union

Townley, B., Morris, T. and Kelly, J. (1985). *CPSA: The Decision to Join: an evaluation of the CPSA's recruitment year*, London School of Economics, unpublished Report

TUC (1989). *TUC Survey of Union Officers*, London: Trades Union Congress

(1991). *TUC Towards 2000*, London: Trades Union Congress

Turnbull, P., Woolfson, C. and Kelly, J. (1991). *Dock Strike: conflict and restructuring in Britain's ports*, Aldershot: Gower

Undy, R. and Martin, R. (1984). *Ballots and Trade Union Democracy*, Oxford: Blackwell

Undy, R., Ellis, V., McCarthy, W. E. J. and Halmos, A. (1981). *Change in Trade Unions*, London: Hutchinson

Upchurch, M. and Donnelly, E. (1992). 'Membership patterns in USDAW 1980–1990: survival as success?', *Industrial Relations Journal* 23(1): 60–8

Van Tine, W. R. (1973). *The Making of the Labor Bureaucrat*, Amherst: University of Massachusetts Press

Visser, J. (1990). 'In search of inclusive unionism', *Bulletin of Comparative Labour Relations* 18: 1–226

Walton, R. E. (1985). 'From control to commitment in the workplace', *Harvard Business Review* 64: 77–84

Walton, R. E. and McKersie, R. M. (1965). *A Behavioral Theory of Labor Negotiations*, New York: McGraw-Hill

Watson, D. (1988). *Managers of Discontent: trade union officers and industrial relations managers*, London: Routledge

Webb, S. and Webb, B. (1902). *Industrial Democracy*, London: Longmans
  (1920). *The History of Trade Unionism*, London: Longmans

Willman, P. (1980). 'Leadership and trade union principles: some problems of management sponsorship and independence', *Industrial Relations Journal* 11(4): 39–49
  (1982). *Fairness, Collective Bargaining and Incomes Policy*, Oxford: Clarendon
  (1989). 'The logic of "market share" unionism', *Industrial Relations Journal* 20: 260–71
  (1990). 'The financial status and performance of British trade unions, 1950–1988', *British Journal of Industrial Relations* 28(3): 313–27

Willman, P. and Morris, T. (1988). *The Finances of British Trade Unions 1975–1985, Research Paper* 62, London: Department of Employment

Willman, P., Morris, T. and Aston, B. (1993). *Union Business: trade union organisation and financial reform in the Thatcher years*, Cambridge: Cambridge University Press

Wrigley, C. J. (1987). 'The trade unions between the wars', in Wrigley, C. J. (ed.), *A History of British Industrial Relations Vol 2 1914–1939*, Brighton: Harvester

# Index of names

# Index of subjects

# Cambridge Studies in Management